KING'S CROSS SECOND MAN

A SIXTIES DIESEL CAREER

KING'S CROSS SECOND MAN

A SIXTIES DIESEL CAREER

Norman Hill

PEN & SWORD
TRANSPORT

AN IMPRINT OF PEN & SWORD BOOKS LTD.
YORKSHIRE - PHILADELPHIA

First published in Great Britain in 2018 by
Pen and Sword Transport
An imprint of
Pen & Sword Books Ltd
Yorkshire - Philadelphia

ISBN 978 1 47387 823 5

A CIP catalogue record for this book is available from the British Library.

Typeset by Aura Technology and Software Services, India
Printed and bound by Replika Press Pvt. Ltd.

Pen & Sword Books Ltd incorporates the Imprints of Pen & Sword Books Archaeology, Atlas, Aviation, Battleground, Discovery, Family History, History, Maritime, Military, Naval, Politics, Railways, Select, Transport, True Crime, Fiction, Frontline Books, Leo Cooper, Praetorian Press, Seaforth Publishing, Wharncliffe and White Owl.

For a complete list of Pen & Sword titles please contact
PEN & SWORD BOOKS LIMITED
47 Church Street, Barnsley, South Yorkshire, S70 2AS, England
E-mail: enquiries@pen-and-sword.co.uk
Website: www.pen-and-sword.co.uk

or

PEN AND SWORD BOOKS
1950 Lawrence Rd, Havertown, PA 19083, USA
E-mail: Uspen-and-sword@casematepublishers.com
Website: www.penandswordbooks.com

CONTENTS

ACKNOWLEDGEMENTS

For photographs I am indebted to :-

Justin Bailey for allowing me to reproduce his view of the parting of the ways between the 'Widened Lines' and the road up Snow Hill Bank to 'The South' at Farringdon, **Paul Chancellor of Colour-Rail** for his advice and assistance, **Revd Tom Gladwin** 'RCTS Hitchin member' who provided the fine shot of new Hitachis coming up out of Welwyn tunnels and through Welwyn North station. Special thanks to **Paul Hepworth** for his permission to show the essential images which he took during his part in the preparations for the new ECML South electric railway of the 1970s and also to **John Broughton**, custodian of the **RCTS** photo-archive, notably for his most speedy despatches from far away Grange-over-Sands.

For the wonders of today's 'websites' I am especially grateful to the patient researches of :-

Nick Catford and his colleagues in their most comprehensive 'Disused Stations' site; **David Hills** and his amazingly detailed researches into 'Derby Sulzers'; **David Hey's** immense collection of everything railway, and quite a few sites dealing with the histories of modern railway traction manufacturers.

I must mention *'Golden Eagle Luxury Trains'* site which grew out of the 1963 'Altrinchamian Railway Excursion Society' who's early 1966 'Flying Scotsman' hauled 'Elizabethan' venture I saw climb past Ashburton Grove cum Emirates Stadium on that memorable Saturday morning. They run exotic rail tours to parts of the world undreamed of.

I must also be grateful for the patience of my commissioning editor John Scott-Morgan in the south and production manager Janet Brookes in the north; in the north also Dom Allen who patiently turned my pencilled scribblings of the lines from Kings Cross into comprehensible route maps. I am grateful also to the patience of my wife, Joy, for not getting out and about so much during these last few months.

Finally I must offer eternal thanks to Driver Roy Head of King's Cross who is unfortunately no longer around to receive them but who I will always remember as the best work-mate I ever had.

Norman Hill
August 2018.

PREFACE

I wanted to be an engine driver when I was 8. I wanted to leave school and do this when I was 15. But things called G.C.E. exams thwarted that plan. Ten years later I realised this ambition when I just beat the age barrier to become a 'second-man', diesel locomotives, King's Cross. Although it was a job which only lasted some four years it was the only job of my many which was more than 'just a job'. I recorded every shift I worked in foolscap diaries; times attended, drivers with, locomotives worked, diagrams booked, what actually occurred. That was just 50 years ago now; but those few years still stand clear in my memory, and some events are still as vivid as if they had happened yesterday.

But as I prepared to write up and share these memories I realised that there could be much more in them than the mere repetition of my shifts worked on diesel locomotives, for those locomotives in the mid-1960s were still a new form of motive power, they had only recently replaced about 150 years of steam power, and although my journeys rarely took me far from King's Cross they took me through over a century of King's Cross Area railway history and into railway places now long gone; the many goods and carriage sidings, forgotten goods and passenger stations, much changed King's Cross station itself. And I was 'second man' at a time when modernisation was actually rewriting railway history, a process which is still the case today when the current Railway Upgrade Plan is busily building a new national railway system, not the least of which is a brand new railway for the East Coast Main Line and the King's Cross Area. I have incorporated brief histories of these now long gone railway places and also accounts of the 'new railways' of 50 years ago and today into my account of the small part I played in the railway modernisation of the 1960s.

"One of Gateshead's big 'Sulzers' an Eastern 'Peak'", sadly failed, opens my account in late 1964. Here, some ten years later, a sister 'Peak' thunders out of Hadley South tunnel and through Hadley Wood station under the new overhead electric wires on the climb out of London, still in front-line ECML service but surely towards the end of her days. (Colour-Rail)

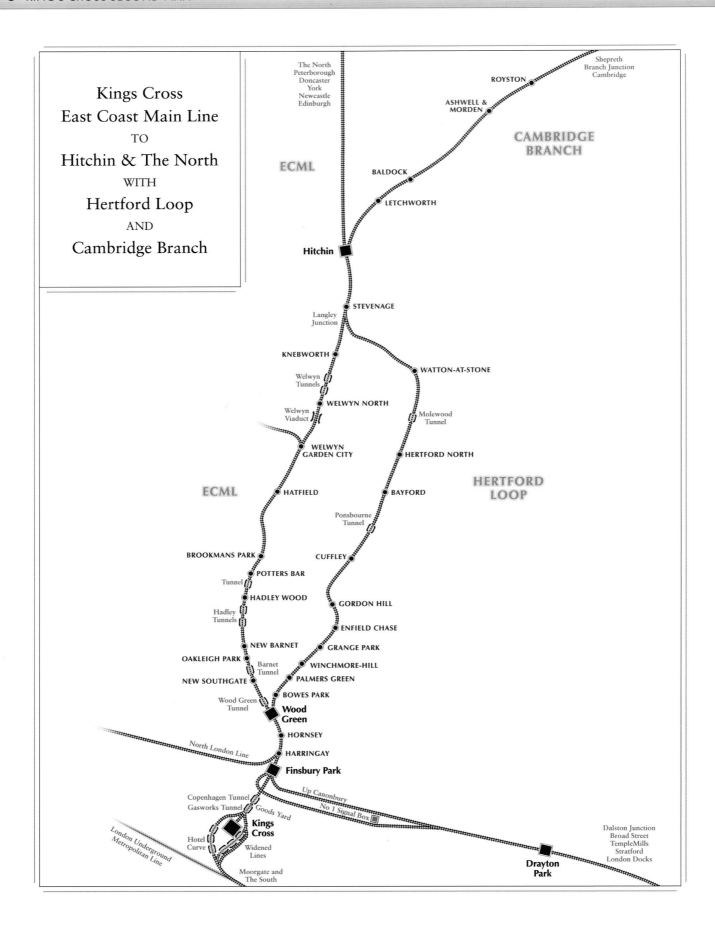

Kings Cross
East Coast Main Line
TO
Hitchin & The North
WITH
Hertford Loop
AND
Cambridge Branch

Gateshead 'Peak' D174, sister to the cause of my initial discomfort on the 'Passenger Loco', drops back past King's Cross box onto a Summer 1965 departure in platform 5; both alert second-man and keen young enthusiast who's 'bunked' onto York Road platform 'keep a sharp look out'. (RCTS)

CHAPTER 1

KING'S CROSS - PASSED CLEANER

One of Gateshead's big 'Sulzers', an Eastern 'Peak' (TOPS class 46), had failed, almost, but not quite, on King's Cross 'Passenger Loco's' exit stops, just enough for its north end bogie to be skewed on the curve of the approach road to the stops out of the shed yard. She had died completely, would not answer to the starter at all. They'd brought a 'Brush-4' (47) down on top of the failed 'Peak' in order to couple them. As there wasn't room for the two big engines to approach the exit stops together, the 'Brush' would then drag the 'Peak' back into the middle of the shed yard before propelling out past the exit stops into the 'milk-yard' - usually the way *onto* the shed - thence 'rightaway' to 'Clarence Yard', Finsbury Park TMD; an apparently easy solution to an inconvenient situation. But when the 'Brush' came up to the skewed north end of the 'Peak' to be coupled, of course the 'Brush's' south end was also skewed on the curved approach to the exit stops, thus while buffers touched on the inside of the curve, a considerable gap yawned between the outside buffers of the two locos. It was somewhere between 1 and 2 a.m. on a mercifully dry November morning in 1964 when one of King's Cross MPD's rawest recruits was sent down from the crew room on platform 10 (today's 8) to assist in the resolution of this situation. "Passed-cleaner Hill," the foreman called into the room where some half dozen shed-duty men whiled away their time, some hoping something would turn up, others, with only a couple of hours to go, fervently hoping the rest of their shift would not produce a job. It was my first duty in the exalted capacity of 'passed cleaner', having only the week before passed out in basic signalling, hand and lamps, and had been deemed capable of preparing and running locomotive steam heating boilers, and, as I was about to find out in no uncertain manner, of coupling locomotives to trains and together. I stood up attentively. "Go down to the 'Passenger Loco'," continued the 'inside foreman', "and act as a rider on a failed engine to Clarence Yard." Even with my 25 years, a lifetime, of railway enthusiasm, I wasn't exactly sure what this order involved, but obediently descended the stairs from the room and walked quickly along to the end of platform 10.

I could see the two big engines standing together just off the shed exit stops as I walked down the platform 10/11 end slope and approached the little knot of men gathered round the junction between the two locomotives. I saw the shed running foreman, the 'outside foreman', and declared myself, name, rank and mission. "Ah, well," said foreman Alf, "before you do your riding you'll have to do a spot of coupling, get in there," he indicated the dark and dirty gap between the ends of the two big diesels with a wave of his 'bardic' hand lamp, "and tie these two together".

I looked into the dark, cramped place beyond the buffers, between the locomotive couplings, lit fitfully in the beam of the foreman's wavering lamp, looked briefly back at the foreman, round the circle of cold, unsympathetic faces, then ducked under the buffers into that black hole, crouching between the two big coupling hooks, also cold and unsympathetic, on each side. "Take the Brush's brake hose off first," came a voice from the outside world as I reached up to do just that; to unship the assisting engine's brake hose from its plate on the engine's buffer-beam, thus making sure that the brakes would remain applied no matter what any idiot in the cab might do, and so further ensuring that the 'Brush' would not move - which eventuality could make conditions between the two engines very much more uncomfortable! I pivoted round, back towards the Brush, and unhooked the 'Peak's hose in turn - just in case she came to life and made an unexpected move back towards the shed! The two fat hoses hung opposite each other like two elephant trunks reaching for a proffered bun, and still further restricting room to work in the cramped gap. I knew that once I'd hooked the engines together I would have to couple the two hoses together when, hopefully, the 'Brush' would then be able to release all brakes and so move the 'Peak' - after I had wriggled out from between the engines! From the shouts of advice directed from the waiting group of enginemen outside it was obvious that they were convinced that I was unaware of this necessary order of events. Closing my ears to the shouts I took hold of the top link of the 'Brush's heavy

'Brush' 'Type-4's became a familiar sight from Land's End to Thurso. A 'Brush-4' rescued the failed 'Peak' during my first eventful shift. Here D1511 is brand new in that handsome two-tone green at Finsbury Park TMD on 20th March 1963. (RCTS)

coupling chain which was correctly stowed on its hook on the buffer beam, heaved it forwards and upwards to drop over the 'Peak's hook, but it didn't reach and fell back with a clang against the buffer beam, narrowly missing my braced knee in the process, then hung, swaying slightly from its attachment on the engine's drawbar, cold, unsympathetic and liberally covered in grease and lube, some of which had already transferred itself to me. I turned my back half towards the Brush, stooped, and again took hold of the first link of the dangling coupling chain; lifted with both hands, offered the coupling across the gap towards the Peak's hook, but the end of the coupling scraped up the curved point of the other locomotive's hook and stopped before it reached the top as the whole chain came up taught, would not reach, was too short. The full weight of the chain became too much for my tensed arms as I expected the chain to drop over the hook and so take its weight off them; but I dropped it again and,

again, it narrowly missed my tensed legs as it clanged back against the buffer beam.

"Unscrew it," yelled a voice from the outside group. "Try the Sulzer's chain," advised another. And, indeed, I did try everything. I unscrewed the great links of the Brush's filthy coupling chain and tried to sling it, again, without success; I heaved off the 'Peak's chain, unscrewed and slung it at the 'Brush's hook, all the time knowing that the chains would never reach because of the way the locos' bogies were skewed on the curved road, the great gap between the far-side buffers; surely 'they' could see that, but who was I, new recruit, passed cleaner, to advise all these experienced locomen who gawped and shouted at me from their own outside world?

"What's goin' on? The whole jobs stopped." It was a new voice above the babble, "Well, why doesn't one of you go in there and give him a hand?" A new face peered in at me as I gripped a greasy coupling once more and prepared my aching, shaking arms for another throw. I recognised Johnny Wissen, a tall young driver, not long passed out, who I'd exchanged a few words with up in the room but never really spoken to - well, on a first night shift, with my peers all on days, I hadn't said many words to anybody! Johnny bent his long height in two and pushed his way into my cramped, greasy and, by now, sweaty, world. He surveyed the scene, dappled by the fitful gleam of the 'bardic' lamps shining in from that world outside.

"I reckon," said Johnny, "that if we both take hold of the 'Brush's coupling, between us we can just about get it on that hook." His head nodded towards the dead 'Peak', looming large over us in the gloom. "Can you get over the other side?"

I doubled myself up once more.

"How long have you been here?" asked Johnny as I crept underneath the cold cruel hooks and those elephant-trunk hoses.

"Dunno, lost track of time," I replied, now facing Johnny across the hooks, between the hoses, with that wretched gap between the far buffers behind me.

"No," said Johnny patiently, "at 'The Cross', on the job?"

"Well," I replied as we automatically took hold of each side of the coupling link, "a month or so's cleaning and this is my first shift passed out."

"After three," said Johnny, did the count, "1-2-and-3 and heave", and the coupling scraped over that cruel hooked point and dropped with a satisfying 'clank' into the shank.

"Well," said Johnny Wissen, "let's screw it up tight and get out of here. A bloke would have to be a sight bigger and stronger than you *or* me to heave that over on his own."

We screwed up the coupling, clipped the brake hoses together and rejoined the group outside, back in the big real world. I followed Johnny Wissen out and, hard on his heels though I was, Johnny was already in full flow, turning the big real world blue, as I straightened up beside him.

"This man," Johnny Wissen was saying, "is working his very first shift, you all must know he hasn't been around for long, yet you send him in there to couple up two skewed engines - on his own - don't even try to help when anyone can see a man with fifty years' service couldn't sling that hook on his own. What a lot of

horrible, useless, b - - - - - - s." Johnny went on at great length using many a pithy adjective along the way; men slowly melted away, most of the crowd had trapped locos to get off the shed, in fact there must, by now, be locos in the station waiting to get onto the shed, even in these wee small hours. The crew on the assisting 'Brush' were already 'making a brake' and preparing to move the sulking 'Sulzer', and Johnny Wissen's audience dwindled down to the engine-movements crew who could move no engines until the Brush had taken the Sulzer out of the way, and were enjoying meantime the spectacle of foreman Alf, mouth agape, being dressed down by a very junior driver in the company of a very grubby, greasy and extremely junior passed-cleaner.

With a sudden loud and satisfying hiss the brakes of both engines came off and the big 'Sulzer' groaned in self-pity as the 'Brush' eased her gently away from the stops. The Brush's driver stopped the movement and climbed down in order to change ends before dragging the Sulzer back into the shed yard and then propelling back into the 'milk-yard' and so gaining the down slow road into Gasworks tunnel. "She'll roll now, Alf," he called to the foreman as his second man walked back into the yard to set the road.

Further intervention by Johnny Wissen and the agreement of a homeward-bound fitter to ride in the Sulzer to Clarence Yard (luckily no union reps witnessed this transaction) saw me and driver Wissen return to the crew room for a clean-up and a welcome 'mash' of tea. Johnny had no rostered second man that night so young driver and even younger passed cleaner stayed and chatted as a team for the rest of the night although no other jobs came their way.

And thus my first shift as 'passed cleaner' at King's Cross M. P. D. I had started cleaning at King's Cross on the 16th of November 1964 after a transfer amidst considerable shows of amazement and incredulity by clerical colleagues and superiors in the Midland Region's Audit Office in Melton House, Watford, together with much head shaking and 'here he goes again' comments from friends and family. But an advertisement for 'second men' at King's Cross Motive Power Depot, British Railways, King's Cross, in our local *Potters Bar Press* offered an invitation to realise a long outstanding ambition - and off I went.

My visions of climbing all over diesel locomotives with hoses, buckets of water, swabs, cloths, heavy duty detergent and the like were soon shattered, perhaps with relief, when the cleaning turned out to consist in merely scrubbing locomotive cab floors and cleaning cab windows in the 'Passenger Loco'; heavy external cleaning of diesel locomotives already being mechanised. The rank of 'engine cleaner' had become a short-term introductory grade to a 'footplate' career, although the honourable word 'footplate' was now much scorned by the ex-steam men - and that included all of the drivers, whether newly passed shed-duty or top-link Newcastle 'lodge' men. But I would soon discover that, as with so many innovations, new methods of operation could not be put in place overnight and in the mid-1960s diesel locomotives were still to a great extent maintained on traditional principals which had evolved during more than a century of everyday steam usage.

And so, after this dramatic introductory shift, things settled into a steady routine of jobs around The Cross, worked in shifts around the clock, 24/7, as they say today, repetitive jobs but never ever boring for me. As a 'passed cleaner' - meaning that I had passed the initial hand and lamp signalling tests, and had a basic idea of the different fixed signals which controlled the movement of trains upon the railway - I assisted in the 'shed duty', No.8 link, where the jobs were rostered under such exciting titles as: 'As Required', 'Relief', 'Ferry' and 'Engine Movements'. By the dieselised mid-1960s these jobs all consisted of much the same activities, generally involving the 'preparation' or 'disposal' and movement of light engines around King's Cross station and centred upon the extremely cramped loco refuelling and stabling shed, known as 'The Passenger Loco', squeezed

The 'Power Box' no longer dominates the approaches in this 1970s panorama as preparation for the 'new electric railway' gets under way at 'The Cross'. A 'Brush-4' brings an express out of 5 while a 'Type-2' cousin is station-pilot, resting in the spur by York Road platform. The 'Passenger Loco' stands on the far right with the exit road coming into the down slow just beyond the covered refuelling road and the end slope from the 'V' of 10/11 beyond again. (Paul Hepworth)

between the north end of the suburban platforms and the mouth of Gasworks Tunnel on the west side of the station yard.

The 'Passenger Loco' was opened in 1924 on land purchased from the Gas Light and Coke Company and replaced the loco-yard built initially in 1876 adjacent to the new suburban platform 11 outside the original west wall of the 1852 station and known as 'Bottom Shed'. 1924 saw the final much needed expansion of King's Cross Suburban, now an 'add-on' station west of the main terminus; the loco-yard was replaced by platforms 13 and 14, and so 'Bottom Shed' moved north to become the 'Passenger Loco'.

'Bottom Shed', and then 'Passenger Loco', avoided the trip out to 'Top Shed', between the tunnels, for engines which could be turned and quickly returned to duty with a minimum of servicing. By diesel days the 'Passenger Loco' consisted of two refuelling roads

and four cramped tracks for stabling between duties. Refuelling was carried out on the two easterly roads which stood each side of a row of low buildings comprising a range of rooms which provided accommodation for loco stores, engine-movement crews and fitters. The most easterly fuelling road was covered by a modern glass lean-to roof providing the only covered stabling on the depot and directly overlooking the slow roads from the suburban platforms as they entered the western portal of Gasworks Tunnel - which it was necessary for every locomotive to enter and reverse from in order to gain access either into or out of both depot and station.

On the far west, south, arrival, side of the 'Passenger Loco', opposite the departure stops, stood the 'outside' foremen's neat modern office whence he could watch all arrivals and departures and plan refuelling, exiting and stabling strategies.

In this 1960s view of King's Cross approaches viewed from the south-east, York Way, the signal box overlooks all, hiding the 'Passenger Loco' while the limited space between the platforms and Gasworks Tunnel can be appreciated. A DMU heads in from the tunnel to the suburban; a station-pilot waits a move in the 'dead-end', otherwise, the Cross is unusually quiet. (Paul Hepworth)

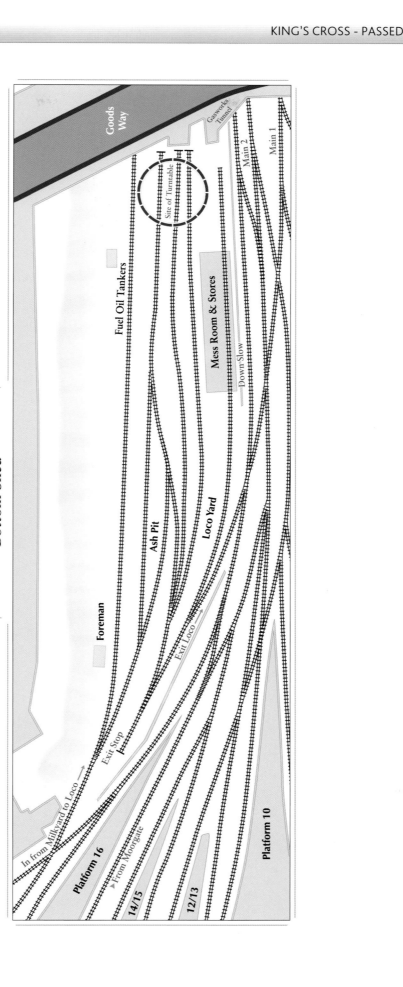

Kings Cross Passenger Loco
Bottom Shed

Another 1970s pre-electrification scene shows King's Cross west side. A 'Brush-2' brings a suburban train from Moorgate out of platform 16 onto the down slow, the 'add-on' suburban station is left of the train, the 'Passenger Loco' right, while a 'Brush-4' powered EC express leaves 5. (Paul Hepworth)

'Type-4' 'Sulzer' 2,500h.p. 1Co-Co1. (TOPS 45/46). With the 'EE-2.000s' the first early B.R. 'big' diesel types, known as 'Peaks' in view of the names bestowed on the first 10 of a class total of 193. The 'Peaks' (45) were the mainstay of the Midland Main Line but Gateshead fielded half of the final 1961 batch (46) of 56 locos, represented here by D179 dropping back to the 'Milk Yard' past the 'Passenger Loco' exit in order to access the depot. The 'outside' foreman's office in the left background. (RCTS)

King's Cross 'Passenger Loco' - steam-days' 'Bottom Shed'; in the 1960s, unusually empty with 'Deltic', 'Baby Deltic' and 'Sulzer-2' nicely posed. A 'Brush-4' stands off in the background and the depot's portable fuel tanks stand in 'the corner'. (Colour-Rail)

As their turn came to leave, the 'Passenger Loco' loco-motives were 'prepared' by a shed-duty crew who then moved the locomotive onto the departure stops, identi-fied the loco to the signal box on the departure phone, then came off the 'loco', into Gasworks Tunnel – twice to get the east side! - then into the appropriate station plat-form to join its train. After coupling up by one of the sta-tion shunters the main line crew stepped aboard to take the train north, and we menial shed-duty lads returned to await our next 'preparation' or 'disposal'. 'Disposal' worked in reverse to 'preparation', incoming main line crews were relieved on arrival in the station by a shed-duty crew who, when the loco was uncoupled and the coaches left the station, either as a north bound train but more usually as empty stock for service in the carriage sidings, took the locomotive onto the 'Passenger Loco' where, under the direction of the 'outside' foreman, it was refuelled, examined by the loco fitters, then 'stood

off' by the 'engine-movements' crew until 'preparation' for its next duty. The intricate art of 'engine movements' will be looked at more closely when I come to practice it myself.

These 'shed-duty' jobs were the remnants of steam days practice and, with steam working completely eliminated south of Peterborough by 1964, operating procedures were in slow transition between the old and new practices and the needs of these two very differ-ent forms of motive power. 'Shed-duty' jobs had been a vital part of the care and maintenance of steam locomo-tives. The long, dirty and arduous process of preparing a steam engine for work; coaling and watering, building a good fire, raising steam, lubricating rods and motion; the equally dirty and heavy job of disposal when a locomotive came on shed after work; cleaning or drop-ping the fire, emptying accumulated ash and clinker from ashpan and smokebox; these all disappeared with

'Deltic' D9007 (TOPS 55 007) 'Pinza', has come off the 'Passenger Loco' into Gasworks and now sets back onto her train in platform 8. (Paul Hepworth)

'Deltic' D9020 'Nimbus' has worked the up 'Flying Scotsman' and now a shed-duty crew take her out of 6 into Gasworks before moving across to the 'Milk Yard' and so into the 'Passenger Loco' for 'disposal' and servicing. (RCTS)

the advent of diesels which could be started up at the touch of a button and be ready to roll after a relatively quick inspection of fuel and lubricating oils, coolant and braking systems, and even more quickly 'disposed' of; engine stopped, locomotive safely braked and stabled anywhere away from running lines.

And yet diesel 'shed duties' in the 1960s were still carried out with the time-honoured methods of over a century of steam practice. On some 'as required' shifts we never turned a wheel and the mess room was full of 'shed-duty' men as we followed those generous, out-of-date steam diagrams on jobs which could be finished in a fraction of the booked time. The plus side of this

was that there were always plenty of spare crews to cover for delays, sudden sickness, and general non-attendance of booked men, which meant that no train was ever cancelled. But with such gross over-manning it was hardly surprising that the railway was still heavily in debt even after Dr. Beeching's remedy and the ongoing 'Modernisation Plan'. Modernisation could not be done overnight and a diversion from the 'main-line' of my own memories of this important time in railway history will make a brief survey of the reasons for this painfully slow transition during the 1950s and '60s, from long established steam railway locomotive practice to today's much simpler diesel and electric operation.

The pioneer 'Baby Deltic' D5900 runs into 6 with what the 'A' discs and stock suggest is an arriving 'Cambridge Buffet Express'. (RCTS)

CHAPTER 2

THE NEW RAILWAY – PART I

In his 2014 account of *The Railway Modernisation Plan* David Clough notes the slow change from steam power in his observation that,

"Sadly, thinking on motive power modernisation was in terms of the way steam had been utilised, rather than how the advent of the diesel might enable a more efficient regime to be brought in." (1)

This "thinking" from steam to diesel was not helped by the fact that dieselisation had come in very quickly in the end, when, in 1957, the caution of two years earlier which had advocated the trial of a few different diesel designs for initial assessment was thrown to the winds in a desperate attempt finally to end the dire financial and economic situation which the railway still laboured under despite the post-war decade of government 'assistance'; nationalisation, de-centralisation, contradictory political acts and general confusion which attempted ineffectually to improve that financial situation under the 'British Transport Commission' in 1948, then the 'British Railways Board' from 1962.

After the Second World War, the Labour Transport Act of 1947 saw the 1948 nationalisation of road, rail and inland waterways. Nationalisation promised a new, centralised national transport system, within which the nation's railways became 'British Railways'. David Clough points to how nationalisation put the BTC into a "political pecking order" where it must now take its turn with the other socially necessary bodies; education, health, etc. for "what could be afforded rather than the railways being free to spend what they could afford" (2) from their own, direct, income, as they had as private concerns.

This centralisation of nationalisation, however, was reversed after only five years when the general election of 1951 saw the almost inevitable replacement of Labour by a Conservative government which saw an inevitable reversal of attitude towards national transport, which led inevitably straight back towards decentralisation in the shape of the '1953 Transport Act', while the need to tackle the escalating debt and yet to modernise was recognised by the 1955 'Plan for the Modernisation of British Railways'.

The 1953 legislation privatised 'British Road Services', and while abolishing the central authority of 'The Railway Executive', retained the six railway regions under the direct authority of the 'British Transport Commission' – which led almost immediately to the formation of the 'Modernisation Plan Steering Committee' - which virtually replaced the 'Railway Executive' in mediating between the BTC and the railway regions via such already existing committees as the 'Technical Committee', an engineering-focused body, formed by the BTC in 1954 together with the 'Works and Equipment Committee'.

'The Modernisation Plan' set out to rebuild the railways over 15 years at a cost of £1,240 million. In 1957, this amount was increased to £1,600 million – providing the BTC did not increase railway charges!

That most professional and popular of railwaymen, R.H.N. Hardy, best known for his reminiscences, both written and spoken, of his years, supervisory then management, in 'running and maintenance' posts throughout the railway, but notably on the Southern and Eastern regions during the last days of steam, points out that, "the 1953 Transport Act had required the fundamental restructuring of public transport in Britain," and such profound changes were bound to have "a considerable effect on railway finances." (3) Of course railway finances were effected throughout the system by this total restructuring; but the particularly profound effect on railway finances was surely the change from steam to modern power and it must be remembered that as the first new untried diesels arrived in 1957 steam locomotives were still being built; indeed the last class of steam locomotive to be built, the 'Standard' '9F' for heavy freight work, was introduced in 1954 and the last one emerged from Swindon works in 1960 by which time diesels were in quantity production. This sudden flood of diesel orders came as a result of an initial BTC enquiry sent out in 1955 in an attempt to fulfil its roll of co-ordination with the regions. This led to a July 1956 report by engineering staff to the 'Technical Committee' entitled 'Selection of Diesel Types'. The report was assembled from the ambitious replies submitted by the six regions to the BTC enquiry and formed part of what David Clough calls "a massive document" (4) produced in April 1957 to show the overall needs of future passenger train motive power provision.

The outcome of this co-ordination between BTC and regions was a total change of mind during 1956 by both 'Technical Committee' and BTC over the plan agreed in January 1955 to test several diesel designs over three years. By the end of 1956 it was agreed to order diesel locomotives without further trial.

David Clough refers to "the avalanche of orders" which had been placed for diesel locomotives with some dozen different manufacturers by September 1957, "Such was the desperation to press forward with the elimination of steam that it was agreed to possibly make use of some companies not at present associated with locomotive building. If ever that was a recipe for disaster!" (5)

Thus the excess of committees produced the excess of orders which in turn produced an excess of diverse diesel locomotives which were totally untried, often unreliable and unsuitable. Of particular note in this respect at King's Cross were the North British 'Type 2' 1,000h.p. M.A.N./G.E.C. powered locomotives which became TOPS class '21', until many were rebuilt as class '29' from 1963 with Paxman engines in a not too successful attempt to improve them. The first ten came to King's Cross suburban services in 1958 under the 1955 'Pilot Scheme' but even before their arrival, the 1957 u-turn decision had seen no less than 48 more of this type alone ordered. When they *did* run they were prone to catch fire and my own memory of them was to see them arrive at Potters Bar station from my booking-office vantage point, and their appearance was often of biblical proportions – the loco roof a cloud of smoke by day and a column of flame by night! They were outlawed from 'The Cross' by early 1960 and sent as far away as possible, to Glasgow and Kittybrewster, Aberdeen, who were already lucky enough to have been allocated 19 of the North British beasts, brand new! They were boldly tried

The North British 'Type-2's (TOPS 21) were not a success at King's Cross although D6103 seems to be doing well as she takes empty coaches past Ferme Park down yard in June 1959. Hornsey loco's pall of smoke beyond shows that steam is not yet finished and also demonstrates one of the great disadvantages of steam. (RCTS)

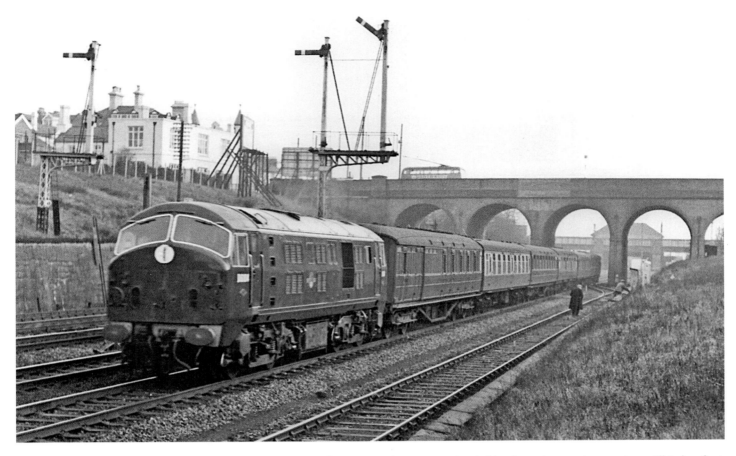

D6104 is also apparently going well down the main through New Southgate on a Cambridge branch stopping service, still in her first year in 1959. (RCTS)

on the 3-hour Aberdeen to Glasgow expresses but were soon replaced by the remaining steam 'A4' 'Pacifics' in their final blaze of glory.

The North British diesels were found to be most successful on crew training and night freight trips; they were all gone by 1969 after just one decade in service.

Even the first 'Brush 2s' and '4's were not at first the great success which they became, the original Mirlees engines on the 'Type-2's replaced by the English Electric 1470,h.p. unit, while the Sulzer 12LDA 2,750h.p. engines in the early 'Type-4's suffered stress fractures and were de-rated to 2,580h.p.

The underlying reason behind this initial chaotic locomotive situation surely goes back to that urgent need for total railway modernisation after the wear and tear of the Second World War, a desperate need almost suddenly realised with the 1953 Transport Act and then applied to the cautious ideas of the 1954 diesel locomotive Pilot Scheme which were soon forgotten in the political panic which drove the essential need to modernise and to stem the growing deficit at any cost.

For the deficit grew from £68.1 million in 1957 to £84 million by 1959 and well in excess of £100m by 1961 (£2billion in 2015 terms) in what R.H.N. Hardy calls a veritable "whirlwind of financial disaster" (6) for the nation's railway system.

After the confusion of the 1950s Hardy's "financial whirlwind" was bound to blow! But in 1960 the whirlwind became a full gale with the acceptance by the Macmillan government of the results of the investigation into railway pay undertaken by the Railway Staff National Tribunal in 1958. The RSNT pointed out how low railway wages were compared with other industries but also recognised the railway's financial plight. General Sir Brian Robertson, chairman of the BTC since 1953, actually accompanied union representatives to talk about the RSNT report with the Prime Minister who appointed C.W. Guillebaud to form the inevitable

'Type-2' 'Brush' 1,470h.p. A1A-A1A. TOPS 31. D5654 drops back past King's Cross 'Passenger Loco' towards the 'Milk-Yard' in January 1969. 34G, Finsbury Park TMD's, allocation of '31's varied between 50 to 60 locomotives during the 1960s. (RCTS)

'Type-4' 'Brush' 2,580h.p. Co-Co. TOPS 47. B.R.'s standard main line passenger locomotive. 54 were allocated to 34G Finsbury Park TMD by 1957 out of an eventual total of 512. D1523 leaves the 'Passenger Loco' probably destined for Finsbury Park TMD, as she is signalled 'right away' down the slow. High visibility clothes were not worn in the 1960s! (RCTS)

committee of enquiry into railway pay. Guillebaud was Reader in Economics at Cambridge University and had considerable experience in reconciliation enquiries in industrial pay claims. On 2nd March 1960 Guillebaud's report recommended wage increases of 8% for railway conciliation and 10% for salaried grades. On the 10th of March Parliament was informed of the acceptance of this deal backdated to 4th January 1960.

The Guillebaud decision added a lump sum of £33million to the growing railway deficit; the "whirlwind" could not possibly be allowed to blow for much longer and drastic steps were soon taken towards quelling the growing escalation of debt when Prime Minister Macmillan's Minister of Transport, Ernest Marples, replaced the British Transport Commission with the British Railways Board in his own 1962 Transport Act and appointed businessman Dr. Richard Beeching, chairman of the huge ICI chemical concern, as chairman of the BRB. Dr. Beeching was charged with the task of changing our railway from a public service into a profitable business, with the now well-known result; a wholesale culling of railway lines published to howls of ineffectual protest in 1963 as *The Reshaping of British Railways* – or, as R.H.N. Hardy sees it, "The Reckoning." (7).

In 1989, looking back at the political prevarications of the 1950s, R.H.N. sees the 1953 Transport Act as beginning, "a period when the nation's transport, was to be virtually without direction or control" and started, "almost unlimited competition between different forms of transport." (8)

Hardy's career in railway management during the crucial years which led up to "the reckoning" found R.H.N. as Assistant District Motive Power Superintendent at the huge Stratford – for Liverpool Street - shed between 1955 and 1959 where he presided over the arrival of their first diesels, which included the troublesome North British types; 10 of the disastrous M.A.N. powered 'Type-2s' (21) already mentioned, and

The 10 1958 North British 'Type-1's (TOPS 16) were notably unsuccessful and after an initial allocation to Devons Road, Bow, became part of Dick Hardy's problem at Stratford 30A where the first of the class, D8401, catches the sun on 15th November 1964. (RCTS)

No work for North British 'Type-1's D8403, D8404, D8407, D8402 and D8406 on a very wet Summer's day, 16 July 1961, at Stratford, although they would survive until 1968. (RCTS)

'Type-1' 'Paxman' 800h.p. Bo-Bo TOPS '15'; 34G Finsbury Park TMD had seven, all stabled at Hornsey where D8233 rests on 18th July 1965. They were a good deal better than the North British 'Type-1's. D8233 survives in preservation on the East Lancs Railway. (RCTS)

the 10 even more lamentable Paxman/G.E.C. powered 'Type-1s' (16) with single cab, similar in appearance to their somewhat better designed Paxman/B.T.H cousins (15) - which we will meet during my short time at Hornsey depot - and the infinitely more successful English Electric 'Type-1s' (20) - 34G had 10 working from Hitchin in the mid-1960s - together with the first of the eventually successful 'Brush' 'Type-2's (31) - which I experienced more than any other type at King's Cross; and the first big 2,000h.p. English Electric 'Type-4's (40); later class members were allocated to Gateshead and came up to King's Cross where I assisted in their preparation and disposal. Hardy tells how the "combination at Stratford of diesel traction maintained under cramped circumstances and steam locomotives in very poor shape had a disastrous effect on (Liverpool Street's) punctuality." (9)

Hardy became District Motive Power Superintendant at Liverpool Street in 1959 and saw the tremendous changes in the very way of life of "drivers and firemen, artisans and technicians, labourers and clerks, foremen and managers" (10) which the railway's modernisation and renaissance really involved.

Indeed, while in every aspect of railway operation new ways had to be thought out and put into practice, surely the greatest innovation came about in the change of motive power, and this is well illustrated by R.H.N. when he says, "Our whole attitude of mind changed, - where could we get traction electricians in the East End of London? - - - we turned our boilermakers into electricians!" (11) For, indeed, men who had spent their lifetime career skills in the service of the external combustion engine - the steam locomotive - must now convert those skills into an entirely new and unknown direction with internal combustion and electric motive power.

And so these 'career railwaymen', the men in the front line, under the leadership of such stalwarts as R.H.N. Hardy, constructed their 'new railway' in the face of considerable hardship, working, they knew, towards the

D5500, the very first 'Type-2' diesel locomotive, stands in Cambridge north bay platform 5 in March 1959, just 18 months old and belonging to Dick Hardy's Stratford allocation. These early 'Brush-2's had no route boxes; not visible here is the under-powered 'Mirlees' 1,250h.p. engine; also no longer visible today is the gantry of semaphores and that steam age essential, the tender/tank filler pipe. (RCTS)

'The doyen' in disguise; D5500 now lives in the NRM at York but is unfortunately displayed in its later TOPS guise in 'BR blue' as 31018. The first 20, 'pilot', 'Brush-2's were known as 'toffee-apples' thanks to the shape of their 'fore-and-aft' action power controllers. (Author)

'Type-4' 'English Electric' 2.000h.p 1Co-Co1. TOPS 40. The first B.R. 'big' diesel, and truly the 'Deltic' predecessor. Some 200 were built but while none were allocated to 34G by the mid-1960s, Gateshead's '2,000's visited. D282 comes off the 'Passenger Loco' and is 'right-away' into Gasworks Tunnel and 'Main2' although I doubt she was going far. (RCTS)

modernisation of their railway and facing, beyond their own recognised problems, "the deep seated problems of which" as Hardy points out, "*so many railwaymen were unaware,* (my italics) and which required quite drastic structural treatment." (12) And, indeed, most railway people did not realise just how dire the railway's situation was, did not realise as they tried sincerely to get on with their jobs, that in persevering with the great changes and new ways that faced them in those jobs, they were actually delivering that "drastic structural treatment" which, as Hardy points out, the railway's "deep seated problems" needed. But then, these railway people who worked the trains, worked the stations, worked the signals, worked the track each day, the workers at the front of railway operation, had little knowledge of the great management turmoil that boiled behind this great drive to modernisation, and "no conception" says R.H.N., "of the drama being played out in the corridors of power at Westminster and Marylebone. There the world was different ---." (13)

And here the two worlds, the dichotomy which exists in all great corporations – the world of those who work and the world of those who instruct them how to work – workers and managers – often disagreeing with each other in their different worlds but who, however, must eventually come together, to form one harmonious corporate world. And in the case of British Railways in the 1950s and 1960s, government, management and workforce must bring about a veritable renaissance in the nation's transport system; a renewal which had never been done before; entirely new ways which must be implemented while the old ways still carried on, 'business as usual', in the face of the great renaissance itself which went forward in spite of, and somewhat because of, the repeated contradictory attempts by alternating political parties to repair the railway, run down and worn out after transporting the nation through two World Wars, but often merely exacerbating the growing financial deficit.

By the mid-1960s, however, the new railway was settling down and David Clough has latterly summarised the situation at about the time when I joined King's Cross MPD, railway pro and con;

"The Modernisation Plan was to be delivered over a 15-year term and it is fair to say that the railways looked markedly different by the latter part of the 1960s when compared to 1955. Train services were cleaner, faster and more punctual." But;

"Financial losses were still being incurred", and, "There was a dubious legacy in respect of the diesel locomotive fleet and a serious weeding-out process of unreliable types was in progress." (14)

But the deed had been done, "the reckoning" paid and, to continue with Hardy who personally experienced and oversaw the railway renaissance, "We had seemingly achieved the impossible, we had made history," (15) while David Clough, concluding his account of this history in 2014, points out that, "Clearly there was still more to do." And indeed there was much more to do in order to break even. In 1964 diesel power was supreme in the King's Cross area, quite reliable, and now accepted and operated by men who had gone through the painful transition from steam power and now recognised the comforts and benefits of the new power which had been effectively "weeded"; but this transformation from steam locomotion and its accompanying railway system, developed over some 150 years, was, as we have seen, a slow and inefficient process; old habits died hard and the new, convenient power was still maintained in the out-moded and inconvenient ways of the unwieldy old power.

CHAPTER 3

SHED DUTY

And so, despite a declared reduction in manpower during 1962-64 from 502,000 to 399,000 - during which time productivity increased by 26%! – a need for 'second men' at King's Cross was advertised in October 1964 and I joined the new ECML diesel railway, its new locomotives still serving their first decade and still maintained to a large extent on steam operating principles. From early 1965, still officially a 'passed-cleaner', I covered diagrams in 'No.8', the 'Shed Duty', link, never moving far from King's Cross, usually toing and froing, 'light-engine', between the station and the 'Passenger Loco' with occasional welcome 'light-engine' trips through Gasworks and Copenhagen tunnels and climbing Holloway Bank to Finsbury Park where the 'Traction Maintenance Depot' was situated on the down side just south of Finsbury Park station, occupying the west side of 'Clarence Yard', a once busy 30 road marshalling yard. 'Clarence Yard', as we usually referred to it – officially 'Finsbury Park TMD' - was the first purpose-built diesel maintenance depot in the country, opened early in 1960, and by 1965 was responsible for the maintenance of some 180 diesel locomotives which worked the King's Cross area, stabled and serviced at the old steam sheds at Hornsey, Hatfield and Hitchin and, of course, King's Cross 'Passenger Loco'.

The view ahead from the cab of a DMU crossing from King's Cross main station to enter Gasworks Tunnel on the down slow, surely following a 'Deltic' which has left its trade-mark 'clag' at the tunnel mouth as it entered 'Down Main 1'. (Paul Hepworth)

The 'distant's off for the slow road into at 'Belle Isle'; Copenhagen's south portals hidden by the fly-over taking up traffic across the main lines into the goods yard. (Colour-Rail).

This local light engine work was the way in which we new second men, in company with our young, newly passed drivers, gained immediate experience with all the East Coast main line locomotives, '350' (08) shunters, 'Type-1' to 'Type 5', we rode them all, they were our everyday fare, and while the 'Type 5' (55) 'Deltics' were, of course, recognised as something a bit special even then, a 3,000h.p. locomotive, unique to our East Coast Main Line, the great 'Deltic cult' which has been woven about them since their retirement, was still in process of fabrication during the '60s; they were just a special kind of variation on the variety of locos which we ferried about at King's Cross every day.

The first break in this routine of shed duty came for me on Monday, 28th December 1964 - and initiated my determination to keep a record of all my jobs - which I did until my final turn on Sunday, 3 March 1968.

At about 14.00 hours on that already darkening December afternoon I signed on for a listed 'Relief' shift with ebullient Bobby Bull, one of the young, recently passed-out drivers who we new second men usually accompanied. At about 18.00 as we sat waiting for something to turn up the foreman suddenly called for me. A '4 link', 'Cambridge', second-man had not turned up for duty and passed-cleaner Hill was the most senior second man in the rest room.

"Go over the Passenger-Loco and join driver Hawker on the 18.17 Peterborough engine," was the instruction and I didn't need telling twice. I descended the end of platform 10 in a much more accomplished fashion to that adopted on that first fateful night some two months earlier and found driver Hawker preparing to leave with 'Type-2' 'Brush' (31) D5676. I believe Jim Hawker was in 'number-2' 'Leeds' Link, but he was certainly way beyond the shed duty links and also used to bigger

Above: Holloway Bank looking north on the up side, 'Brush' cousins run the last lap into King's Cross; 'Type-4' D1632 - TOPS 47050 ex-D1632 last at Tinsley (Sheffield) - up the main on a 'Cambridge Buffet' and a 'Type-2' telling 'porkies' with a suburban set up the slow; Holloway carriage sidings on the down side beyond and the cattle/car dock stood on the up side, extreme right. (Paul Hepworth)

Right: Looks north continuing the view from the DMU, approaching Finsbury Park on 'Down Slow 2'; the goods roads branch left to join the down Canonbury lines which run under the main lines beyond the far downside signal gantry, to pass Clarence Yard and the TMD and run together into Finsbury Park down side. (Paul Hepworth)

machinery than 'Brush-2s', and he was the first 'running man' I had worked with. He was a pleasant, good-natured man with that certain 'main line dignity' which you didn't find among the younger, newly passed, shed duty drivers. He greeted me civilly and said he believed the train heating boiler, my job, was alright. I took the hint and dived into the engine room to fire up my first 'Spanner' 'in the field', the simplest of the locomotive train heating boilers. It was already running, Jim had set it going, and it circulated grumpily, maintaining a good head of steam, ready to go, as were we. Jim dropped D5676 down onto those fateful exit stops where I had wrestled with the failed 'Peak', but this time, in great anticipation - my first 'running job' - I jumped down and reported our presence and intent

Looks south, an unfortunately misty panorama from Finsbury Park down side; the Canonbury lines come in left from under the distant main line and are joined by the down goods roads from Holloway Bank (previous picture) while the remains of Clarence Yard sidings stand beyond; 'No.2 box' is centre right and Finsbury Park TMD, 34G, stands behind 'No.2' right. (Paul Hepworth)

Finsbury Park TMD. The six roads seen from the fueling points and the approach from Finsbury Park down side. Three 'Deltics' receive attention in the company of lesser locomotion. (Colour-Rail)

The standard B.R. shunt or 'pilot' 'English Electric' 6KT powered 350h.p. 0-6-0 diesel-electric loco-motive; D3619 is ex-works at Doncaster and won't shine like this for long. Finsbury Park TMD's (34G) allocation was 35 in 1965. They became TOPS class '08'. (Colour-Rail)

The very first of the 'Deltic's (55) was D9000 'Royal Scots Grey', allocated to Haymarket (Edinburgh). In 1981 D9000 was saved to become 55022 (the TOPS system couldn't handle 55000!) and in that guise the preserved pioneer worked the 'Norseman' special between King's Cross and Newcastle via the Durham coast on Saturday, 11th September 2010. Here 55022 sweeps through Hatfield on the return leg to London. (Author)

to work the 18.17 Peterborough on the exit-phone to the signal box who soon let us out into Gasworks tunnel mouth from where we reversed onto our train on one of the suburban platforms, platforms 11-16 in those days, a movement I had by now made many times; but this time I was going to proceed into Gasworks tunnel at the head of a booked passenger train, through Copenhagen, and then venture beyond Finsbury Park, northwards, first stop Hatfield!

Of that first momentous outward journey I recall sitting in that right hand seat, enthralled as we blasted full throttle to the top of the bank at Potters Bar and then on outwards through the dark Hertfordshire countryside to Hatfield, on to Hitchin, then calling at stations; Biggleswade, Sandy, St. Neots, Huntingdon, which had, until then, just been a blur seen from a speeding express's carriage window as we dashed northwards on the annual trip to my mother's family in County Durham.

At Peterborough we were relieved by Peterborough men, and took our break in the crew room situated on the station. We were eventually told that our return working was approaching and stepped onto the platform into bitter cold and suddenly fast falling snow. We relieved a pair of Doncaster men on Immingham's 'Brush 2', D5543, which arrived at the head of 3E29, a fitted, refrigerated fish train from Grimsby, and agreed with them that the fish had no need for refrigeration that night! They left us with the always hoped for message passed on to relieving crews, "she's alright mate", and we settled into the gratefully well heated cab with a green signal in front of us and the guard's green lamp giving us 'right away' from his brake way behind us as we set off briskly into pitch blackness beyond Peterborough, relieved only by the reflection of 5543's lights on the thickly falling flakes. These fish trains were fully fitted and despite their 'class 3' designation were given express treatment. And so, with Jim concentrating on the signals as they leaped out of the increasingly thickening snow, we bowled along in fine style at a steady 75/80 m.p.h. until somewhere in the vicinity of Huntingdon up came the yellows and we were turned in, slow road, and then brought to a stand in a countryside illuminated only by that sultry glow from 5543's fitful lights. "Well, with this lot falling, mate," said Jim, "you'd better get down and find out why they've turned us in and stopped us."

During training in 'Rules and regulations', rule 55 had been impressed upon us more than any of the many others. Rule 55, 'Detention of Trains on Running Lines', dealt at length with steps to be taken when a train is stopped at a danger signal; but on this night, in the middle of the snowbound fenlands, I got down immediately to go to the lineside telephone which was situated a little down the embankment, away from the up slow signal which itself occupied the less than 'four feet' between sleeper ends and embankment top. I went forward through fresh white snow between the sleeper-ends - and then, without thought, stepped down the embankment in order to walk directly across to the telephone in its snow-topped black and white striped box - into snow which swallowed me up to the waist ! As I floundered about Jim leaned out of the cab and asked me seriously how I was doing. Now one of my regular young shed duty drivers would no doubt have found this highly amusing, but Jim kept a straight face and so preserved my dignity as I eventually floundered to the phone to find out from the Huntingdon signalman that our delay had nothing to do with the weather but was caused by a broken rail on the up fast. I returned carefully along the sleeper ends and spent the rest of the trip standing, thawing out, close to the heaters at the back of the cab. We weren't kept much longer and proceeded into the snow-filled night, never seeing any sign of a broken rail nor anybody out to attend to it, in fact nothing stirred in the bleak, black night except the Huntingdon signalman who gave us a wave as we ran by, then on through the lights of the deserted station. I didn't, thankfully, need to make another trip to the phone, but the rest of the journey was accomplished in a stop start manner that eventually brought us into snowy King's Cross Goods around 3.00 a.m.

After this eventful introduction to 'running' I returned to 'shed-duty', light-engine work around 'The Cross' and Finsbury Park. But on Tuesday, 5th 1965 I recorded another loco landmark when I drove a locomotive for the first time; not a humble 'Type-2', nor even a 'big Brush' 'Type-4', (47) but the biggest of all - a unique 'Type-5' 'Deltic'. I was on '7 Relief', 06.40 to 15.40, for the first time with driver Johnny Hopwood, a smart, dapper young driver, with a very pleasant, chatty disposition and so easy to get on with. Our train duly arrived behind its 'Deltic', - which one, unfortunately, on this momentous occasion, I have not recorded - we greeted the incoming main line men and let them go home, and Johnny casually waved me into the driving seat. How much surprise registered on my face I can't recall, but Johnny asked me if I'd driven and when I said that I hadn't he remarked that it was about time I did. So I sat in the hallowed left hand seat for the first time and waited eagerly for the empty coaches in front of us to leave when I pressed a starter button for the very first time, bringing to life that unique 'Deltic howl' from the rear of the two 'Napier' engines; station 'standing orders' required that when running 'light engine' only one 'Deltic' engine must be run, and of course, using the rear engine reduced cab noise. Johnny stood next to me, straddling the well leading into the nose compartment as I dropped the loco air brake off, gingerly pulled the long controller back, expecting 1,750 horses immediately to gallop us along the platform - and met the first 'Deltic' idiosyncrasy - nothing happened at all! I would find that this was the usual way with all 'English Electric' control equipment, the controller slides straight round the quadrant without the guiding power notches of 'Brush' equipment and power does not develop immediately, especially when using only one 'Deltic' engine. Johnny told me to shut off and start

again and eventually, with the controller halfway round the quadrant and our 'Napier' exhaust howling into the heights of King's Cross's great station roof, we moved sedately along the platform to come to a hastily braked stand at the 'country end' signals. When the 'dolly' (the disc shunt-signal) came off Johnny piloted me as I eased the giant diesel over the station yard layout; out across the confusing maze of conflicting crossovers, 'dolly' to 'dolly', to stop in the murky mouth of Gasworks tunnel, select 'back gear' - steam talk for 'reverse' - and wait for Johnny to call across the cab, 'Right back' when the 'dolly' behind us came off, then, gradually becoming familiar with the controller's idiosyncrasies, I reversed the beast gently round past the suburban platforms and into the 'Milk Yard', the most south-westerly corner of King's Cross station, from where a final 'dolly' signalled us forward into the 'Passenger Loco'. Once past the entry 'dolly' locos left the control of the signal box and points for movements inside the loco-yard were set by hand pulled levers; on arrival from the 'milk yard', the second man pulled the points and the locomotive shunted, at

'Deltic' D9012 pauses at Grantham northbound on 24th March 1981 in the last months of her life; 'Crepello', by then TOPS numbered 55012, was withdrawn that September. My several runs to Grantham and beyond were all made in 'Brush-4s' but I often 'shedded' 'Crepello'. (RCTS)

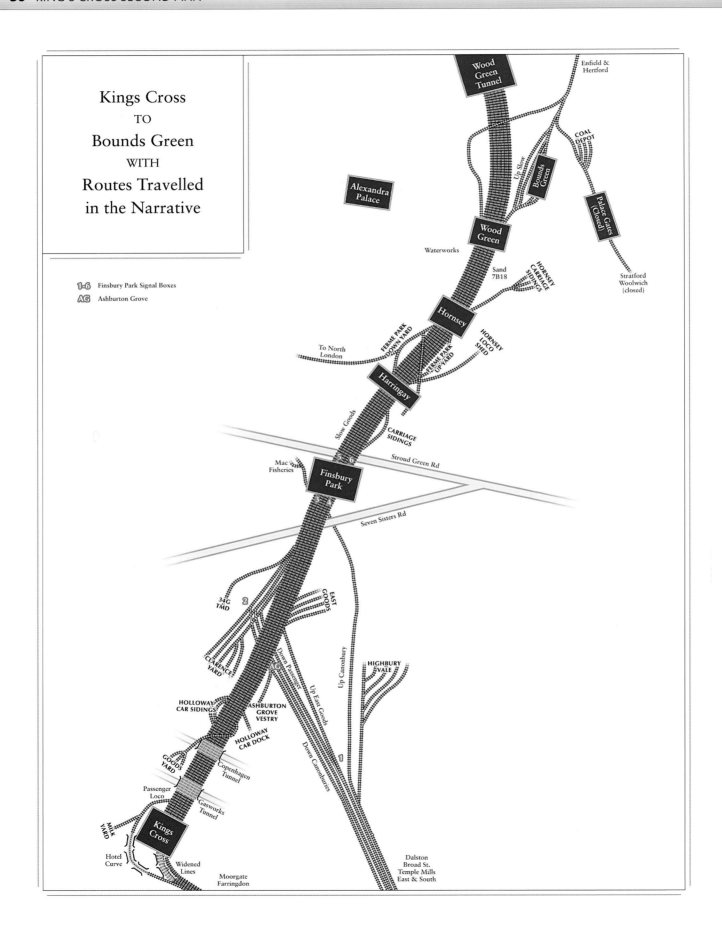

Kings Cross
TO
Bounds Green
WITH
Routes Travelled
in the Narrative

1-6 Finsbury Park Signal Boxes

AG Ashburton Grove

the shed foreman's direction from his office on the west side of the yard entry, to enter one of the two refuelling roads on the east side of the 'loco'; the furthest, the only covered road, overlooking the down slow departure roads from the suburban platforms as described above. On this first driving turn, Johnny duly got down and 'second-manned' me, trustfully walking in front of the big 'Deltic' which I kept in check with the air brake, hardly daring to touch the controller which I'd coaxed into a position which gave just enough power to move us when I dropped the brake off, as Johnny pulled the appropriate hand point levers to set us into the relevant refuelling road.

The next day, Wednesday, 6th January 1965, I was booked 'As Required' 08.00-15.00. Just one hour into the shift, the 'requirement' suddenly took on a new interest when the foreman told me to travel out to Hornsey, walk to Ferme Park up yard, find and join driver Dawkins on the 'Provender Runround' engine. The 'runrounds' were goods transfer runs between the local yards, by the 1960s mainly between King's Cross Goods Yard and Ferme Park yards, the huge up and downside marshalling yards situated each side of the main running lines between Harringay and Hornsey stations. These through yards were opened in 1887/8 and took mineral and through freight loads away from Clarence Yard down-side and East Goods up-side yards, the 1876 'dead-ended' yards south of Finsbury Park, relieving and assisting the ever increasing flow of nineteenth century GNR goods traffic. A flyover across the running lines provided access between the yards. Although this traffic had declined remarkably post-war, Ferme Park was still busy in the mid-'60s although already a shadow of those halcyon days when both yards were packed with trains of wagons, and six-wheeler shunt engines, the yard 'pilots' – 'modern' 1920s Gresley J50s and ancient Stirling GNR J52 saddle-backs - almost as old as the yards they worked – which shunted eternally, sorting and reforming the arriving trains into other, departing trains, according to final destinations throughout the land.

Harringay station looking south towards Finsbury Park. A 'Brush-4' occupies the dead end from Ferme Park up yard and has the road to access the fly-over and cross to the down side. Far right is the Harringay curve access to Ferme Park down yard from the North London line. (Paul Hepworth)

Ferme Park fly-over connected up and down yards and also up and down sides of the ECML. (Colour-Rail)

Seen from the Ferme Park fly-over in the 1970s, a DMU hurries along the main line between Harringay and Hornsey. On the right is the north end of Ferme Park up yard with the old steam and diesel loco shed just visible in the background, rebuilding into Hornsey TMD for the new EMUs. (Paul Hepworth)

In diesel days pilot duties were undertaken by the boxy little diesel 0-6-0s known to us as '350's (08) referring to the horse-power of the six-cylinder English Electric engine which trundled them round the still plentiful pre-Freightliner goods and marshalling yards of British railways. Just about 1000 of these tough little units were built between 1953 and 1962 and King's Cross District fielded just 31 in January 1965, shunting in the yards and working the 'run-rounds' between the yards at an alleged maximum speed of 15m.p.h.

On that winter Wednesday I travelled out to Hornsey and carefully crossed the running roads on the boardwalk – no high visibility jackets then - to the north end of Ferme Park up yard where, after a lengthy search of the up yard pilots, I eventually discovered driver Jimmy Dawkins and his toothy grin aboard D3716. We spent some time assisting the single-manned yard pilots in shunting and while most shunting signals were given from Jimmy's side, I soon discovered that, with controls duplicated each side of the cab, a 'pilot's' second man, where provided, could be expected to take over on occasions when a shunter directed from his side, although, with a 'greenhorn' aboard, Jimmy came across the cab whenever such a move was needed, for shunting was a dangerous art, calling for speed and precision by both loco crew, who must quickly alternate between carefully judged fore and back movements at the shunters' direction, (without 'nipping' him!) and the shunters themselves who deftly hooked and unhooked between wagons with their long hooked poles - taking care not to be 'nipped'!

We made one return trip to King's Cross Goods Yard that day, and I was initiated into the bone-shaking experience of piloting a string of unbraked wagons at '350' top speed along the ECML South's London Area goods roads; we perched on small round 'bar stools' although it was often more comfortable to stand as each and every rail joint sent its own distinct vibration up through the trundling wheels, along the whole length of the locomotive frame and from head to toe of any human frame which was in contact with it. We were finished at 17.30 on that Wednesday - office hours - and I had begun to learn another kind of humble but essential loco driving skill.

On the following Sunday, the 10th of January I started a week of nights, and after spending Sunday night 'As Required' without being required at all, I was booked 'Engine Movements' 22.00 'til 06.00 for the Monday night - and thus initiated into another facet of the engineman's art. 'Engine Movements' consisted in keeping the locomotives on-shed tidy and manageable. When refuelling and basic checks had been completed on arriving locomotives they had to be 'stood off' from the two refuelling roads to await departure for their next duty. The shed running (or 'outside') foreman oversaw this order and management of the 'Passenger Loco'; he must know and observe the rosters of arriving locomotives and so arrange them on the shed roads in such a way that earliest departures were stabled nearest the exit stops, no easy task in the 'Passenger Loco's' cramped conditions. Assisting him in this constant rearrangement of the shed were the 'engine movements' crews; two drivers and two second men during the day and just one pair during the hoped for peace of the night. For my first 'Engine Movements' shift I was paired with Horace Yates, a driver in his sixties who was condemned to end his driving days permanently rostered on 'Engine Movements' as the result of an accident he suffered years previously on the footplate of a 'Pacific'. Gresley 'Pacifics' had linked regulator levers each side of the cab and, as I heard it, Horace's fireman confirmed a signal which Horace couldn't see from his side as being 'off' and then opened the regulator from his, right hand, side, thus lifting the left hand lever straight into Horace's eye. Horace lost the eye - and the rest of his main line career. How long he had been confined to the 'Passenger Loco' on 'movements' by 1965 I don't know, but in consideration of the bitterness and resentment many would have felt at such deprivation I discovered during that first night of 'engine movements' that he was a most patient and understanding 'old-school' man to work with. We were quite busy into the small hours when, with nothing moving and the yard tidied to the foreman's satisfaction, that gentleman retired to his office on the west side of the loco yard and I 'mashed' a can of tea with Horace who then also disappeared to an unknown place of rest which he had established somewhere in the old building, while I spent until after 3 a.m. alone in the engine movements crew room, the only sounds the crack and tick from the cooling engines of the most recent arrivals on the shed, the occasional rumble of the 'Brush 2' (31) station pilot, marshalling vans out in the station and the 'Milk Yard' for the morning departures - and perhaps the whispers of the many Great Northern and LNE engine men who had rested briefly between their arrivals and departures and their preparations and disposals in King's Cross 'Bottom Shed' and 'Passenger Loco'.

Soon after three Horace returned refreshed and we had another can of tea until the first 'Deltics' came onto the refuelling roads off the first up sleeper and mail trains, and the foreman returned with instructions regarding the placement of these first arrivals after refuelling. We were then kept busy until the 6 a.m. EM crews relieved us.

It later occurred to me that I was fortunate in serving my first 'Engine Movements' shift on nights, for it gave me time to learn the layout of the yard; the names of the roads; 'shed road', 'back road', 'ash-pit', 'pit road' (the old turntable pit was still *in situ*), 'the corner', etc., and which levers to heave over or back in order to set a route into or out of each road. And there were times, Bank Holiday

weekends in particular, when the cramped nature of the 'Passenger Loco' and the need for quick turn-rounds made 'engine movements' a busy and demanding job, in fact at such times the two pairs of drivers and second men became one team of four men, following the harassed foreman's instructions, each man nipping in and out of cabs, moving engines, pulling points, whichever action was most convenient to the moment in each necessary manoeuvre needed to move locomotives into and out of the various roads, and all managed in concert with engines arriving and departing the depot. I loved it! But it would not have been at all easy to serve one's first, unpractised, 'engine movements' turn at such a busy time without knowledge of roads and switches.

'Engine Movements' turned up quite often after this, welcome as a change to the regular diet of 'relief' or 'as required' shifts, but my next break from 'shed duty' turns occurred during week commencing Monday the

The 'Passenger Loco' from the end of platforms 7/8. A 'Brush-4' enters the covered road while a sister is stabled with a 'Baby Deltic' on the 'ash-pit'. A 'Deltic' stands beyond on the 'pit road' and a 'Brush-2' on the 'back road'. Exit was unavoidably into Gasworks tunnel. The exit road runs behind the low wall while the 'stops', the scene of my first eventful shift, are just out of shot on the left. (Colour-Rail)

15th February when I changed turns to oblige a second man in number 5, 'empty coaches', link, even though it meant my working two successive 'late turn' (14.00 to 22.00 approx.) weeks.

'277 diagram' was typical of the many 'mixed' jobs found in the King's Cross local, lower link, rosters. How these rosters were worked out – manually, with pen and paper, no computers - in order to incorporate every local light engine, stock and suburban passenger working was, and still is, a mystery and a wonder to me. A breakdown of '277 diagram' will illustrate the 'colourful' variety of these jobs in the days before multiple units replaced the need for every train to have a separate locomotive on the front. The 'highlight' of '277' was the 17.20 'fast' inner-suburban peak hour trip with a 'Brush 2' (31), from King's Cross suburban station, non-stop to Potters Bar, then Brookmans Park – my home town and site of my first booking-office job respectively - and terminating at Hatfield at 17.49.

However, before we made this epic sprint some intricate preparations were made. After signing on at 14.15 we rode out on the 14.30 suburban service to Hornsey station where we crossed the running lines and the top, north, end of Ferme Park up yard, to Hornsey shed; today the site of Hornsey EMU traction depot, much enlarged and extended to stable and maintain brand new 'Siemens' 'Desiro' electric units to work the Govia 'Great Northern' suburban services, which are planned in 2018 to connect to Govia's 'Thameslink' services to Brighton and other southern destinations.

At Hornsey for the 1965 277 diagram we reported to the foreman who allocated us our locomotive and told us which road it was stabled on among the many locomotives on-shed, an old ex-steam shed, but offering much more cover and room to manoeuvre than the 'Passenger Loco'. Having prepared our 'Brush 2', we were booked off the shed at 15.35 when we ran light-engine to Bounds Green to pick up our first

Hornsey steam shed about 1960 with the first cuckoos in the nest. The '350' is grimy enough to blend in, but the new 'Brush-2' looks distinctly alien next to the faithful 1922 G.N.R. vintage 'J50' tanks. (Colour-Rail)

Hornsey TMD in September 2016. A new 'Bombardier' 'Electrostar' 387119 joins the mix of GN EMUs in the crowded sidings . A year later the depot is twice the size and prepared to receive a new allocation of Siemens 'Desiro City' EMUs. (Author)

set of coaches. Now, to run down to Bounds Green carriage sidings from Hornsey loco, both on the up side, involved running into Ferme Park up goods yard, changing ends, crossing to the down yard over the fly-over, then running down through Wood Green (nowadays Alexandra Palace) station, crossing the main lines again by the fly-over onto the Hertford Loop, - 'the down Enfield' - then, after changing ends again, back across onto the 'up Enfield', then switching onto the access road into Bounds Green sidings, (nowadays the TMD for the East Coast electric '91' locomotives and their Mark IV coach sets) where we picked up our empty coaches. After this excursion we were booked to leave Bounds Green at 16.10, arrive at Finsbury Park at 16.20 where we became a passenger train, departing

at 16.24 and arriving into King's Cross at 16.30. The timings were quite tight, but it was important that we met them and left Finsbury Park on time as the evening peak got under way. Such diversions and manoeuvres were common place in the days before fixed sets and multiple-units, with a cab at each end of the train, and when locomotive top-and-tailing was, to my knowledge, unheard of; therefore, at a terminus every train must have its arriving locomotive detached and run round, or else another attached at the other end, before it could proceed. By the 1960s, however, all off-peak suburban services were worked by diesel multiple units, while morning and evening peak trains in and out of King's Cross, Moorgate and Broad Street were still locomotive worked.

An 'English Electric-4' brings a down ECML express along the level between Hornsey and Wood Green (Alexandra Palace) by Waterworks box and sidings. (Paul Hepworth)

Looking south from Wood Green (Alexandra Palace), a DMU for Welwyn Garden City approaches the station on 'slow-1'. The nearest lines are the up goods and slow roads from the Hertford loop and Bounds Green, with 'turn-outs' to the up slow, then the up main and down lines. Hornsey carriage sidings may just be glimpsed between the signals. (Paul Hepworth)

Above: Looking north from Wood Green (Alexandra Palace), a DMU approaches up the slow with the Hertford Loop fly-over behind and Bounds Green sidings on the right, accessed from the fly-over. (Paul Hepworth)

Left: Looking back to Wood Green from above Wood Green tunnel's south portal, a DMU comes down the main, the Hertford Loop fly-over in the background. (Paul Hepworth)

Upon our arrival into King's Cross on '277 diagram' with the 16.30, therefore, we were detached from the front of our train which now became its rear, and upon its departure we followed it down to the platform end departure signals where we waited until we were 'called forward' by the station yard 'dollies', then reversed onto our 17.20 'flyer' to Hatfield. We returned more slowly from Hatfield, departing at 18.15, running all stations to Oakleigh Park, then a dash to Finsbury Park, arriving King's Cross at 18.54 when we were uncoupled, ran round the train and out into the station yard again, then backed down onto the 19.55 Cambridge departure where we were relieved by a homeward bound Cambridge crew.

But the diagram was not yet over! After our relief we then travelled out as passengers again, by the 20.03

Looks south from the end of Finsbury Park platforms 2/3; the line forks in front of 'No.4 box' where the DMU has departed for King's Cross and the left turn joins the up Canonbury line out of platform 1 past the box, the way to walk to the distant East Goods Yard. A 'Deltic' charges north down the main. (Paul Hepworth)

departure to Finsbury Park station from where we tramped back off the end of the up platform towards King's Cross between the up coal road and the up 'Canonbury' – in the dark – no 'high visibility' clothing then - to East Goods Yard, the remains of the huge 1876 40 road up-side marshalling yard complimentary to Clarence Yard on the down side. In East Goods we relieved a set of Hornsey men aboard a 'Sulzer-2' (24) at the head of 3N01 empty sleepers which they had brought from Hornsey sidings. We eventually took 'N01s' into King's Cross and stood behind them, keeping them steam-heated, as the overnight passengers boarded and so turned 3N01, empty coaching stock, into 1N01, an overnight sleeper departure. Where this sleeper's far away destination was I know not for at 22.15 it was the turn of a couple of Hornsey men to relieve us, when King's Cross '277 diagram' was completed and we were

able to walk round to the crew room, put our bill into the list office and go home.

I worked '277 diagram' with driver Freddy Halls from Monday to Friday - rest day Saturday - that week, with much interest but without incident until the very last, Friday evening, the 19th February 1965, when, as Freddy took D5607 on our 'flyer', full throttle through Potters Bar tunnel, the brakes began to apply - someone had pulled the emergency cord! Well, Freddy didn't want us stopped in the tunnel, whatever, and was able to run the ejector to keep enough vacuum in the train-pipe long enough for us to run to a stand in Potters Bar down slow platform where I jumped down to see what had occurred. I was confronted by two irate passengers complaining that the door of their compartment had blown open as we exited Barnet Tunnel and approached Oakleigh Park station when the cord was pulled - an

'English Electric-2' D5907 leaves Barnet Tunnel on the main line with a down evening fast suburban service in October 1961 just about where a door was alleged to have opened on my 'Brush-2' powered 'Hatfield Flyer' in February 1965. (RCTS)

action which produced no reaction in the brake system until we were in the tunnel. Really, the incident should have been reported immediately by the guard, which report would have resulted in a long examination of, and delay to, our train. In the event the guard, who, while I was listening to the passengers' complaint that we did not stop earlier, had found and reset the appropriate emergency valve, found nothing further amiss and declared us fit for departure, while Freddy, stood at the cab door, confirmed that all was well with the brake our end and agreed that we were ready to go - so I jumped aboard and away we went - at 17.43, only a couple of minutes lost, leaving indignant passengers, open-mouthed, on the platform! The incident was not really handled correctly but the confrontation on the platform reminded me, ironically, of my several years of first time employment in the booking office of that very same, Potters Bar station, in my old home town, some nine years previously, as also did arrival at the

next station, little old Brookmans Park, where I also worked for some time in the booking office, alternating shifts with gruff but easy-going Mr. Hubert Daniels, station-master; every station had a station-master in those days. We terminated at Hatfield where, although I, of course, did not know it at the time, I would eventually return to booking office work.

These occasional trips away from shed duty seemed destined to be accompanied by incident for me, and this remarkable destiny continued in what promised to be a pleasant late afternoon trip out on the Saturday of the week after my 'Hatfield Flyer', '277 diagram'. Having waited since booking on at 14.00 'As Required' with merry Mickey Loughran we were told to catch the 16.40 local out to Oakleigh Park and there relieve a crew working the breakdown train; the huge 45 ton area breakdown crane itself, and the attendant cluster of vans carrying the breakdown crew and their equipment, and take it down to New Barnet, where a cross-over allowed us to

Yet to be named 'Gordon Highlander', 'Deltic' D9016 comes up through Brookmans Park in June 1963; here, and in Potters Bar booking office in 1956–7, I started work. (RCTS)

propel the train over all tracks to the up side, run round, then run back up the slow road to the breakdown train's home in Clarence Yard sidings, adjacent to the TMD.

This circular trip was frequently made by the breakdown train on a Saturday when the monster crane would be used to re-rail any wagons which had come off the road during the previous week or so's shunting in the local goods yards; it was good practice for the breakdown crew and kept the yards tidy. On this Saturday the train had set out earlier and the loco crew's shift was finished when we reached them around 17.00. We took over 'Sulzer-2' (24) D5070 and soon ran the train through New Barnet station on the down slow, stopping just clear of the cross-over north of the station and waiting until main-line traffic permitted the New Barnet North signalman to set the cross-over right across the main lines behind us, pulled the ground 'dolly' off and Mickey gingerly propelled the giant and its attendants, across the main lines into the up yard where we changed ends, uncoupled, and ran round the train.

I coupled us up at the south end, and we awaited the road to proceed up the slow. It wasn't long before the 'dolly' came off, Mickey dropped the air brake off and eased D5070 towards the turnout onto the up slow road. We hadn't gone far when frantic shouts took me across to Mickey's side of the cab as he brought us to a sudden stand. I got down and joined one of the gangers as he came forward from the train, saying that they'd seen a bouncing movement from one of the monster crane's leading bogies. We carefully examined the bogie and wheels and all seemed to be stood square and firm on the rails - so we climbed back up, loco and van respectively, and Mickey moved us slowly away again as I hung out of the cab door - and I can hear the bumping and banging now as that set of wheels lifted from the railhead and the whole fabric of that mammoth crane shook from side to side as Mickey again brought things to a shuddering stand. Well, luckily we were still clear of the yard turn-out - and even more luckily she hadn't come off when we were propelling over the cross-over, when the

An unusually clean '350' D3309 makes unusual power for the area breakdown crane, emerging from the north end of Wood Green tunnel on the 18th of June 1962, reminiscent of my fateful breakdown crane trip in February 1965. (RCTS)

New Barnet North box during its last 1970s days. A 'Deltic' brings an ECML express up the main. The up slow can just be seen behind the box and the yard where the area break down crane derailed is beyond. (Paul Hepworth)

A clearer view of New Barnet's northern approaches in 2017. A suburban '313' EMU approaches the station up the slow; the North box stood off the up platform end behind the train and the cross-over came across all running lines beyond the bridge abutments. The nearest line is the last remaining yard road which still runs the length of the station. (Author)

whole East Coast Main line would have been blocked! I well remember the calm and resigned approach of the gang as they surveyed the derailed bogie and decided they could 'easily' lift it back on with their own jib.

Well, it was about 17.30-18.00 dusk when the crane came off and around 21.30 when the gang declared that they were quite sure that we could move out. They had raised the crane's great jib, somehow chained the bogie- and eventually lifted and shifted the whole lot back onto the railhead. We both held our breaths when we got the road, Mickey gently eased the controller open and the leviathan moved once more; easily and without further trouble out onto the slow road and through to Ferme Park up yard. From Ferme Park we crept along the goods

road through Finsbury Park station, then along the 'Up Canonbury' line - today's Moorgate line towards Drayton Park – to isolated Finsbury Park No.1 signal box, where we ran round, crossed onto the 'Down Canonbury' – from Moorgate today - which burrowed under the main lines and took us back to join the down goods road just south of Finsbury Park station, the access point into both the TMD and the remaining Clarence Yard sidings where the breakdown train was stabled.

I record a finish time of 22.30 in Clarence Yard TMD where we stabled D5070. And so the end of an eventful shift which finished later than expected due to an accident which could have had much more serious consequences. I had a day off on Sunday, 28th February.

A 'Brush-4' leads a main-line departure out of a scaffolded King's Cross platform 5 past the box in the 1970s. The 'Brush-4' could be seen throughout British railways on every kind of train until HSTs replaced them on main line passenger workings at the end of the 1970s. (Paul Hepworth)

With just a few 'running' jobs, 'shed duty' from March through to June 1965 took its routine course, with my never getting very far but never bored, working on every type of ECML locomotive. Among the few journeys I made, an early morning Cambridge return with '4-link' driver Ernie Hemmings on Tuesday, 16th March was remarkable in that we had a 'Brush-4', D1535 (47), one of the most successful main-line diesel-electric types, which eventually ran trains, almost literally, on railways from Lands' End to John o' Groats. They were still being delivered in 1965, and while I'd ridden quite a few each way light-engine between station and 'Passenger Loco' - and indeed one played a part in my very first eventful shift as related at the opening of my narrative - this was the first time I experienced one at work, and on such a lightly loaded train the acceleration and running of an extra 1400 horses compared with the usual 'Brush' or 'Sulzer' 'type 2' was quite something; D1535 made light work of things and rarely needed a wide controller once

she'd got things moving. With the 1967 'rationalisation' 'Brush-4's would become regular power on Cambridge turns and even on empty stock workings.

A couple of 6 am turns at the end of the same week and at the other end of the motive power scale saw me on King's Cross Goods Yard's 'No.6 Pilot', or the 'North London Pilot', which proved to be another new experience on a job that could prove to be pretty hair-raising - at least to a relatively new second man. Based on the far west side of the Goods Yard and the ruins of 'Top Shed', the 'North London' '350' pilot hauled loose coupled wagonloads up and down the steep incline to and from St. Pancras Junction, exchanging a still considerable traffic with the old North London line which then provided a western cross-London route for through traffic, just as the Canonbury lines from Finsbury Park connected us to the 'Eastern' through Temple Mills Yard and so on through to London's still busy docks, while the other way across London was via the 'Widened Lines', (see below pages 77ff.) diving down under King's Cross station's east end from York Road via Farringdon and the Snow Hill Bank to Blackfriars; this route took Hornsey men, as I would soon find out, across to 'The South', thus providing an eastern connection round London; they were the nearest thing London's railways then had to today's recently completed 'London Overground' lines and the still building 'Crossrail' project. Apart from inner suburban peak services to and from Moorgate, these lines were totally freight worked by the 1960s, and long gone were the days when various diminutive tank engines worked peak passenger services between north and south London.

But the short transfer from the Goods Yard up to St. Pancras Junction was more in the nature of a 'run-round' turn than a 'pilot' and so required a second man. The 'North London' could be a trial - both for the 350 horses hauling the wagons on the ascending trips, and for the 2 crew members flogging those horses. Driver Harry Nipper was as sharp as his name and I recall how he said, so seriously, during our first diesel-roaring, motor-howling, walking-pace ascent with 17 wagons, that it was sometimes necessary for the second man to jump down and throw sand under the wheels! I stood ready to do this, to Harry's undoubted amusement, on each subsequent grinding ascent. It was not until some time later that I realised that Harry had been what is politely known as 'taking the Michael' out of a naive new second man.

On the 26th of April I started my ten day 'boiler instruction' course at the Eastern Region training school over on 'The Eastern', at Ilford and Stratford depots. By the mid-sixties the sudden transition from steam to diesel traction found British Rail using a brand new fleet of diesel powered locomotives to haul a fleet of steam age, steam heated, coaches, which, of course, was fine and irrelevant during the summer, but with the arrival of winter those coaches needed to be heated. Any alternative heating system to steam would involve the astronomical cost of converting the coaches - although it could be argued that astronomical costs had not stopped British Railways modifications so far - together with an astronomical length of time needed to carry out the conversion, so the logical solution had been thought through at the outset of the diesel replacement programme, for once, and all the early diesel locomotives of 'Type 2'

and upwards carried an oil fired boiler which generated steam to supply the winter needs of passenger train heating. The boiler was housed in a small space, usually just inside the locomotive engine compartment, adjacent to one of the cabs, and was the special preserve of the second man, giving him a winter time *raison d'etre* when he really did become a 'fireman', raising and supplying steam to heat the train - although the nearest he came to the super-human efforts of his steam locomotive predecessors was in opening the cocks to allow water into the boiler and to permit the 'finished article', the generated steam, to pass from the boiler into the train pipe; fuel oil was supplied automatically from the locomotive's supply, and, once fired at the touch of a button, the whole generator - in theory - cycled away on its own, automatically, allowing the fireman to return to his other duties on the right-hand side of the locomotive cab.

Although the need for steam heating with diesels had been anticipated, there was little attempt at standardisation of steam generators - as the boilers were correctly termed - so that four varieties were in use in the mid-1960s, supplied by; Spanner, marks I and III (what happened to the mark II I do not know !), Stone, and Clayton companies, and it was necessary for we second men to go to school to learn the operation of these generators.

So for nine o'clock on that Monday morning I made my way via Liverpool Street to the Eastern Region's boiler school, located in Ilford EMU depot, where boiler theory was taught under the able tutorship of driver-instructors Bill Lincoln and Ian Martin. Five days were spent at Ilford where operating theory and faults and failures were taught with the aid of exploded schematic diagrams and drawings; these classroom days interspersed with much more interesting practical classes at Stratford Works where a special unit in the depot had been fitted out with examples of the several varieties of steam generators, on which we practiced the theoretical skills acquired at Ilford. I think there were about a dozen of us on the course from various depots and most of us had already had some experience of train heating boilers; at King's Cross it had been necessary to test the boilers through the recent winter months during engine preparation and my few trips on suburban passenger trains had involved the care of 'Spanner Mk1s', the simplest boilers, as fitted to the 'Brush-2' locos. I surely took the opportunity to get round the famous 30A Stratford, largest loco depot in the country, when I could, dieselised though it was; but my clearest memory of the boiler course after over 50 years is of big old Bill Lincoln's way of finishing off his expositions at Ilford, fixing us with a gimlet eye and asking in a stentorian below, "Now, is that quite clear !" a habitual rhetorical question, to which we gave variously worded and amused rhetorical affirmatives. The true extent of our understanding was demonstrated the next day at Stratford when the generator boilers could be rigged with every manner of fault and failure – sometimes created their own - for us to diagnose and put right. Bill and Ian were, of course, ex-steam loco men who had found a useful niche in the new diesel age.

We finished our boiler instruction on Friday, 7th May 1965 - just in time for the end of steam heating for the next six months! - with a "Now is that quite clear!" questions and practical test at Stratford, and broke up soon after midday for a full weekend off during which time we could, if we so wished, digest our new found steam generating knowledge!

Our rostered hours at King's Cross were arranged broadly in three weekly lots of eight hours; 'mornings', 06.00-14.00, 'afternoons', 14.00-22.00, with a 'rest day' off during the week, and 'nights', 22.00-06.00, with Sunday guaranteed off, so we could see roughly where we'd be from week to week through the year; but

a certain amount of 'latitude' was taken by the roster office in observing these weekly hours; thus, my week after completion of the boiler instruction course was listed as '06.00-14.00', but actually saw me starting the Monday morning the 10th of May at the 'graveyard' hour of 02.30, on '2 Relief' with young driver George Godbold. We expected to relieve a 'Deltic' on one of the first sleeper/mail arrivals, but this was not to be and by 04.00 we hadn't 'turned a wheel'. At 04.10 I was suddenly ordered to take up '270 Diagram' with driver Harry Tomkinson. '270 Diagram' was akin to '277' which I'd worked for a week back in February and detailed above; but '270' did not include the luxury of a suburban passenger run, and was, indeed, an 'empty coaches' job, involving e.c.s. trips between King's Cross and Hornsey Carriage Sidings where the main-line ECML coaching stock, including sleeping-cars, was stabled and serviced. Hornsey Carriage Sidings were situated on the up side north of Hornsey shed, today's recently extended EMU traction depot, and empties from King's Cross for Hornsey made quite a trek, running all the way down from King's Cross to Wood Green then across the Enfield Loop fly-over as related above on 277 diagram; but empty coaches, having arrived on the 'Up Enfield'. must be propelled into Bounds Green sidings where the loco 'ran round' and the empties were then taken up the

'Sulzer-2' D5050 brings empty stock into King's Cross in 1966. D5050 was the first of 34G's allocation of 25 mighty 'Baby Sulzers'; but they were all sent north in the Summer of '66. (RCTS)

goods road to Hornsey where they were propelled - a tricky move, especially during night-time, guided only by the pin-point 'glow-worms' of light from the shunters' lamps – into the carriage sidings.

On that May Monday morning we were booked to leave King's Cross at 04.30 and allowed a half hour for the circuit to Hornsey, where we unhooked, 'stood off', had a mash of tea, and left for King's Cross with a freshly prepared empty train at about 06.30, ambling gently back in procession with other stock, 'run-round' freight, and light-engine workings, along the up slow and goods roads and eventually arriving back into 'the Cross' at about our booked time of 07.10.

In King's Cross our 'coaches' became an East Coast express, and the passengers boarded while we patiently awaited its departure, when, released from the buffer stops, we followed our 'dollies' out into the station yard and 'stood off' on one of the dead ends, taking the chance to have our meal break until the 'dolly' came off and we were directed onto our 08.35 departure - for Hornsey Carriage Sidings - via Bounds Green - due at

12 noon! On arrival into the carriage sidings we were relieved by a Hornsey crew and, booked 'home passenger', our shift was finished.

270 diagram was a typical empty coaches diagram and shows just how much non-productive time was spent in the provision and maintenance of coaching stock on the 'old railway'.

To do this job we had an 1160 horse-power 'Sulzer-2', D5055, and I feel sure that this was the diagram on which I first gained a special regard for those boxy little 'Bo-Bo' locomotives – which have latterly become known as 'Rats' by less discerning enthusiasts; 151 were built by British Railways and Beyer, Peacock from 1958, eventually to become TOPS class '24', while no less than 327 uprated units, TOPS '25', mainly for the Midland Region, followed from 1961. They were all powered by the gutsy, 'tickety-tock', 6-cylinder Sulzer 6LDA28 engine of 1,160h.p. (24s) or 1,250h.p. (25s), and soon gave me the impression that they could haul anything that was hung on behind them! Finsbury Park/Hornsey had an allocation of 25 of the original 1,160h.p. jobs in

'Brush-2' D5644 brings another train of empties into 6. Empty coach workings were the preserve of the 'Type-2's until the 'locomotive rationalisation' of 1967. (RCTS)

'Type-2' 'Sulzer' 1,160h.p. Bo-Bo, TOPS '24'. 'Sulzer-2' D5094 comes out of 8 (7) into the sunshine to wait access to the yard in order to pick up another set of empties. D5094 and D5095 were an odd couple at 34G after the main batch from D5050 to D5072. (RCTS)

1965; D5050-D5072 and D5094-D5095. They worked the empty stock diagrams and the inner suburban peak passenger trains, while Hornsey crews had them for the cross-London transfer freight trips, as I would find out later in the year.

'Brush-2s' were nominally more powerful than the 'Sulzer-2s' with their original 'Mirlees' 12-cylinder JVS12T engines uprated from 1250 to 1365 horse-power, although, in the mid-60s, these 'Mirlees' units were being steadily replaced by the even more powerful – and musical - English Electric 12SV power plants of 1,470h.p. But, in spite of these extra horses, a 'Brush', it seemed to me, never 'got away' with the same gusto as a 'Sulzer', especially on the peak time inner-suburban passenger workings which the two classes shared, although outer suburban, Cambridge and Peterborough jobs were the preserve of the 'Brush-2s', their 'star turns' being the 'Cambridge Buffet Expresses' which, with seven coaches including a 'Gresley' buffet car, were

booked 80 minutes London to Cambridge, calling at Welwyn Garden City, Stevenage, Hitchin, Letchworth and Royston, against 100 minutes for the fastest stopping services. The 'Brush-2's handled the buffets comfortably, often showing a fair turn of speed, especially with the whistling 'English Electric' 1,470h.p. engines. The 'Sulzer-2's 'top jobs' were Hornsey's often heavy – as we shall see when I go to Hornsey - cross-London freight transfers out of Ferme Park up yard and they did seem more suited than the 'Brush-2's to this work.

No engineer, however, I can only give here my own impressions gained from working with these locomotives and even the cab control equipment seemed to play a part in locomotive performance.

Compared to the art of applying power to the external combustion steam engine, the control of internal combustion powered diesel-electric locomotives is relatively simple; on a steam locomotive the actual amount of steam used to power the locomotive

'Brush-2' D5615 is relegated to the slow road with an up 'Cambridge Buffet Express' approaching Potters Bar on the 15th of April 1967. (RCTS)

In 1960 Stratford's 'Brush-2' D5579 was given an experimental 'golden ochre' livery. This and D5578's 'electric blue' unfortunately came to nothing. In August 1961 D5579 stands at the north end of platform 3 at Cambridge; Platforms 7 and 8 now stand in the space occupied by the suburban coaches on the right. (Colour-Rail)

from the reservoir of steam available is balanced by thoughtful and expert use of the regulator (throttle) in conjunction with the 'reverser' (gear-lever), which is infinitely variable relative to an internal combustion gearbox, and regulates the travel of the valves and thus the quantity of steam permitted to enter the cylinders to power the pistons and so, finally, the locomotive's driving wheels, while, on a diesel locomotive, as on any internal combustion road vehicle, the amount of fuel used from the available reservoir to power the locomotive is controlled by the throttle lever or pedal – known on a locomotive as the 'controller' - which, once opened, allows diesel fuel to pass, as the steam in an external combustion engine, through valves to power pistons in cylinders; but this application of power is, of course, completely automatic, there is no need for the diesel driver to be aware of the amount of fuel which he is permitting to enter the cylinders by use of the 'controller'. But this method of simple power control varies between diesel-electric types, the cab control equipment depending upon the type of electrical transmission and traction motors, the 'final drive', which receive the electricity from the generator – or more recent alternator - driven by the diesel engine.

The two main diesel-electric control systems which I became familiar with were by 'Brush' and by 'English Electric'. Brush control equipment was utilised on the 'Mirlees' and 'English Electric' engined 'Brush-2s', (31s), the then new 'Sulzer 12LDA' powered 2,750h.p. 'Brush-4s', (47s), and also the last (1963) batch of 'Type-4' 'Peaks' (46) - also fitted with 'Sulzer 12LDA' diesel engines and allocated to Gateshead depot - one of which gave me the dramatic introduction to diesel work as outlined at the opening of this account - and on these types the controller stood atop a plinth on which the controller openings were marked, for the controller passed through four distinct 'notches' to achieve 'half-throttle', after which the lever moved freely to full power. The 'English Electric' controller was a much more purposeful looking instrument protruding from, and sliding in, a slot in the side of a semi-circular quadrant, and could be moved easily from 'closed' to 'full-power' without any check - although such action was not to be recommended on 'English Electric' locos! Locomotives which I experienced with this equipment were the 'English Electric' 'Type-4s', (40s) and both types of 'Deltic', 'Type-5' (55) and 'Type-2' 'Baby

Deltics' (23). The earlier '6LDA' engined 'Sulzer-2s', however, were powered by B.T.H. traction motors and the control desk differed somewhat from both 'Brush' and 'English Electric' layouts; the control 'desk' was set apart from the rest of the controls to the driver's right hand, the controller itself a short, knobbed lever, angled invitingly upwards towards the driver's right hand rather than standing directly in front of him, and sliding across the full width of the 'desk' in such a way that the driver swivelled his seat into a snug 'cockpit' position left of the control 'desk' and to clatter and 'Sulzer-knock' through the tunnels up to Potters Bar with an evening peak 'block-ender' set full of homeward bound commuters, that controller pulled right back but within easy reach of my right hand, was an experience always especially remembered; a great difference was in that that controller really could be shifted from closed to wide-open, 'full-power' in one fell swoop - as I discovered for the first time on that morning of the 10th of May 1965.

Our 04.30 departure consisted of a mixture of sleeping cars, mail vans and passenger coaches which was made up from the overnight arrivals and marshalled into sections for convenient attention at Hornsey by the station pilots, and by the time we reversed out of Gasworks tunnel onto the front of the train in one of the centre platforms, 5 or 6, we were well out of the platform, and our guard was obliged to make his way between the tracks to reach us in order for his routines; take driver's name and tell us the load, something like "18 on". The first signal we could see was at the tunnel mouth and when it came off I had to look back to the signal box for confirmation that the platform starter was off; a signalman gave me 'right' from the box, a porter gave me 'right' from the platform, I gave Harry 'right away' across the cab and he promptly and without hesitation dropped the air brake off - and gave 5055 'the lot', swinging that long controller from one end of the quadrant to the other. Used to the 'Brush 2' gradual move away with the controller in 'notch 2', usually going to 'notch 4' then 'full power' as we probed the recesses of Gasworks Tunnel, I was truly amazed to see this treatment meted out to our little loco, and her reaction, experienced for the first time, was quite spectacular too, but one which I would soon get used to; there was a micro-second's pause while silence reigned and

Some say they have no good looks at all – some call them 'Rats' but 'Sulzer-2' (24) D5067 is beautifully posed at home, at rest on No.2 road, just outside the old steam shed at Hornsey on 11th February 1962 - and I was a total 'Baby Sulzer' enthusiast! (RCTS)

time stopped, then 5055's 'Sulzer 6' gave a mighty roar of protest, the 'tickety-tock' tick-over became a loud and determined clatter, the traction motors gave a howl of protest as this great charge of electricity hit them, and we moved slowly and surely over the station yard and into Gasworks Tunnel where, having cleared the brief dip down under the course of the Regents Canal, which with a Brush marked the first opportunity for full power, our 6LDA was snarling at the tunnel walls and roof in great voice while the traction motors continued their banshee scream as we tackled the initial climb through Copenhagen Tunnel and onto Holloway Bank. But our volcanic main line progress was short lived as we were soon signalled across to the down goods road, and as Harry eased the controller the clamour of hard-pushed diesel engine and traction motors was replaced by the squeal of tortured flanges as we negotiated the

cross-overs and progressed slowly along the down, west, side of Finsbury Park station to take our place in the stop-start procession of traffic wending its way between the various yards and sidings, and so to our crossing of the main lines at Bounds Green where we ran round and took the heavy train on its last lap up to Hornsey station on the up goods road before reversing into the carriage sidings.

I worked many a '270' type e.c.s. diagram after this, eventually doing a bit of supervised driving as drivers got to know me; but on the day after working '270' diagram, Tuesday, 11th May '65, again booked for '2 Relief' at 02.30, this time with 'downright Yorkshire' driver Dennis Cadywould, we were sent across to the 'Passenger Loco' to prepare 'Brush-2' D5663 and take her to the 03.50 'newspapers', '250' diagram, departure, a job which would become a rostered turn when I arrived in '4A link', as will be seen. When we reversed onto the train we were duly met by driver Bob Graves with instructions that I was to stay with him as his second man hadn't turned up. Bob took D5663 away sharply at 03.50 at the head of a train of parcels vans all loaded with Tuesday's newspapers; we were first stop Hatfield and then called at all stations to Hitchin. At each station a gang of porters and newspaper men awaited us and off-loaded their quota of newspapers for distribution by road to the local newsagents. Together with most of the mail traffic, this newspaper traffic is now long lost to the railways and entirely catered for by road. After unloading the last of our 'newspaper round' in Hitchin station at around 05.30, we shunted the empty vans into Hitchin down

yard north of the station and left D5663 on the adjacent Hitchin depot. Much of Hitchin down yard and the then diesel depot are still in place today, now used by Network Rail engineers, the yard stabling an interesting collection of track maintenance machines, often including one of Network Rail's two seven vehicle rail grinding machines. However, on '250' diagram in 1965 we appreciated the proximity of the diesel shed to the yard as, after leaving D5663, we had to sprint across the road, luckily quiet at that time of morning, in order to catch the 05.56 to Hatfield for the next leg of our diagram. This 'Hitchin sprint' would become a regular early morning exercise when I went into '4A link' with my regular driver, Roy Head.

Hatfield up side platform in 2013 showing the down slow running in on the line of the original curve. Before the 1970s renewal the steam shed smoked on the right in the now cordoned area while carriage sidings and the St. Albans branch wandered off through the then sparser forestation. (Author)

Hatfield up side in 2017. The car park was once the bay platform where many down inner suburban steam trains terminated, crossing and block-ing the main lines when arriving; Lord Salisbury's personal waiting room stood between the bay and the platform buildings and up to the 1970s served as a class room. Old Hatfield town lies beyond. (Author)

Hatfield's 'staggered' up platform today, number 1, seen from the down island which serves main line platform 2 and slow road platform 3, so different to the Hatfield who's booking office I returned to in 1968. (Author)

Looking north along Hatfield's up platform; an up express leans to the curve through Hatfield behind a 'Brush-4' shortly after the station's rebuild and easing of the curve. The bay platform stood on the right here before the footbridge came, with Lord Salisbury's waiting room, latterly MIC and first aid school room, just before the platform buildings. (Paul Hepworth)

At Hatfield, once the busy focus of three branch lines, we crossed to the down-side and the sidings on the remains of the old steam shed which still served as a signing on point, although the closure of the branch to Dunstable only one month before left very little work for Hatfield crews and they would soon be brought into King's Cross. We found 'Brush-2' D5646 stabled in the sidings and duly gave her a preparatory look round while she ticked over and built her air before moving to the exit where I phoned and waved to the 'bobby' in Hatfield No.3 box. He soon let us out onto the down slow to run down light engine to the next station north, Welwyn Garden City, where we were crossed over and attached to our coaches for the 07.15 King's Cross passenger departure.

We were able to have our break at Welwyn Garden City before we took our commuters all stations to Potters

Bar then Finsbury Park, and 'home' into 'The Cross' at 07.50. But the job was not yet done, and those masters of logic and statistics in the list office had decided that to round off our hours we could run down, light-engine, to Finsbury Park, at this most busy time of the morning, cross to East Goods Yard and work '3E09' empty parcels vans back into 'The Cross'. This was accomplished by 09.00 and we were finally relieved out in the 'dead-end' between the tunnel mouths at 10.40 when '250 diagram' was successfully completed and Bob and me could go home.

Wednesday, 12th of May 1965 was my day off and I started back on Thursday 13th, refreshed, at 01.00 hours on - list office logic again - '1 Relief' diagram with driver Pat Blades. This time, '1 Relief' it was, and I continued on my rostered shed duty jobs until Thursday, 3rd June, when, towards the end of a week of night-time

The southern approaches to Welwyn Garden City in the early 1970s; an express comes down the main behind a 'Brush-4'; the 'new-railway's up-side colour-lights are ready to replace the traditional semaphores at the south end of up island platform 1 and 2; the yard is just visible on the left beyond the platform 1 turn-out. (Paul Hepworth)

Looking south into Welwyn Garden City yard today; the yard is often host to engineers' trains and here the locomotive on the weekly Lafarge Stevenage aggregates train has run-round ready to return to Peterborough. In the 1960s the yard was busy with freight and also stabled suburban coaches. (Author)

Looking south again from Welwyn Garden City island platform 1 and 2 today, the yard is left; far right, a 313 suburban unit at the start of its journey to Moorgate climbs to the 1977 fly-over which replaced the necessity for departing trains to cross all running lines on the level. (Author)

Welwyn Garden City station looking north, across to down platforms 3 and 4, in the 1960s. The DMU has terminated and is moving out of 4 past the box, as we did with peak time loco and coaches, to access the cross-over and so to come back across the main lines into up platform 2 for London, where patient passengers wait. (Colour-Rail)

'engine-movements', 22.00-06.00, I changed turns with a colleague for '17 Relief', 19.25-03.25, just for that one night. But no sooner had I booked on than I was directed to join main line, '2-link' driver, Horace Fairy and go to Peterborough. The train was 4N07, a semi-fitted freight from the Goods Yard, but we relieved a King's Cross crew in the station on 'Brush-2' D5588 which we took light-engine through Gasworks Tunnel then reversed into the yard, following the hallowed path of over a century of tired steam engines en-route from station to Top Shed.

We hooked on and departed well enough, 20.45 off the Goods Yard, with me hanging out of the cab window to catch the guard's green lamp waved from his brake at the end of the train, and hastily getting my head in before we ran into Copenhagen Tunnel. We were due into Peterborough Westwood Sidings at 22.30 - but

things didn't quite work out like that - once more my 'journey jinx' struck. D5588 gave up somewhere in the vicinity of Stevenage, a sudden blue warning light on Horace's desk, followed immediately by the engine's complete shut-down. I have the failure time at 21.25 but unfortunately did not time the subsequent events. Horace brought us to a careful stand and I got down and phoned Langley box from the nearest signal phone and met our guard who then went back behind the train – rule 55 observed! Horace investigated the engine room but was unable to make a restart and I told Langley that we needed assistance. And that assistance eventually came in the form of a 'new', very recently refurbished locomotive, another new type of traction for me – an 'English Electric-2' always known as 'Baby Deltics' (23).

Now this much scaled down version of the legendary 'Type-5' 'Deltic' had first appeared in 1959, some

Welwyn Garden City looking across from down platform 3 to up platform 2 today. The overbridge is now enclosed otherwise little has changed. (Author)

two years before their mighty cousins, and carried a 9-cylinder 'delta' form English Electric engine of 1,100? b.h.p. - the '5s' had two 18 cylinder 'Deltic' engines of 1,650b.h.p. - each! The ten 'Type 2' 'Deltics' never enjoyed the success of their big '5' cousins, even on the much lighter work which they were, of course, employed on; from the first they were most unreliable and were all withdrawn from service in 1963; but were returned during April 1965, soon after my start as a second-man, re-engined and with new 'noses', just one month before our failure with D5588. All 10, while officially allocated to Finsbury Park TMD, 34G, worked - would it be fair to say 'out of the way'! – out of Hitchin shed. I hadn't seen one in London, and D5909, coming to our rescue at Langley on this 3rd of June was my first sight of a 'Baby Deltic'. D5909 came by us on the up, crossed behind us and actually propelled us from Langley to Hitchin; with Horace and me both anxiously savouring a new experience, sitting powerless in the front of D5588 and

watching the slow approach of Hitchin station, Horace finding it very difficult to keep his hands off the useless controls as we rolled into the down platform. We detached D5588 and yet another of these 'new' locos, the first at that, D5900, took D5588 onto Hitchin loco, then came back onto the train.

Horace and I took our seats in D5900's rear cab, Horace couldn't drive as he hadn't 'learned' the 'Baby Deltics', and Hitchin men took us without further mishap to Peterborough. Our return working was 3E23, a fitted fish train, probably from Grimsby and companion to 3E29 which I rode through the snow with Driver Hawker back in December 1964. However 3E23 was long gone when we finally got to Peterborough on that considerably warmer June night, and we went home 'on the cushions' on one of the first 'mails', arriving into King's Cross at about 03.00. I was on 'Engine Movements' on that Friday night, then back to the continuing round of shed duty turns.

'Type-2' 'English Electric' 1,100h.p. Bo-Bo, TOPS '23'. On the 11th of July 1965 'Baby Deltic' D5905 is at Hitchin where the whole class of 10 were usually stabled after refurbishment. (RCTS)

In May 1961, before withdrawal for modification, 'English Electric-2' 'Baby Deltic' D5901 stands contentedly at Hitchin's up platform on smart coaches, probably 'Cambridge Buffet' stock, ready to go to London. The steam shed still stands behind the platform. (Colour-Rail)

CHAPTER 4

HORNSEY EXILE: HORNSEY 5 LINK

It was during that same week, week ending the 5th of June 1965, that I had news of my transfer to Hornsey shed. Still officially a 'passed cleaner' and always likely to be taken off 'second-man' duties, I joined several King's Cross colleagues of my seniority and applied to go to Hornsey where our seniority would put us in a regular 'second man' link.

My transfer became effective from Monday, 14th June 1965, and on that date I became a 'Hornsey man', allocated to 'Hornsey 5-Link', rostered that week for 11.00-19.00 and actually signing on that Monday at 12.56 for '357 Diagram' with Driver R.C. Smith. '357 diagram' had a similar mixed make-up to Kings Cross '277'

detailed above. We went out to Bounds Green carriage sidings where we relieved a Hornsey crew and shunted coaches with 'Sulzer-2' D5056 until running light up to Finsbury Park carriage sidings at about 16.00. Most of the inner-suburban coaching stock, the 'modern' six-coach sets known as 'block-enders' and the remaining old articulated 'quad-art' sets, was stabled in Finsbury Park sidings, situated on the up side just north of the station.

Arrived in the sidings we swapped 'Sulzers' with another Hornsey crew and took D5050, already hooked on to a set of empty coaches, through King's Cross York Road and 'The Widened Lines', into Moorgate where,

The main lines pass between Finsbury Park 5 and 6 boxes while beyond 6 – on the up side stand the carriage sidings with the weekday evening suburban e.c.s. line-up. A medley of 'Type-2's wait to take their coaches into London while the shunting staff take a break. (Colour-Rail)

D5071 exits Finsbury Park carriage sidings with suburban coaches for King's Cross or Moorgate. (Colour-Rail)

after release, we waited in the spur outside the platforms until it was our turn to reverse onto another set of incoming coaches which became our 17.52 passenger departure calling most stations to Hatfield. From Hatfield we returned, empty coaches again – so many empty coach movements were necessary on this transitional railway - to Potters Bar where we reversed the coaches into the up siding for a next morning up peak working, (King's Cross '332 diagram', see below, page 115ff, June 1966) and finally ran light-engine back to Hornsey shed by about 20.00.

Most of the rest of my first week at Hornsey consisted of similar empty coach workings with Hornsey drivers, who I found to be an amenable enough 'family'. In retrospect I've wondered that some kind of antagonism wasn't shown to we King's Cross 'birds of passage', by both Hornsey drivers and their regular second men, after all we were going to return to the 'big main line shed' and, it could be said, we were only using humble

Hornsey as a stepping-stone; but I cannot recollect any such attitude, if anything it was a kind of 'if that's what you want, you can have it!' feeling, and everybody was happy.

Friday of that first week introduced me to Hornsey's 'top link' work - and a dramatic demonstration of the big difference in the top jobs as worked by King's Cross and Hornsey crews. I signed on at cross-London and was immediately assigned to go with Driver Melton for my first run 'down the south' as Hornsey's ex-London goods jobs to Feltham and Hither Green yards were colloquially referred to. This particular trip was to be to Feltham, the Southern Region's ex-London and South Western Railway yard opened in 1918 where freight to and from the south-west of England was exchanged.

The power for these cross-London goods trains was almost always provided by the hardy 'Sulzer-2s', and we departed Ferme Park up yard at 12.25 with D5061 in charge of our long loose-coupled goods train. Now the

Coaches from several evening peak services were stabled in the suburbs and the loco ran back light to London. This might well have been the case for D5603 passing Potters Bar golf course on the up main in typical mid-'60s style. (RCTS)

important term here is 'loose-coupled' meaning that the brakes on the train went right back to the very beginnings of railways - there weren't any! The only brakes on the train were the engine's air brake at the front and the guard's screw down brake in his van at the rear. Of course, such trains are now a thing of the past, all freight trains today consisting of long air-braked bogie vehicles, but in the mid-sixties 'loose-coupled' was a normal operation. Controlling such a train called for particular driving skills; such trains had to be treated with respect; they must be started off carefully so that no sudden snatch broke a coupling hook - or knocked the guard off his feet! Loose coupled trains had to be run at a cautious speed which suited the curves and gradients of the route, and the drivers' knowledge of that route, especially at night time, had to be especially keen; stopping a loose-coupled train was a slow and careful operation - and the drivers of these trains always hoped the signalmen were aware of this, especially when running on absolute block (passenger train) lines - as we were soon to find out on that Friday afternoon.

From Ferme Park we made made our way along the up goods road through Finsbury Park station and continued left onto the up Canonbury, descending to isolated Finsbury Park No.1 box and on to Dalston Junction from where we continued westwards along the North London Line, through the complications of Willesden Junction, looked down on Old Oak Depot as we crossed the Western main line at North Acton, then followed the most westerly of the electrified lines of what is nowadays the very much refurbished London Overground as it approaches its western terminus at Richmond. And it was as we rolled towards Acton Central that Bob looked across the cab at me and said, as I sat there completely oblivious to the fact that, "we're not stopping, mate, screw the brake on." We were ambling along slowly enough - but I noted the position of the stubby straight air brake lever at Bob's left hand - hard on! And the next signal was also horizontally on, protecting the level crossing at Acton Central, its gates firmly shut against us, and growing steadily larger as we approached, traffic plainly passing in both directions. I leaped out of my seat and quickly screwed down the parking brake on the cab back, then dived through the engine room, passed the loud idling tick-over of D5061's 6LDA, and screwed on the brake in the back cab. We were still rolling steadily towards the crossing when I returned to the front, Bob started a series of hoots and wondered if the guard was aware of our dangerous progress and had applied his own brake at the end of the train. I leaned out of the cab and looked impotently back along our motley, clanging collection of wagons; there was no sign of activity or acknowledgement from the distant brake van and looking forward again we had now passed the stop signal and could plainly see the non-stop streams of unsuspecting traffic blissfully unaware of the inexorable advance of some 300 tons of unstoppable goods train. And then we stopped! Anti-climax now I suppose but a blessed relief at the time. The road mercifully levelled and the train just came to a shuddering stand with a last tired squeal from D5061's locked flanges; and I stood in the middle of the cab, Bob sat in his seat, left hand on the loco's air-brake lever, right hand on horn lever, and we looked at each other in a silence broken only by the casual 'tickety-tock' of the idling diesel. We were just before the signal box, situated on the up side, and when we'd gathered ourselves together it was obvious that my job was to go and see the man in that box and explain why we had run by his signal - and almost demolished the crossing - and whatever road vehicles we would have come in contact with in the course of that demolition process! Bob decided that under the circumstances he would go, so I watched from the cab as he crossed to the box, climbed the steps and disappeared inside. He soon reappeared and came back, and as he reached the engine the traffic stopped and the crossing gates opened in our favour while, on looking back, the home 'board' was now 'off' and the guard giving right from his brake - that's all we saw of him! Bob had been suitably penitent and explained that the train just 'got away' with us; the signalman had realised this and agreed to make no more of the incident, which could have been so much, much worse if we had been propelled much further by those 'troublesome trucks'.

And so that big difference between driving an express passenger train at speed, and a humble, loose-coupled goods train. A train travelling at 100 m.p.h. and more needs constant vigilance from the driver, but will certainly stop - after a reasonable distance, of course - when the brake, acting the full length of the train, is applied. A weighty loose-coupled freight train, however, although travelling so much more slowly, demanded a different and most precise kind of skill, and with brakes only available at the front and rear of the train, even with the utmost care, especially on down grades, there was no guarantee that application of the brake would hold the train - as had been demonstrated that afternoon on my first cross-London goods job from Hornsey.

So I unscrewed our parking brakes and we proceeded gently through Richmond, where we joined the Southern Region, and on through Twickenham, Whitton Junction and so into Feltham yard at 14.25, just two hours from Ferme Park.

We had an hour before we left with our return freight, so we relaxed over a 'mash' of tea and our lunch before leaving Feltham at 15.27, routed back to Willesden and then via Gospel Oak, through Upper Holloway to the Harringay curve which led us directly up from the North London line into Ferme Park down-side at 16.30, half the time our interrupted outward trip had taken via Dalston. From Ferme Park down we ran light engine over the fly-over and were back on Hornsey shed by 17.00 where we had another 'mash' in the crew room before taking D5061 into Hornsey carriage sidings; an empty coach trip had been worked onto the end of our diagram, illustrating again the tremendous amount of empty stock movements necessary in those days in order to service, maintain and place passenger coaches; today the servicing of restaurant and buffet cars, the replenishment of water tanks, etc., are all taken care of in King's Cross station platforms, with visits to Bounds Green depot for heavier maintenance being kept to a minimum. So our last job on Friday, 18th June 1965 was to take a rake of coaches from Hornsey carriage sidings into King's Cross, leaving the sidings at 18.30 and relieved in King's Cross at 19.35.

D5061 went on to lead a most colourful life, first going from King's Cross to Haymarket, Edinburgh, in the mass Exodus of 'Sulzer-2s' from the King's Cross area which we shall come to in the Summer of 1966. But, by strange coincidence, she is one of four 'Sulzer-2s' - or '24's as they became in the TOPS classification - to survive into preservation, and is at present with the North York Moors Railway where she is currently (mid-2018) awaiting overhaul. Her survival is due to her allocation to Derby

Research Centre upon withdrawal from service as 24061 in November 1975, as departmental RDB968007. In 1979 this fortunate 'Sulzer-2' was taken to Doncaster works where she was given the engine from less fortunate sister D5063 (by then 24063), renumbered as 97201 and decked out in a dark blue livery with smart orange side panels and named 'Experiment'. During the 1980s between trials at Derby and working special research trains, sometimes in company with big 'Sulzer-4' cousin 97403, ex 46035, originally D172, now named 'Ixion', one of the later, Gateshead allocated 'Eastern Peaks' of the type which memorably opened my story, also surviving into departmental service. D5061/24061/97201 attended a number of heritage railway galas. Again officially withdrawn in July 1986 D5061/97201 was destined for Vic Berry's scrap yard

in Leicester – but turned up on May 31st of the following year at the Coalville Open Day! The loco then languished at Leicester for several years but her charmed life continued when, after the closure of Vic Berry's, she was purchased by The Midland Railway Centre at Butterley where she opened at their 'Diesel Spectacular' in July 1991. In 1992, now D5061 again, the loco went to the North Tyneside Railway and finally came to the NYMR in 1994. I was so very pleased to travel behind old D5061 – original number, no name, and suitably grubby plain green – on the NYMR in May 2012, 47 years after our near miss at Acton!

After this first June week at Hornsey my seniority moved me up from Hornsey '5-link' into '4-link' - which proved to be the only link I was pleased eventually to move out of!

'Sulzer-2' D5061, authentically shabby but apparently a quite contented 'rat', waits to relieve steam at Grosmont on the North York Moors Railway on the 30th of May 2012. I have memories of D5061 and a close call at Acton back in June 1965. In mid-2018 D5061 awaits overhaul. (Author)

The diesel I second manned in the 1960s, D5061, poses next to the streamlined flank of an immaculate 'A4' 'Pacific', a steamer I wanted to 'second-man' in the 1950s. (Author)

And the 'Pacific' in question, spotless 60007 'Sir Nigel Gresley', named after the designer of the LNER 'Pacifics' who's statue now stands, unfortunately to one side of, rather in the centre of, the twenty-first century King's Cross concourse. Based on the NYMR, 'Number 7' is currently (mid-2018) under overhaul at the NRM York. (Author)

CHAPTER 5

HORNSEY (FINSBURY PARK) 4 LINK

Hornsey '4-link' was based on Finsbury Park station along with King's Cross '6-link', so both Hornsey and King's Cross had crews at Finsbury Park. 'King's Cross 6' was also known as the 'suburban link' and the King's Cross '6-link' second men at Finsbury Park were certainly more gainfully employed than were their Hornsey '4-link' counterparts. In early 1966 I would return to 'The Park' in 'King's Cross 6-link', but in that Summer of 1965 'Hornsey 4-link' introduced me to the joys of 'Ferry' and 'Relief' diagrams which

were a rough equivalent of King's Cross 'shed duty' but, without the many locomotive movements necessary in the terminus, there was often precious little 'ferrying' or 'relieving' to be done, and these positions were further examples of the unavoidably slow and wasteful transition from steam to modern traction working, representing left-over firing turns from the now gone days of steam locomotive operation.

The signing on point at Finsbury Park was situated on platform 1/2, (rebuilt and lengthened in 2013

Finsbury Park station downside; local platforms 6 and 7 in 2016. Today's automatic doors ensure that only doors onto platform 7 are opened but in 'slam-door' days passengers boarded and alighted both sides, calling for great precision on the part of despatching porters! Platform 8 is far left and serves only trains from Moorgate. (Author)

The remaining 1870s yellow-brick blends well into the twenty-first century Finsbury Park. The up and down main lines run between platforms 4 and 5, down platforms 6/7 are beyond and farthest is platform 8. Up platforms are right of the camera. (Author)

Finsbury Park up platforms 2 and 3 mirror 6 and 7 on the down side. In June 2013 platforms 1 and 2 are modernised, losing the old Hornsey/King's Cross loco S.O.P./restroom in the process; Moorgate trains now call at platform 1 beyond the new building, extreme right. (Author)

Above: Main lines from the north through Finsbury Park in the 1960s. No.5 box presided over the down roads; a 'Brush-2' hurries up the main between No.5 and No.6 which regulated up main line approach routes into King's Cross. (Paul Hepworth)

Below: A reverse view of the previous photo with the down main occupied by a 'Deltic' hauled express roaring north through the station. Taken from the south window of Finsbury Park No.5 box looking towards the station, No.6 across the main lines on the left. (Paul Hepworth)

'Paxman's D8231 and D8232 bring 'Ashburton Pullman' empties up through Finsbury Park platforms 2 and 3 in 1969 and are about to pass the joint Hornsey/King's Cross loco crew room on platform 1/2. (RCTS)

to provide still more capacity for today's busy King's Cross and Moorgate up-side suburban traffic) and consisted of a long and often cheerless ex-waiting room, with timekeeper's office at one end, benches set along the long walls and at joined mess tables which ran the length of the centre of the room, with a mediocre coal fire at the far end in Winter. It was a dismal contrast to the mess room overlooking platform 10 (today's 8) at King's Cross, always full of the busy noise of men coming and going from along the length of the East Coast Main Line, Peterborough 'Bungits', Doncaster and Leeds 'Tykes', Northumbrian 'Geordies' signing on after their lodge break in the Great Northern Hotel, locomen meal breaking, laughing, moaning, barracking in a really cheerful, lively atmosphere, night and day. And Hornsey '4-link' second men spent far too much time in that bleak room at Finsbury Park just waiting for something to turn up. There were a few e.c.s. jobs in the link and on occasion I was taken off to cover other empty

coach jobs and the occasional inner-suburban peak passenger job on both Hornsey and King's Cross diagrams, while '4-link's '707 diagram' introduced another job which at least brought change from the monotony of waiting to 'ferry' the occasional light engine, usually up the 'Canonbury' to 'No1 box' in order to reverse, run under the main lines and so gain Finsbury Park down-side, usually then to access Clarence Yard TMD with another reversal.

Hornsey '707 diagram' covered a period of 24 hours divided roughly into three variable shifts, and provided crews for the 'Snow Hill Banker', a '350' (08) 'pilot' which was outstationed at Farringdon on the 'Widened Lines', as the augmented lines through from King's Cross to Farringdon and Moorgate and the south have been known since 1868 when the Metropolitan Railway's original up and down roads, cut between Paddington and Farringdon in 1862 and extended on to Moorgate in 1865, were doubled.

King's Cross York Road platform. It's 1973 and D5610, now in blue and TOPS numbered 31187, prepares to descend to Farringdon and Moorgate when driver Les Coulson has climbed aboard. (Paul Hepworth)

'The Hole' - The subterranean way down to the 'Met', 'The Widened Lines', Farringdon, Moorgate and 'The South' from York Road platform. The haze was much thicker in steam days. (Paul Hepworth)

In 1863 Great Northern trains gained access to the Metropolitan lines via the narrow, steeply descending burrow of a tunnel driven from York Road platform on King's Cross station's east side down to King's Cross Metropolitan station. Trains from the Metropolitan climbed equally steeply up into platform 16 (1960s numbering) on the far west side of the station round the 'Hotel Curve'; but 'steeply up' was a different proposition to the gentle descent from York Road and the ascent in a hard-working steam engine, endured for a century by footplatemen working both cross-London freights and passenger trains, was both extremely uncomfortable and extremely unhealthy; even our 1960s diesels working trains from Moorgate were obliged to climb from 'Hotel Curve' under full power in order to lift the train into platform 16.

By early 1866 another tunnel climbed steeply south from a junction with the Metropolitan lines east of Farringdon station and ran under Smithfield and Snow Hill to a connection with the London, Chatham and Dover railway's Ludgate Hill terminus, so commencing cross-London services, both passenger and goods. The obvious congestion and pollution of such an intensive steam-hauled service resulted in the 1868 'Widened Lines'. But increasing goods traffic meant that congestion continued on the 'Widened Lines' until a goods depot was built adjacent to and below Farringdon station. The depot opened in 1874 and the area it covered was extensive - in fact the extent of the nineteenth century City goods depots; the 1874 Farringdon Great Northern Railway goods depot, the already (1869) built Great Western goods depot, apparently still extant today under Smithfield Market, and the Midland's nearby Whitecross depot of 1878, nearly all underground – is – in twenty-first century terms - awesome!

After joining the 'Met', 'The Widened Lines' ran through 'King's Cross Metropolitan' station which would become King's Cross 'Thameslink' in 1986 when the through line from Bedford to the South was opened. A B.R. train heads for Moorgate in the early 1970s. (Paul Hepworth)

The dingy 1970s King's Cross 'Met', as LUL trains pass and a light 'Brush-2' runs through to Moorgate, is now replaced by the modern 'City Thames Link' station actually built on the site of the 1874 L.C.&D.R. 'Holborn Viaduct' station. (Paul Hepworth)

King's Cross Platform 16, probably late afternoon as the commuters are few and a DMU rather than a full throttled 'Brush-2' comes up from the 'Hotel Curve', while a station-pilot has possession of soon to be busy platform 15 above left. St. Pancras overlooks. (Paul Hepworth)

The Great Northern Goods Depot presented Farringdon Road with a 300 feet frontage and stood 60 feet high. Designed by the G.N.'s chief architect Richard Johnson, it formed part of the mid-nineteenth century rebuilding of the 'Farringdon waste' as the area was known, (apparently, to call the Farringdon Road area 'infamous' in the early part of the nineteenth century was to pay it a compliment!) and was comparable to the 'roaring waste' of King's Cross before the Great Northern arrived there in 1852. Road access to Farringdon goods station proper was from a ramp diving underneath the south end of the building into the maw of cranes, hoists and traversers of the goods station proper; rail access was from the northerly, King's Cross direction; indeed, the Snow Hill Banker's 1960s spur was surely situated just to the north of the old goods yard access, although I recall no sign of such access by then.

The depot paralleled the whole western length of Farringdon station and it seems that in 1965 the remains could surely still be viewed through the dark arches on the west side of Snow Hill Tunnel, for, although the depot closed in 1956, it lay dark and derelict parallel to the tunnel, together with the great building above it, not demolished until 1988 when the dull grey buildings which replaced it, and which today overlook the 'Thameslink' trains, were built at the end of the '80s. Again I cannot recall seeing anything beyond those

dark-shadowed tunnel arches as we rolled back down to the station and into our short spur on the return trips from Snow Hill top. What were plainly visible, however, were the remaining sidings south-east of Farringdon station which were then still used to stable Metropolitan underground stock, while the two sidings which remain today are used to stable the occasional 'Thameslink' units, although the whole Farringdon station area is now (mid-2018) completely changed once more, and will yet change still more as it prepares to become the hub of London's 'Crossrail' and, as such, the busiest railway station in Europe, situated in the main below ground at the centre of the most fantastic feat of precision tunneling ever undertaken.

At present (mid-2018) London Underground's Metropolitan, Circle, and Hammersmith and City lines run into platforms 1 and 2 in Farringdon station, while the

The steep 'Widened Lines' approach to Farringdon from King's Cross. LUL 'Met' trains pass. The spur which accommodated the Snow Hill banking engine is on the left middle of this 1970s picture and access to Farringdon Goods was surely where the lorry is parked beneath the road access ramp. (Paul Hepworth)

The notable D5061 comes up the bank into Farringdon on the 'Widened Lines' with a trainload of tractors in 1961. The Snow Hill banker waits to assist in the spur beyond the third tractor. D5061 gave me a few anxious minutes with a Feltham freight in June 1965 and has survived into heritage working on the North York Moors Railway where in 2018 she awaits overhaul. (Colour-Rail)

Farringdon station. A Moorgate bound DMU in platform 3 passes a north-bound 'Brush-2' and its train in 4. The LUL 'Met' lines are on the left at a higher level. (Paul Hepworth)

'Widened Lines' run into platforms 3 and 4, adjacent to but somewhat lower than the LUL platforms, and are now used solely by the cross-London 'Thames-Link' services from Bedford to Brighton and 'The South'; but in the 1960s the 'Widened Lines' curved left from just east of the station and paralleled the Metropolitan – London Underground - lines as far as Moorgate; the morning and evening Moorgate trains were by then the only passenger trains to run over the 'Widened Lines'. From the same junction the cross-London lines turned right – south - and immediately entered the wide, two road, Snow Hill tunnel and the steep climb up Snow Hill Bank, the route of Hornsey's south-easterly bound cross-London freight trains which went to various Southern goods yards including Hither Green, the south-eastern counterpart of south-western Feltham which I have already visited in the eventful journey of 25th June 1965 described above. Snow Hill Bank ascended through the tunnel at a fearsome 1 in 40 which, as I would discover, tested even the omnipotence of the sturdy 'Sulzer 2s', and so the need

for the 'Snow Hill Banker', a '350' 'pilot' which stood expectantly in the short spur next to the down (northbound) road just outside, north-west of, Farringdon station. Southbound goods trains ran through the station and came to a stand just on the bank inside Snow Hill Tunnel when the points from the banker's spur would be switched, the 'dolly' come 'off' with a threatening crash, and the 'banker' rolled out of its sanctuary, through the up platform, buffered up to the rear of the waiting freight and then assisted it full-throttle to the top of the bank and into that mysterious territory, known officially in 1965 as 'British Railways Southern Region', but to GN enginemen as 'The Sarf' - the pre 1923 London, Chatham and Dover Railway route. Emerging from the tunnel at the top of the bank beneath Holborn Viaduct, the goods continued its leisurely way, passing the site of the original L.C.&D.R. 1865 Ludgate Hill terminus, crossing the Thames at Blackfriars and wending its way deep into Southern territory, while the banker ground to a halt just beyond the crossover points, from where a brief bustling

Moorgate B.R. 'Widened Lines'. D5615 has arrived with empty coaches for an evening commuter train. When the train departs D5615 will run out into the spur and awaits the arrival of the next e.c.s. which will form D5615's train.(RCTS)

Looking towards Moorgate on the left and 'The South' branching right at the south end of Farringdon 'Widened Lines' platforms in the 1960s. (Justin Bailey)

In this 1970s scene a 'Brush-2' brings a train into Farringdon from Moorgate and the grim portal of Snow Hill Tunnel looms on the right at the foot of the bank. The track was lifted in 1971 and relaid for the 'Thameslink' line in 1986. (Paul Hepworth)

birds-eye view of Farringdon Road and its environs below, right-side, and a higher view of the L.C.&D.'s 1874 Holborn Viaduct station over on the left beneath the Old Bailey's glinting Scales of Justice, with the great dome of St. Pauls Cathedral completing the background beyond, a fine City view which could be enjoyed briefly until the points clashed across, 'dolly' clanged off, and we crossed to the down road and dropped back down the bank and back into our spur to await the next southbound goods.

I did not realise as I perched on my 'bar stool' during my shifts on the 'Snow Hill banker', vibrating gently in 3-4 time with the grumbling rumble of our trusty English Electric '6KT' engine, that I was in the midst of such a truly amazing amount of London's, and indeed, Britain's railway history.

Today's electric 'Thameslink' trains make an effortless climb of Snow Hill Bank over a completely renovated line which passes close by the site of the old L.C.&D. 1874 Holborn Viaduct station and actually uses the original street level façade as the entrance to today's modern 'City Thameslink' station. 'City Thameslink' is situated under Ludgate Hill beneath the site of the L.C.&D's original 1865 Ludgate Hill terminus at the intersection of the south end of Farringdon Road and New Bridge Street on the approach to the Blackfriars Bridges where today's 'Thameslink' line makes its physical link across the Thames on the original L.C.&D.R. railway bridge.

I worked my first turn on the 'Snow Hill Banker' on Wednesday the 6th July 1965 when I was paired with driver Johnny Barrell, a pleasant and confident young driver who I would meet again on the Friday of that week, but, as we shall see, on that occasion, not in quite such a pleasant mood. Wednesday's shift started at the strange hour of 17.14 and finished at 01.40. We hitched a lift to Farringdon in the back cab of a 'Brush 2' taking empty coaches into Moorgate for an evening peak departure, then walked across to the spur and boarded and started our stabled steed, D3693; for the banker was unmanned during the evening peak and, indeed, it was some time before our first freight came through and Johnny demonstrated my first Snow Hill banking procedure. The train appeared quite suddenly, the 'Sulzer's' '6LDA' idling, 'tickety-tock', and the long line of wagons clanking behind. As the brake van stopped just beyond Farringdon up platform our points switched over, the 'dolly' came off with a clash, and Johnny took us out of

the spur, across the down line and buffered us up to the rear of the brake-van, when the guard appeared briefly on the brake's veranda and took the train's tail lamp off its bracket - we were now the rear of the train. On the left hand side two bare wires stood out prominently at cab height from the mass of covered cables which disappeared into the tunnel; Johnny pressed these together and then answered the series of hoots which immediately echoed back down the tunnel from the train engine. The wires touched together completed a circuit which lit up a signal in front of the train engine which then 'crowed' its intention to start, which it did as soon as we acknowledged with the '350's shrill whistle and Johnny dropped the brake off D3693, pulled the tram-like controller wide open and we howled through the tunnel and up the bank buffered up close to the rear of the train and so assisting up the bank. At the summit we came out of the tunnel, apparently just beyond the site of Snow Hill station although I confess, not then knowing my history, I never noticed that site. On that Wednesday evening Johnny shut off and we watched the goods train's guard replace his tail-lamp as the train went on to pass the site of Ludgate Hill station, cross the Thames at Blackfriars and disappear slowly into the mysterious 'Sarf'.

For the first time I gazed out over that impressive view from Snow Hill Bank top as we waited to cross over and return to Farringdon; way below us stretched the busy south end of Farringdon Street while on our left the lines to and from Holborn Viaduct came past us from their turn-out from the lines ahead of us and curved round into Holborn Viaduct station, quite imposing from our lower position, the evening sun flashing from Justice's scales over The Old Bailey beyond and in front of the towering dome of St. Pauls.

The cross-London freights ceased in 1969 and today's sophisticated, air-braked traffic now uses a much rebuilt and refurbished North London line with links south from Willesden Junction to Acton for the west, or Kensington, Clapham Junction and Wandsworth Road for the south and south-east. Holborn Viaduct station finally closed in 1990, two years after 'Thameslink' electric passenger trains again connected north and south through the Snow Hill Tunnel, and Holborn Viaduct's Victorian frontage is now incorporated in the new City 'Thameslink' Link station opened in 1990.

My maiden mid-week evening shift on the banker with Johnny Barrell was followed by two more on

Thursday and Friday but with a much newer and less experienced driver than Johnny. I shall call him Ron. We got through Thursday alright, somehow, but Ron had a different way of handling D3693; for, while Johnny opened up to full power and left it that way all the roaring way up the bank, Ron kept an eye on the ammeter and eased the controller whenever the amps needle swung round into 'overload' - which it did - constantly! Johnny had just let her charge on - with no ill effects, and that this was the way to handle the engine was proved on the Friday evening when, as my short note recalls, we "stalled on bank." The train was heavy and as we toiled upwards the ammeter stayed stubbornly in 'overload' with Ron easing the controller back all the time so that the engine's note dropped to a sullen rumble and we ground along, slower and slower; Ron looked worried but still eased the controller back - until we finally came to a shuddering halt. Well, Ron didn't seem to know what to do and pulled the big air-brake lever on while I thought about train protection and the hallowed 'Rule 55' - should I get down and walk back; but where was the guard? Surely he didn't think we'd reached the top yet? But the van's veranda stood vacant just in front of us, still devoid of tail lamp. Ron seemed to have his attention fixed on the train ahead and leaned out his side window just before the door opened with a crash - and in climbed Driver Johnny Barrell, very angry and telling us many unprintable things. Taking Ron's place at the control desk he loosed a series of shrieks from D3693's whistle, and when an answering cadenza echoed down the tunnel from the front of the train he dropped the brake off and gave D3693 full throttle as his mate opened up their 'Sulzer' on the front. And so we reached Snow Hill summit, where Johnny shut off and left us as swiftly as he had arrived, returning to the front of his waiting freight, while we waited for the 'dolly', then returned, engine grumbling, side rods clanking, nothing spoken, down the bank to our base in the spur.

The next week saw me pottering about between Finsbury Park carriage sidings and King's Cross on an afternoon empty coaches diagram. This was followed by 17 days leave divided between friends in Bournemouth and the annual visit to cousins in County Durham, and it was a bit of a jolt to return on Wednesday, 4th August, from tramping the northern hills and dales to sit in Finsbury Park's 'signing-on point' cum-rest-cum-waiting room on four days of virtually jobless 'Ferry' duties.

It was a slight improvement to be rostered from Monday, 9th August for full five days on the day-time 'Snow Hill Banker' - Monday to Friday 08.05 'til 16.50 - but I was also told that I would move into Hornsey '3-link' on the Tuesday of the next week, my position in the roster giving me a Monday rest-day and so a long weekend off.

D3310 was the allocated banking steed at Farringdon for that last August week in 'Hornsey 4-link' and I have not recorded the driver's name. However, we were together for the week with rostered weekend off, and we got on well enough because it wasn't far into Monday when he let me 'have a go', so that by Tuesday I was no longer nervous of the electric shock I expected when I pressed the 'right away' wires together to signal the train driver, nor of winding the controller round to full power as soon as we'd exchanged whistles, although my first couple of tries resulted in a certain amount of rebounding from the brake van's buffers, and I hope the guard was sitting down! About midday on Wednesday we'd sat for some time between freights when my mate announced his intention to 'go shopping' and wouldn't be long, upon which he climbed down and disappeared into the station. And of course, scarcely had he gone than a 'Sulzer 2' growled into the up platform, duly stopped its freight beyond the station, when the points switched over and our 'dolly' dropped 'off' with a clash like the fall of a guillotine. I ambled D3310 out of the spur and buffered up to the brake, exchanging a casual nod with the guard as he unshipped his tail lamp, then automatically pinched the signal wires together, exchanged toots with the train engine, pushed the controller to 'full', then sat rigidly on the left-hand 'bar stool' with hand white-knuckled on the wide-open controller and eyes glued to the ammeter needle as it stood stubbornly in 'overload' and we blasted through the tunnel up Snow Hill Bank until at last the blessed daylight outside the tunnel enabled me to slam the controller shut and pull down on the long brake handle to bring my clanking steed to a stand over Ludgate Hill, quite neatly, I thought in retrospect, just beyond the return crossover and 'dolly'. 'Dolly' came off and I dropped D3310 gently back through the tunnel and into the light of the station where my driver casually awaited me. It happened again on Thursday and Friday and I cannot help but think that my driver's 'shopping' was contained in a glass, but his 'shopping' did my confidence a world of good – and I managed to overcome the strong urge to take D3310 on with the freight into the mysterious 'South'!

CHAPTER 6

HORNSEY 3-LINK

On Tuesday, 17th August 1965, rest-day Monday, I moved up into Hornsey shed's 'number-3' or 'Acton-link'. As the name implies, most of the diagrams allocated to '3-link' included trips to Acton yard, in the vicinity of my 'runaway' on the Feltham trip with driver Bob Melton and D5061 a couple of months earlier. A return trip from Ferme Park to Acton Yard took about three to four hours depending mainly on how long we were stood off at Acton before the return train was ready. Rostered hours were made up by light engine movements or else by the inevitable empty coach trips which were tacked on to all kinds of jobs at both Hornsey and King's Cross; so many empty stock movements were necessary in those days, and working out how to cater for them all (without a computer!) was surely a job as miraculous as working out the rosters for the men and the locomotives which worked them.

Membership of 'Hornsey 3 link' and above included teaming up with a regular driver, a practice which could found lasting friendships - and also longstanding enmities! My own first 'regular mate' was Peter Welch who I did not meet until my second week in the link as he was 'road learning'; he had only recently come into the link himself and was uncertain of some of the routes travelled by '3-link' diagrams; a driver must know a route perfectly before he drives on it and must sign a route sheet in order to confirm that he has that knowledge. In order to learn and then sign the route, he must travel the route with other drivers and visit and study the busier junctions, yards and sidings on the route until he feels that he can sign with confidence. And this is what Peter was doing during my first week in the link when I made four daily, 10.00 'til 18.00, trips to Acton with various drivers on various 'Sulzer 2s' on 397 diagram - which finished off with an inevitable empty coach trip from Bounds Green sidings into King's Cross.

An interesting variation on '397' diagram occurred on the Saturday of that week when it became '396' diagram, still going to Acton but rostered from 09.30 'til 17.30. I was with driver Jimmy Hayes who possessed an unshakably optimistic and easy going attitude which, under this day's circumstances was just as well, for the real interest in the day started when the foreman allocated us our locomotives - yes, two, "they're all I've got, mate, and you'll need both of them," said the foreman to Jimmy and indicated two 'Paxmans' standing off across the shed yard. Now the 'Paxman' was a new and untried beast to me, they rarely came into King's Cross station and appeared to be the sole property of Hornsey men - and from what I'd heard, they were far from being their favourite property! They were rated in the diesel loco classification as 'Type 1', i.e. those mustering but 800 to 1000 horse-power in the diesel hierarchy, the 'babies' of the fleet, although we referred to our 'Type 2s' as 'Baby Brushes' and 'Baby Sulzers'; but it appeared that even in the 'baby diesel' league the 'Paxmans' did not cut the mustard. They were generally known as 'Paxmans' (TOPS type '15') because it was an 800 horse-power, no less than V-16 cylindered 'YHXL Paxman' engine which inhabited the locomotive's long bonnet extending in front of the single cab; in fact in appearance they very much resembled the excellent 1000-horse English Electric 'Type 1s', which became TOPS type '20', many of which are still in both national and heritage service to this day. The 'Paxmans' were B.T.H. built and the Paxman engine generated the electricity which drove the 'Bo-Bo' bogies through B.T.H. traction motors. And we had two of these beasts to play with on that fine August Saturday morning.

With an undaunted "come on mate, let's tie these two together first", Jimmy set off across the tracks and I followed on more slowly, revising what I'd learned about 'coupling locomotives in multiple'. The two locos stood near enough next to each other on adjacent tracks. The good news was that they were facing in opposite directions and could be coupled nose to nose, i.e. we'd have a cab front and back when they were coupled. The pair were D8233 and D8235 and subsequent notes and events suggest that D8235 was on the south end. Jimmy threw me a key and told me to "jump in and get one goin', mate." I climbed aboard D8233 - the only member of the class to be preserved and currently (2018) under heavy overhaul by the 'Class 15 Preservation Society' on the East Lancashire Railway - and quickly worked out what did what so that my 'Paxman' roared into life just seconds after D8235. We waited for air, unscrewed the parking brakes then crossed D8235 in front of D8233 and buffered them up nose to nose, then we made what we thought was a very professional job of coupling the pair up, not only brake hoses and hook, of course, but both jumper control cables which would ensure that the two locos would work as one unit - which they did - after a fashion! Jimmy climbed into D8235's cab and dropped the airbrake off and opened up while I walked across to the shed exit phone. Well, the two 'Paxman' engines answered with a suitably synchronized roar - but with a motion which was far from synchronized; D8233 wanted to go home, into the shed, while D8235 tugged in the other, correct, southerly, direction! Jimmy shut off sharply and with a few similarly sharp words, both sacred and profane, he got down and we set about realigning the jumpers so that the two locos were eventually reconciled with each other and we finally departed

Ferme Park up yard with 8T75 at 11.20 instead of the scheduled 10.25. We were some 40 minutes late arriving into Acton yard but, punctuality not being as rigorous for freight as for passenger trains, especially on a Saturday, we were back into Ferme Park down by 15.30 with our return working and back on Hornsey shed at 16.00. However this 'smart running' earned us another job, and, after uncoupling D8233, we had a 'brew' then set out again with D8235 alone, to work a special short goods, south-east by devious lines from Dalston, via Hackney and Stratford to Devons Road, Bow; but we were stopped somewhere in the depths of Hackney where the 'bobby' directed us to leave the train in a siding - the yard at Devons Road to where the 'special' trip was 'especially' consigned being closed for the weekend! We ambled back light engine to Hornsey, stabled D8235 next to her sister, D8233, and finally booked off near enough on time at 17.30.

'Paxmans' D8232 and D8231, coupled nose-to-tail but cab leading, approach 'Potters' Bar on the up slow with empty wagons on 5th of June 1968. On our trip to Acton in August 1965 we were able, fortunately - and eventually! - to couple D8233 and D8235 nose to nose. (RCTS)

That Saturday's extra job had introduced me to part of another new (to me) London goods route which Hornsey men worked. This line went on from Hackney to Stratford, and the vast Temple Mills yard, adjacent to the main line from Liverpool Street, then from Stratford a goods only line ran through to Canning Town and London's docks which at this time had returned, temporarily, to their peak of pre-war prosperity. During the second half of the 1960s, however, this prosperity would see the beginning of a downturn as the new 'container' method of handling sea-freight called for new and mechanised docking facilities which took shape, initially, at Tilbury. These new modern methods of handling the country's imports and exports demanded that the railway must fall in line and reorganise its own methods of carrying goods, a reorganisation already unsuccessfully attempted at strategic points throughout the railway system with the creation of huge marshalling yards such as Temple Mills, Whitemoor and Tees Yard. These complex concentration depots actually catered for decreasing quantities of freight, in disappointing discord with the expectations of the 1955 'Modernisation Plan', and became yet another expensive failure, with the new yards often almost empty. The late 1960s saw the introduction of the first 'freightliner' trains by which containers could be transferred virtually directly from ship to rail and vice versa, and this quickly brought about the end of the 'loose-coupled' goods train and led, by the 1980s, to the carriage of every conceivable commodity on the fully air-braked 'freightliner' trains which now make up today's goods trains. New container ports were built along the east coast until today's busy container ports at Tilbury, Harwich and Felixstowe increasingly enjoy the centuries old trading prosperity which London had lost by 1980. The Royal Victoria Dock was the biggest dock on the Thames in the mid-1960s but today the whole vast site of London's docks has been redeveloped into the new prosperity of that great new residential and commercial area which remembers its maritime roots by its name only, 'Docklands', served by the 'Docklands Light Railway', the automated, driverless, railway, opened in 1987, which for much of its route follows the way of that original nineteenth century goods only docklands railway which I travelled for the first time on '399 diagram' during a week of 'afternoons', starting on Monday, 23rd of August 1965.

After signing on at 15.40, '399 diagram' eventually took me all the way through to the Victoria Docks along a railway run entirely on the 'permissive block' system, very different to today's driverless 'Docklands Railway'. But '399' diagram began, typically, with a local suburban job; we prepared a 'Sulzer 2' on Hornsey loco, ran light engine to now long gone Broad Street station, which had been served from the 'Great Northern' lines by morning peak arrivals and evening peak departures via the Canonbury spur and Dalston Junction since 1875. Broad Street stood on the west side of and high above Liverpool Street station, terminus of 'The Eastern'; in fact when we stood outside the platforms at Broad Street on the up side, waiting to drop down onto our return train, we had a grandstand view of busy Liverpool Street below us.

But by the 1960s Broad Street traffic was a shadow of its former self. The Broad Street branch left the busy west-east North London line between Richmond and Stratford at Dalston and was virtually an overhead railway, constructed almost entirely on viaducts. The branch was opened in 1865 to ease congestion on the North London Railway which carried 6.5 million passengers in 1861, and so popular became the new line that it was quadrupled in 1874, and Broad Street became the NLR's City terminus, the third busiest in London after neighbouring Liverpool Street, and Victoria; its initial seven platforms were increased to nine by 1913. In 1896 the North London carried no less than 46 million people. But trams, buses and eventually London Underground saw the gradual reduction in traffic into Broad Street, and despite electrification in 1916 during the economies of the First World War, traffic continued to drop off, slowly but inexorably, until, in 1963 closure was proposed under the Beeching modification plan. An angry petition by regular City commuters saved it. The daily North London off-peak service into Broad Street was provided by 1957 B.R.E. Eastleigh built three-car North London EMUs (which would become TOPS class 501).

On that summer evening at Broad Street we picked up the 17.05 all stations passenger train to Gordon Hill - but we only took the passenger train as far as Hornsey station where we were relieved. Again I have to wonder at the ingenuity with which all these many and varied train movements were put together and crafted around the men and locomotives which worked them – without the aid of computers. We walked over to Hornsey shed and prepared a 'Paxman' for the docks trip, booked off the shed at 18.35, pausing in Ferme Park up yard to collect a brake van and guard and go forward at 18.55 to Victoria Docks where we were expected to arrive at 19.45.

Branching south-east from Stratford, the docklands line consisted of up and down running roads paralleled by many loops and sidings. There were many signals on the docklands line, all mounted on huge gantries which straddled the whole layout; but they weren't the conventional signals for a running road but consisted of forests of shunt or 'calling on' signals, much shorter than the conventional signal. The line was worked on the 'permissive block' system which allowed more than one train to stand at a danger signal and busy periods found queues of trains, 'on the block', moving in one great slowly crawling crocodile along this access into and out of London's docks.

On Monday afternoon I was with Ernie Hancock and we had D5065 for the passenger leg of the diagram from Broad Street. On arrival at Hornsey only a driver waited to relieve us, his name unrecorded, and I stayed with him and D5065 all stations to Gordon Hill where we stabled the train and returned light engine to Hornsey, arriving at 18.25. Ernie waited for me on D8229 - it seems second men were a rare commodity that day – and we were off-shed at 18.45, ten minutes down, picked up our guard and brake and joined the queue to the docks where we arrived right time at 19.45. We left on our return trip as booked at 20.30 with 4S16, a semi-fitted freight and an easy task even for a 'Paxman', due into Ferme Park down yard at 21.10. Our actual arrival was at 21.20 when we stood D8229 off in the down side yard as directed by the yard staff, 'stabled' her and booked off duty at 21.50.

On the next day I was again with Ernie but he was acting as 'pilotman' to my new regular driver Peter Welch who turned out to be a stocky affable man of about 40, with a long journey to and from work, he lived in Clacton from where I believe he had recently transferred, thus his need for London road learning. So we three relieved Hornsey men on D5055 in Ferme Park for our Broad Street trip, then went to the docks and back with D8230. I did the same with driver Peter Smith on '399 diagram' on Wednesday and Thursday and found myself with my new mate, Peter Welch,

on Friday the 27th when our actual working bore little resemblance to our booked '399 diagram'; the opening Broad Street passenger working was worked by Finsbury Park 4-link 'ferry men', while we took a ride on the 16.16 up passenger from Hornsey to Finsbury Park station where we crossed the station and walked down into Clarence Yard TMD to collect freshly serviced Sulzer '2' D5064 which we ran back via Bounds Green to stable on Hornsey shed by17.20. We met driver Stan Wilson, assigned as our pilotman for the trip to the docks but while we had a 'brew' the foreman came to tell us that the docks run was cancelled! We therefore became 'as required' until about 19.15 when we set out for Hornsey station again, to catch the 19.25 into King's Cross and then to walk round to the goods yard to find '350' D3723 attached to a heavy string of wagons and vans which the guard almost apologetically told us were just within a '350's working limit. Directly behind us, first in the load, were empty fish vans bound for the 'Macfish' depot situated adjacent to Finsbury Park down goods roads. But our first port of call was a halt on the goods road next to Clarence Yard while a waiting 'Paxman' came onto our rear and took away most of our wagons, heading for Canonbury, Dalston, then east to Temple Mills yard. Peter had been obliged to work the screaming D3723 flat out to get out of King's Cross Goods and we were glad to be relieved of the Temple Mills wagons which Peter doubted we could have started again on the grade from Clarence Yard into Finsbury Park. As it was, D3723 ambled easily into the 'Macfish' sidings where a shunter unhooked us and we indulged in a spot of shunting, placing and replacing the new arrivals with other empties against the loading dock, a team effort requiring 'both sides' driving, and I was thankful for my King's Cross 'runround' jobs experience. I think it was here that Peter decided we were 'o.k.'!

'Macfish' shunting completed I went to the nearest signal box telephone for orders, expecting to be told "light engine Hornsey depot," but we were directed to run up into King's Cross to pick up vans for Holloway sidings, situated on the down side before Clarence Yard. It was by then about 21.00 so we couldn't really grumble – but we did!

We arrived into King's Cross east side 'arrival' platform, number 1, and then followed the 'dollies' zigzag across the station yard, in and out of 'Gasworks', to the west side where we could access the 'Milk Yard' next to the suburban platforms and pick up a string of parcels wagons, a regularly formed train known as the 'odd stock', which took miscellaneous 'crippled', empty and generally unwanted vans out of the way of King's Cross and stabled them in the outlaying yards, usually Holloway down-side carriage sidings, where the 'pilot' sorted them into their various categories for onward disposal – often only as far as Waterworks sidings, on the down side, just south of Wood Green (Alexandra Palace) station. Again D3723 had to work hard through Gasworks Tunnel although these vans were all 'fitted' (through braked) and we had a clear run into Holloway, then ran light-engine to Ferme Park down side, where we were 'stood off' in a spur by the yard staff and directed to 'stable' D3723. And here was a big advantage of the diesel locomotive over steam, 'stabling' did not require us to feed and water the beast, nor to throw out her fire and empty her smokebox – just to turn the engine off and make sure the parking brake was firmly 'screwed down'. The locomotive key must be returned to an MPD, but the secured loco could be left without attention until it was required for its next duty.

I have dwelt in detail on an apparently mundane job but the variety, the mobility, to be actually riding – and driving - these many types of diesel motive power made it a constant source of fascination. And so it proved again on the Sunday after our rest day off on Saturday, 28th August. I signed on with Peter at 16.35 for the mysterious '365 Additional diagram', a diagram with a subtitle in fact, 'No.2 Late Ballast', which made us quite sure that we would be destined to ride out somewhere to relieve the bored crew of a Sunday ballast train on an engineering possession. For, despite what I've said about the job never palling, it cannot be denied that ballast trains were tedious work; once arrived on site a ballast train moved very occasionally on the orders of the site inspector as the relaying gang gradually loaded or unloaded the rail ballast to or from the hopper wagons. We hoped that when we arrived the job would be nearly completed when we would take the ballast wagons into Ferme Park or some local yard for stabling. In the event we never saw a ballast train that night but were nevertheless kept busy 'odd-jobbing' throughout the shift.

As soon as we'd signed on the foreman sent us out into the shed to find and prepare 'Brush 2' D5609

which we took into King's Cross where we picked up 3E11 empty coaches. These were destined for Hornsey Carriage Sidings, which of course involved the usual trip down to Bounds Green in order to cross to the up side; but a variation on this standard theme involved a call into Holloway sidings and a spot of shunting and re-marshalling before we eventually headed north then south. After reversing 3E11s into Hornsey sidings we were directed back to the depot where we put D5609 away at 19.50; just right, thought we, for 'a brew and a bite' in the mess room. The 'shed gaffer' pounced on us straight away, however, and immediately sent us off to the station where we boarded the 20.22 up passenger as far as Finsbury Park, where, the foreman had told us, we'd find ourselves in for a bit of 'class A' express running. Our 'express' was the return working of a Clacton day excursion from Welwyn Garden City, a type of train, once so popular throughout the railway during the Summer months since the earliest days of the railways, but an 'endangered species' by the mid-1960s; today it is good to see that the excursion train has been revived, initially in the shape of rail enthusiasts' specials, often hauled by preserved steam locomotives; but these enthusiast specials have also formed the basis for more general excursions to popular destinations throughout Britain, and such day and even longer touring excursions have become extremely popular.

On Sunday, 29th August 1965 our return excursion from Clacton, 1Z17, arrived at Finsbury Park behind D5854, worked by fellow Hornsey men; whether they had had a day out to the seaside with Eastern pilotmen or had just brought the train across from Stratford I do not now know, but their shift was finished on arrival at 'The Park' where we relieved them. Another point which intrigues today is my record that D5854, one of the last, 1961/2, batch of 62 out of a total of 263 'Brush 2s', was an Immingham loco, transferred away from Finsbury Park in January 1965. Wherever she lived, however, Peter took us away from Finsbury Park right time at 20.56 to romp down the main line for all of 20 miles to the train's final destination – Welwyn Garden City, terminus of most of our inner suburban commuter trains. From Welwyn Garden City we took the empty coaches, 3Z17, forward another 20 miles or so to Hitchin where they were to be stabled on the up side north of the station alongside the Cambridge Branch in aptly named 'Cambridge Branch Sidings'. Access to the

One of the last batch of 'Brush-2's 'D5824' trundles a long string of empty wagons along the main line at Walton just north of Peterborough in July 1963. I worked excursion empties with her shed-mate D5854 just two years later. (Colour-Rail)

sidings was, as it still is today, from their north end, off the Cambridge Branch itself, and for down trains involved running onto the branch then setting back across the up road into the sidings. In Hitchin station a Hitchin driver joined us as pilotman, as Peter did not know the road over the branch. Having crossed over, set back into the sidings, stabled and run round the coaches, we ran back light to Hornsey loco where we finally 'stabled' D5854 at 23.45 and left for home before midnight; Peter on his long drive to Clacton while I boarded a late train for Potters Bar, retracing my steps of some four hours earlier.

I stayed in Hornsey's '3 link' until the second week of October 1965 when seniority took me back to King's Cross. September saw me working Hornsey jobs similar to those outlined above; mainly trips to Acton Yard or the docks, the occasional cross-London goods and suburban passenger working and, of course, those eternal trips with empty coaches between King's Cross and the various carriage sidings, skillfully woven into both King's Cross and Hornsey diagrams. I worked with Peter more frequently as he became familiar with and signed for more routes but was often rostered with other drivers. I especially remember one such occasion on Monday, 27th September, the start of five nights rostered with Peter on '409 diagram' which we spent aboard a 'Paxman' and which took us what seemed like all night to make just one return trip to Temple Mills where we were booked to spend no less than four hours in that vast flood-lit waste of almost empty sidings waiting for our return working.

On the Monday night, however, Peter did not come in and instead of being allocated another driver for '409' I was paired with driver Arthur Simons who's second man had not reported for duty to work '411' diagram with him. This proved to be a completely different job to '409'; it was, in fact, a night trip 'over the south' to Hither Green, a Hornsey top link diagram. Arthur

Welwyn Garden City today; from the north end of down platform 3 across to up platform 2. In 1965 we would have had to take our empty coaches to platform 1, beyond 2, and so through to the distant up yard for stabling. (Author)

was very tall and very slim and a pair of sharp eyes twinkled mischievously in a long face topped with a mane of grey hair; he must surely have been approaching retirement but turned out to be a pleasant and very able companion. We prepared 'Sulzer 2' D5071, I rang out, and we dropped down into Ferme Park up where we were 'hooked up' to 8T18, a pretty substantial loose-coupled freight. We were booked away from Ferme Park at 20.15 but after his wait for a second man, it was actually 21.30 when Arthur eased our train out of the up yard and I leaned out and exchanged regulation lamp signals with our guard, thus ascertaining that he was with us – and that the train was complete. We wended our way through King's Cross York Road and dropped through the tunnel onto the 'Widened Lines' to Farringdon where it was a change to be *in front* of

the 'Snow Hill banker' which assisted us up to Holborn Viaduct and Arthur then took us across the Thames and continued into the mysterious dark suburbs of south London, the cab briefly bright as we clattered through stations to Elephant and Castle which we ran through at quite a rate, Arthur demonstrating his many years of loose-coupled train experience; then I sat straight with sudden alarm as a red colour-light signal stood bang in front of us! But Arthur kept D5071's controller wide open as we careered to the left of the signal and continued at a grand pace; I looked across the cab at Arthur who gazed straight ahead but with his long face, silhouetted cadaverously in the cab's fitful light, wreathed in a grin of demonic mischief! "It's always a shock first time through Loughborough in the dark" he chortled. This was Loughborough Junction where we veered

Cambridge Branch Junction. This photo was taken from the north end of Hitchin down yard, now stabling for engineers' track machines. It looks across the ECML main line to the Cambridge branch curving away beyond and the sidings on the extreme right. (Author)

eastwards from the southerly route towards Croydon, and headed for Lewisham where our course turned south-eastwards onto the Tonbridge and Hastings line. Hither Green, however, lies just some three miles from Lewisham and we ran slowly into our appointed siding at 22.30 – some 45 minutes late. We left with our return trip at 00.30, arriving back into Ferme Park downside at about 02.00 when we ran light engine over the flyover and back to Hornsey depot where we stabled the trusty D5071 and signed off after a trip over another new and interesting route for me.

I worked the next four nights with Peter on the Temple Mills '409' diagram with D8231 each night.

Friday night, the 1st of October 1965, saw us finish the week with a sudden burst of activity when, upon arrival at Temple Mills at 22.10, and having unhooked and been stood off for the long wait until our 02.23 return working, we were in the midst of the most serious nightly discussion over whether to have our tea and grub straight away or else to leave it for a couple of hours, when a knock on the cab door introduced the yard foreman with instructions from Hornsey for us to return immediately and help out a chronic shortage of local locomotion. We arrived back into Ferme Park by 23.45 and headed out almost on the stroke of midnight with a trip for King's Cross goods where we arrived at about half past; and about half an hour after that we picked up another short trip and D8231 clonked her way steadily back to Ferme Park. We spent the rest of a busy night on transfer trips across the fly-over between Ferme Park up and down yards and we did find time to have a 'mash' before making a final return trip to King's Cross goods between 03.30 and 05.00. We finally stabled D8231 in Hornsey loco at about 05.30, some two hours into overtime, which meant that we could not sign on at our 16.30 booked time on the Saturday night as it was a rule that twelve hours rest must be taken between shifts.

Our job on Saturday was simply described as 'Spare', but when we booked on at 17.40 we were immediately directed to D5065 waiting in the loco yard to work a special weekend trip to Hither Green which road Peter now signed. We took D5065 off shed at 18.10 in great haste to pick up our 'special' in Ferme Park up yard; but it was the waiting game again, why I do not now know, but we eventually left at 20.10, and I again went 'over the South', rolling into the weekend quiet of Hither Green yard at 21.30. There was nothing for us to take back on a Saturday night and I was pleased to take us back light-engine to Clarence Yard sidings, into what remained of the original yard since the TMD was built, consisting of five roads standing between the TMD and the main line and still used for stabling odd wagons and vans, a train of which we picked up and worked to King's Cross goods – via Bounds Green, thus arriving in the goods yard at 23.50 when we unhooked and ran home light engine to Hornsey where we arrived at 00.40.

After Sunday off, my last week at Hornsey, 4th to 25 October 1965, was rostered for early mornings and introduced me to more railway history. I was assigned to work '368A diagram' from Monday to Friday with a rest day on Thursday. The diagram consisted of two distinct parts centred on two separate railway locations, both now long gone. After signing on at the curiously precise time of 05.53,'368A' men prepared a loco to leave Hornsey depot at the equally precise time of 06.28 and then ran light-engine to 'Holloway car dock', a two road platform and loading dock situated on the up side of Holloway Bank south of Finsbury Park and opposite the down side Holloway carriage sidings. As recently as 1963 'Holloway car dock' had opened on the site of 'Holloway cattle dock' which had served the long gone Caledonian Road cattle market. Cattle for the market had arrived at Holloway dock since 1855 when the new Caledonian Road market replaced the old Metropolitan Cattle market. But with the increase in road haulage and the general decrease in the transport of livestock during the first half of the twentieth century, the 1930s saw

the end of the 'cattle dock', which, some 30 years later became the 'car dock', the London terminus for the Perth 'Car-Sleeper Limited', a clear sign of the times – inward bound cattle for slaughter exchanged for cars and their passengers outward bound for pleasure!

The down 'Car-Sleeper Limited' left Holloway at 21.20 each night between the 25th of April and the 2nd of October during 1965 with the cars in vans and their passengers in sleeping cars, arriving into Perth at 05.45. The up sleeper, 1A67, left Perth at 20.30 and arrived into Holloway dock at 05.30 when Hornsey '368A' men then took the empty coaches and car vans, 3A67, round to Hornsey carriage sidings, leaving Holloway at 07.08, - the precise timing because 3A67 had to pick its way across Holloway's tortuous set of cross-overs, blocking the main line on the bank completely in order to reach the down slow roads just south of Finsbury Park station. The last consecutive up working in 1965 left Perth on Sunday night the 3rd of October while two final workings on the nights of Thursday the 7th and Sunday the 10th October finished the 1965 season; coincidentally, therefore, I worked the penultimate Car Sleeper empties for 1965.

On Monday morning the 4th October I was with driver Ron Nicoll aboard 'Brush-2' D5602 and we left Holloway dock some seven minutes down to join the e.c.s. procession along the down goods road, over the Hertford loop fly-over, run round in Bounds Green sidings, finally to reverse into Hornsey carriage sidings at 08.20. We returned immediately to Bounds Green, light-engine via Ferme Park fly-over and the queue to Bounds Green for the second part of 368A diagram. Now the usual visits to Bounds Green sidings involved running round and immediate departure for Hornsey carriage sidings; but on this, my last week working from Hornsey depot, the second part of 368A diagram was listed as 'Palace Gates – shunt as required'. Well, Palace Gates was a completely unknown venue to me, but it became a reality on that Monday morning when a shunter met us in Bounds Green sidings and walked ahead of us setting the road as we slowly crossed to the most easterly side of the sidings where previously unnoticed coal bunkers and lines of hopper wagons marked Bounds Green Coal Concentration Depot. The road out of the coal sidings ran on to turn a corner which hid a most surprising sight - a very substantial and imposing, but very derelict, dilapidated and mysterious two road station, invisible from the carriage sidings; and this was Palace Gates station. Ron told me that the intriguing lines, which still headed invitingly eastwards out of the station, eventually joined the 'Eastern', and trains had until quite recently (1963) run from Palace Gates to North Woolwich on the Thames, beyond the docks line which I had travelled during my short time at Hornsey. Our job at Palace Gates was to sort out the coal hoppers under the direction of the depot shunter, placing full wagons for unloading and preparing empties for departure; empties which I will become acquainted with during 1967 on the outward leg of King's Cross '4A-link's 258 diagram to Cambridge. The longer moves took us into the up platform of the silent station before setting back, and I recall that I gazed upon its decaying grandeur, its hollow, empty booking hall and waiting rooms, intrigued by this now defunct railway, completely unknown to me until this last week at Hornsey depot.

The name, Palace Gates, was itself a bit of a puzzle as the only palace in the vicinity was Alexandra Palace which stood, and still indeed imposingly stands, on the far, west, down-side of the East Coast main line, while Palace Gates, on the easterly side, could hardly be said to stand at the gates of Alexandra Palace. However, more recent research shows that the name was nineteenth century wishful thinking on the part of the Great Eastern Railway which hoped to win a share in the rich revenue which travel to the new Alexandra Palace in the 1870s brought to the Great Northern Railway. Alexandra Palace, known variously through the years as the 'Peoples Palace', and 'Ally Pally', was North London's answer to South London's Crystal Palace, a further example of the later nineteenth century's advance in philanthropy as a centre for social recreation, education and entertainment. Originally built in Hyde Park for the Great Exhibition of 1851, the huge Crystal Palace was moved to Penge Peak, Sydenham Hill, in 1854 - in pieces, on carts, horse/ox drawn! - where it stood until it was destroyed by fire in 1936. Alexandra Palace was completed in 1873 and the Great Northern's Alexandra Palace branch from Finsbury Park was opened on the very same day. No sooner was it built, however, than Alexandra Palace was itself destroyed by fire, but its more conventional bricks and mortar construction as compared to Crystal Palace's cast-iron and plate-glass meant that it was rebuilt by the end of 1875. Ironically,

in the year of the Crystal Palace destruction Alexandra Palace became the first regular home of BBC television and the transmission masts are still used today, as are the original studios, preserved as a television museum, while the Victorian theatre is also still to be seen. The two great halls are now used for conventions, concerts and exhibitions including the annual London Model Engineering and London Festival of Railway Modelling exhibitions. The Palace is today a fine sight on the down side of the East Coast Main Line just south of Alexandra Palace station – known as Wood Green in the 1960s - and the point where the Hertford Loop trains cross the main line on the fly-over which is even today used as access to Bounds Green TMD, now established on the site of the carriage sidings, often mentioned here.

The Great Eastern's first attempt to come west was made in 1866 when parliamentary approval was granted for a branch from Seven Sisters on the G.E.'s Enfield line to cut across and make an end on junction with the Great Northern branch then approaching Highgate, although Alexandra Palace was the final destination proposed, and indeed achieved, when the palace was completed. The Eastern's plans were abandoned in 1869 in view of an unavoidable steep gradient up to the proposed junction, and costs in general. However, the success of the completed Great Northern branch caused the Great Eastern to think again in 1874, but now to build a less ambitious line terminating adjacent to the G.N.'s Wood Green (today's Alexandra Palace) main line station. This branch was duly opened in October 1878 terminating at the new 'Palace Gates - Wood Green' station; the addition of 'Wood Green' to the title no doubt intended to show that the station was not actually at Alexandra Palace – yet!

During the first two decades of the twentieth century a half hourly service ran between Palace Gates and Liverpool Street with one hourly train to North Woolwich. In 1929, with Great Northern and Great Eastern Railways combined into the London and North Eastern Railway since the 'grouping' in 1923, the spur to Bounds Green sidings and so to Bowes Park station and the Hertford loop, was laid in, and subsequently the spur provided a convenient through route for 1930s excursion traffic. These opening decades of the twentieth century were the busiest years for the Palace Gates Branch, but increasing North London road traffic and the arrival of London Underground's Piccadilly Line at Wood Green in 1932 started the gradual decline in the branch's passenger numbers, although, during the Second World War the Palace Gates to Bounds Green spur provided an important link between East and North. In 1947 the regular Liverpool Street service was withdrawal and by 1950 the service had become peak time only to North Woolwich. The branch closed completely to passenger traffic in January 1963, and to goods in December 1964. The last train from Palace Gates on the 5th of January 1963 was powered by Stratford's 'Brush 2' D5619. Stratford had provided the motive power for the branch since Palace Gates' own two-road steam shed, a sub-shed of Stratford in B.R. days, closed in 1954. Palace Gates shed was home to about six Great Eastern tank engines, no doubt T. W. Worsdell's, then most certainly from the 1880s, S. D. Holden's neat little 2-4-2 tank engines - initially known as 'Gobblers' for their prodigious coal consumption – a name which stuck even after valve gear modifications improved consumption - which worked the Palace Gates passenger trains until their withdrawal in the 1950s when A. J. Hill's 'standard suburban' 'N7' 0-6-2 tanks took over, although during the branch's last steam days the North Woolwich trains were worked by the hefty Thompson 'L1' 'Concrete Mixers' - for the considerable 'clank' from side rods - 2-6-4 tanks. Diesel power during the branch's last days was provided by Stratford's 'Brush-2s' and it was with a King's Cross member of that class, D5602, that I discovered the derelict Palace Gates station on Monday and Tuesday mornings of my last week at Hornsey depot.

By that first week of October 1965 the long shunts from the coal depot into and out of Palace Gates station represented the last traffic on the branch. The coal concentration depot was opened in July 1958 and utilized until 1984 by which time most of Palace Gates station had been demolished although the northern platform ends were still accessed by two roads from Bounds Green TMD; these platform stubs have now disappeared beneath a children's recreation ground adjoining flats which cover the remainder of the station site, but the two roads are still extant beyond a high wall and are still used for stabling by the TMD – two humble dead ends which still provide a visible – and still working – reminder of a once busy, now virtually forgotten London branch line and East to North railway link.

On Friday morning I worked both parts of '368A' with Ron Nicol again, aboard 'Paxman' D8229 and we were near enough right time away from Holloway, although it was surely a struggle for D8229 up to 'The Park'. The car-sleeper terminal eventually moved to King's Cross Milk Yard until the demise of the East Coast car-sleepers in 1988.

The temporary, seasonal, nature of the Perth 'Car Sleeper' probably explained the 'A' of '368A diagram', and with no 'Car Sleeper' running on Monday, Tuesday or Wednesday nights during that last week, only the second part of 368A diagram was worked on Tuesday and Wednesday mornings (Thursday off). On Tuesday morning with D5602 again and driver Tony O'Dell, we were sent initially from Hornsey shed to East Goods Yard, where we marshalled '3E09' parcels vans – a variation on the final move on King's Cross '250 diagram' back in May (P.69), but we left them in Finsbury Park at about 09.00 and ran light engine to Bounds Green for the Palace Gates shunt. On Wednesday morning, again with Tony O'Dell, we did nothing until about 10.30 when we walked over to Ferme Park down side and relieved King's Cross 'run-round' men on '350', D3708, with which we jolted down the goods road and crossed Wood Green fly-over to drop back into Bounds Green and Palace Gates, for me, for the last time.

On Saturday, 9th of October 1965 I was booked again with ever cheerful Tony O'Dell - even at 04.55! The title of our job was 'Enfield Shunt' – which apparently didn't happen on Saturdays so we were amended to 'As Required'! At 07.45 I was required to leave Tony and join driver John Cheasman and prepare 'Sulzer-2' D5069 for our first empty coach sortie from Hornsey sidings into King's Cross. I stayed with John for the rest of his diagram which ended in King's Cross station at 15.15 when we were relieved by King's Cross men, making a long day for me.

Sunday, October 10th was my last day at Hornsey and I was pleased to be booked on for the last time with my regular driver, Peter, on an 06.00 'Relief' diagram. We were sent to Hornsey sidings to mobilise and work the carriage pilot, an unusual job even on a Sunday, for the carriage pilots had their own small links of 'stop drivers', in a similar situation to those based at Finsbury Park, who had for various reasons elected not to go forward through the promotion links. We moved and marshalled coaches with D3722 until 13.00 when we said our 'Cheerios', shook hands, and booked off – as far as I can recall, never to see each other again!

CHAPTER 7

RETURN TO 'THE CROSS' – NO8 'SHED DUTY' LINK

My rostered diagram on return to King's Cross on Monday, 11th October 1965 was the hardly exciting '5 Relief', timed to start at the equally uninspiring time of 04.45. The diagram title indicates that I had not advanced workwise beyond the point last Summer when I moved to Hornsey, in fact I had worked this very same '5 Relief' diagram on Wednesday, 9th June, just four days before my move away. But I was now, in October, officially allocated to 'number-8 link' at King's Cross – more commonly known as the 'shed duty gang' – as a 'second man' and could not be put back cleaning; I was also allocated to a regular driver, one Sam Duff who I didn't know at all, hardly surprisingly as he had only very recently arrived at King's Cross, transferred from the closed Peterborough East shed. Sam was road learning King's Cross during this first week, and so, as had happened when I arrived at Hornsey, I did not meet my regular driver for a week after my return to King's Cross.

On Monday morning I was almost immediately sent across to the 'Passenger loco' to join amiable, driver Alan Cooper on 'Brush 2' D5588 for '255 Diagram', which commenced at 06.30 with a light-engine run out to Potters Bar where we crossed to the up siding to pick up a rake of suburban coaches to form the 07.53 all stations passenger train onto the 'Widened Lines' and Moorgate. We returned with empty coaches up the steep climb through the round 'Hotel curve' into King's Cross platform 16 where we were relieved at 09.00 by Hitchin men. We then had a break and a 'brew' in the crew room before relieving Hornsey men on 'Sulzer 2' D5059 standing behind the 10.20 departure when we moved out into the station yard and reversed to pick up the almost inevitable train of empty express stock for Hornsey carriage sidings via Bounds Green. From Hornsey carriage sidings we finished the shift by running light to Finsbury Park carriage sidings where we stabled D5588 and called it a day at 13.30.

I was rest day on Tuesday, 12th October and covered '255 Diagram' with Alan on Wednesday, Thursday and Friday. On Saturday I finished the week with Alan on 'No. 5 Run Round' diagram which took us, initially, at 04.45, to the goods yard to mobilise '350' D3712 and work a busy succession of transfer trips between King's Cross and Ferme Park yards until we were relieved by a King's Cross crew at 13.15.

I worked on Sunday, 17th October and met Sam for the first time. He now signed for King's Cross station area and had learned locomotives the like of which, he said, he never thought he'd work on. We signed on at 06.15 for '5 Relief' and it was return to the 'Deltics' when we relieved Haymarket's D9010 on the 07.30 sleeper arrival. Sam put me straight 'in the seat', declaring that he reckoned I knew as much about the job as he did, which, of course, with his considerable number of years driving on the M.&G.N., was by no means true. Sam was a softly spoken Belfast man and you couldn't possibly not get on with him. He had come to 'The Cross' in company with another refugee from Peterborough East, Ted Wilson, and of course to come as trained drivers from the rural but mobile M.&G.N. to the shed duty gang at King's Cross involved a complete change of environment for them. Ted was a short pleasant man and soon earned the nickname of 'Rommel' from the way he shortened and adjusted the peak of his cap. Sam had moved to Hatfield and as my own home was at Potters Bar, we often travelled to and from 'The Cross' together.

After our first meeting on the Sunday relief job it was three weeks before I saw Sam again and I settled back into King's Cross shed duty work, but was pleased to be often rostered on empty coach and peak time suburban passenger diagrams. In this way I started to get to know the drivers in the lower links and many became 'characters' who I usually – but not in all cases! - fondly remember to this day – and always will. Driver Jack Crate was an enigmatic 'character' who I met on

Saturday, 23rd October when I was booked on with him at 14.30 to work the afternoon 'Provender Runround' diagram; I had worked the morning 'Provender' back in January. How this 'trips' diagram retained a name which probably originated in Great Northern Railway days I do not know; the word 'provender', of course, refers to animal fodder and it is probable that the original 'Provender Run Round' diagram was a trip job initially dedicated to the movement of the considerable amount of this commodity which was delivered, stored and trans-shipped into and out of the warehouses of the vast 'Railway Lands' area which surrounded the goods yard and steam shed, 'Top Shed', west of the running lines between Gasworks and Copenhagen tunnels. 300 dray horses were employed on road deliveries from King's Cross goods depot alone in the 1890s.

Whatever their origins these morning and afternoon 'run-round' diagrams were still booked as the 'Provender Run Round' in 1965 and on that October afternoon I walked with Jack along platform 1 into York Way by the Moorgate platform, turned left off York Way into the old potato market, on the very site, although I unfortunately didn't know at the time, of the first, 1850, pre-King's Cross, G.N.R. terminus, Maiden Lane. Then we were actually above Gasworks Tunnel crossing the main lines, and then down into the still considerable goods yard which I had run into quite a few times on run-round and transfer jobs from Ferme Park and other yards. We reported ourselves to the yard-master who gave Jack a '350' 'spoon' (key) and directed us across the yard to our 'pilot', D3723, standing over by the huge waste of land which Jack pointed out reverently as the site of 'Top Shed', 34A, King's Cross' famous steam depot unfortunately demolished in 1963. We awoke D3723 and moved through the weekend quiet of the goods yard towards the yard exit at 'Five Arches', the huge range of brick arches which spanned the whole yard by 'Goods and Mineral Junction' box guarding the yard entrance/exit, and awaited orders.

The first locomotive stabling point was built on the eastern side of what was to become 'Top Shed' in 1850, at that time adjacent to Maiden Lane station which served as the Great Northern Railway's London terminus until completion of Gasworks Tunnel and the grand new King's Cross station beyond, two years later.

The 'Railway Lands' and 'Top Shed' grew enormously over the following century but with the advent of diesel power, was succeeded in 1960 by Finsbury Park TMD, code 34G, located in and usually referred to as 'Clarence Yard' and described here earlier (P.29).

By 1965 no vestige of 'Top Shed' remained; unlike many steam locomotive sheds this most famous example was never used to stable the steam engine's diesel successors.

As we sat on our 'bar stools', with D3723's diesel grumbling expectantly, Jack regaled me with stories of his steam firing days at 'Top Shed', illustrating his tales with such semi-serious observations as, "Oh, yes, Norm, when you're here during the night you'll hear their ghostly whistles still echoing round these arches in this very goods yard." This followed by a loud burst of genuine Jack laughter; and on that Saturday afternoon in late 1965, as we sat in our 350h.p. diesel shunter awaiting our first move, driver Jack Crate brought the whole area of 'Top Shed' and 'King's Cross Goods', 'The Railway Lands', back momentarily to hot and dirty, smoky, steamy, vibrant, life.

Jack was of average height, always immaculately groomed, suave, yet favoured steam-day overalls rather than the new green uniform, as did many drivers, brought up as they were amidst the grime and grease of steam locomotion; but the big surprise came when he spoke, in a mellow, measured voice, in accents which would have been the envy of any BBC radio announcer; a precise, 'received English' which, let's face it, you didn't expect to hear from a railway engine driver. He smiled readily and punctuated his conversation with a loud, gusty laugh. I don't know where Jack lived and I don't think anybody knew anything of his life outside King's Cross depot; I do remember, however, an occasion in the rest room when one of the wags asked Jack why one so obviously sophisticated (that's not the way the inquisitor put it!) drove railway engines. Jack became unusually serious and said very slowly and surely, "I drive railway engines because I want to drive railway engines and that's that." And as the old smile returned and the eyebrows rose quizzically if not defiantly, the assembled company realised that "that" really was "that". Whatever his background Jack was a most dedicated railway and locomotive man and was a pleasure to work with.

Out on the road I soon discovered that Jack sang as he drove, in a good, tuneful and uninhibited tenor, 'Sound of Music' songs being particular favourites, and, after working several shifts with Jack, I realised that 'My Favourite Things' was THE word perfect favourite.

That afternoon we worked some six hours on transfer trips between King's Cross and Ferme Park yards, spine-jolting trips which I was now becoming used to, and we even had one 15m.p.h. jaunt out to Hornsey carriage sidings with parcels vans – via Bounds Green flyover of course.

Another regular job which I first worked at this time and which I soon came to like for its diversity even though it rarely took us beyond Gas Works tunnel, was 'station pilot'. There were two station pilots – usually 'Brush-2's - known familiarly as 'Number 1 Shunt' and 'Number 2 Shunt'; 'Number 1' was in attendance in and about the station and station yard 24/7 while 'Number 2' withdrew during the night. The job consisted in moving stock around the station, and in those days, with parcels trains, mail trains and the constant necessity to move empty coaches and vans from platform to platform, the two station pilots were kept busy for much of

the day and night, moving under instruction of the station shunters and foremen who co-ordinated the pilots' movements between arriving and departing trains with the signal box, always coming to the 'shunt' driver to tell him how many vehicles were to be moved and where to; sometimes a complex move, dropping off and picking up, would take a pilot from the 'arrival side', east side, of the station, platform 1, via several other platforms, eventually across to the 'milk yard' on the west side of the station, and after the shunter's quick summary of the planned moves it was a matter of following the dollies, weaving from road to road via Gasworks Tunnel which it was often necessary to enter before reversal into a designated platform. As drivers got to know us, and if they decided we were competent, they became willing to share the driving and this was particularly so on the station pilots when we often drove for half the shift each. This station shunt never palled.

Returning to 'The Cross', I also discovered a 'new' locomotive type, one which I had already briefly

The ubiquitous 'Brush-2' – we had some 50 to 60 of them. D5626 is 'No.1 shunt', night station-pilot, at 'The Cross' and the dolly is off for her to leave the top of 10 for her next move. (RCTS)

encountered back in May when D5909 assisted our failed 'Brush-2', D5588, as related above. This was the infamous 'Baby Deltic', ('23'), which had now started to re-appear in London on the peak time suburban jobs but which I initially came across on relief jobs, the routine light engine trips between the station and the 'Passenger Loco'. The 'Baby Deltics' shared the same endearing characteristics as their big cousins, emitting a similar ear-splitting howl from their single 1100 horse power 'Deltic' engine, and showing the same reluctance to move until the controller was halfway round the quadrant, when a smart sleight of hand easing off – but not too much! – was needed as she 'got hold of 'em'. But while the mighty twin-engined 3,300h.p. 'Deltics' became, literally, legends in their own time, the humble Type 1 'Babies' were unpopular from the outset, although, as I mentioned earlier, I came to like them – on passenger trains! My first experience was with D5907 which I took from the suburban side of the station into the 'Passenger Loco' on Wednesday, 20th October with driver Jimmy Geeson, while, in a reverse move ten days later, with driver Vic Beckett, we prepared and took D5908 from

the loco to the Saturday night 00.03 suburban departure, unusually loco hauled instead of DMU worked.

On a particularly wet Sunday night the 7th of November 1965 I started a week of nights following a 9 til 5 week which had included three days at Ilford training school on a train heating boiler revision course. I signed on at 23.00 for an 'as required' turn with Sam who I had not seen since a similar early morning shift three Sundays before. After sitting and yarning for an hour in the cosy crew room I was suddenly summoned to go with another driver Sam, tall and serious, sparsely but pleasantly spoken Sam Gardner of '4', 'Cambridge', link, initially to Finsbury Park and Clarence Yard TMD to pick up a locomotive, and then to run down to Dalston Junction where we were to take over a 'block cement' train, 4N39, from the Southern and take it as far as Peterborough on its long haul to York and then across to Uddingston freight terminal south-east of Glasgow.

These 'block cement' trains ran regularly from Cliffe cement works near Dartford in Kent. Cliffe had quarried cement since the 1860s, it closed in 1970 and is now a wild life centre. The trains consisted of 30 special

During the first, unreliable, 'Baby Deltic' years, in October 1961, D5901 looks to be in fine form as she tears up the main south of Hatfield on a Cambridge line train. (Colour-Rail)

'Presflo' cement wagons into which the cement was loaded and unloaded with compressed air as a fine powder. The 'bulk' 'Presflo' trains had worked in various diagrams since the 1950s and were the first precursors of the 'Freightliner' trains which appeared later in the '60s and became the basis for the whole concept of today's freight train working.

Thirty loaded 'Presflos' weighed around 800 tons but those who worked them proudly proclaimed them as '1000 tonners'. The trains were usually worked from Cliffe by Southern, Hither Green, men with a pair of 'Type 3' 'Cromptons' (33) – a 1960 1,250h.p. Sulzer engine development of our 'Sulzer 2's with Crompton instead of B.T.H. traction motors. The 'Cromptons' usually worked as far as York where a big old 'English Electric 4' (40) took the train on to Glasgow Uddingston. With the arrival of the 'Freightliners' Uddingston became one of the first Freightliner concentration terminals and was renamed Gushetfaulds. Gushetfaulds in turn closed in the 1990s with the opening of Coatbridge 'Euroterminal', and has recently (2014) reopened – as a huge 'First' bus depot!

Why we were to take the cement train over at Dalston on this particular night we did not know and, unfortunately, in retrospect, didn't ask.

We boarded, therefore, the 00.03 local to Finsbury Park and walked down to Clarence Yard Depot through the steadily falling rain where the foreman in his snug office allocated us 'Brush 4' (47) D1533 which stood out in the yard and which we prepared in the soaking wet, a condition I would begin to get used to before this night was finished! We arrived at Dalston Junction by about 01.30 and were put back into the spur just north of the junction box.

The Uddingston cement trains started their long trip from Cliffe at 02.30 (although my notes give this as the time at Dalston) and they came to us via the North London line to Dalston Junction East where they would draw past the junction with the Canonbury, then run round before continuing up the bank to Finsbury Park and our ECML. On this wet November night, however, we would come out of the spur, couple up to the other end of the train and then proceed to Finsbury Park and so on northwards - that was the plan – easy!

4N39 arrived at Dalston Junction at about 04.15 with a rumble and a rattle and the tick of idling 'Sulzers'.

If 02.30 was the Cliffe departure time, somebody had made some typos somewhere and the train wasn't really late at all, and we'd sat in that spur for almost three rain-trickling hours for nothing. We'd both dozed off - while some could sleep during the briefest of night time layovers, this was one of the very few times I dropped off; Sam also dozed in his seat – and as the track shifted and the 'dolly' came off we stretched stiffening limbs and I donned my waterproofs again and prepared to couple up in the still steadily falling rain. We buffered up, Sam eased up tight and I squeezed in between; I'd done a bit of coupling-up since my first fateful shift and thought little of it as I undid brake hoses on the brake-van - there was, thoughtfully, one at each end of the train - and on D1533, slung and tightened the chain over the hook and brought the two brake hoses together – they would not clip. I tried again. Sam appeared, wondering why I was taking so long, shone his lamp in, when I could see that the lug on the brake-van's pipe was bent and would not engage with its counterpart on our hose. "Better tell the bobby," said Sam and I joined him in the soaking rain and went up to the box.

As in all signal boxes it was warm and clean and snug and I must have made a strange sight as I stood and dripped on the door-mat – you didn't walk on a signal box floor with wet or dirty boots – and explained our predicament. The signalman considered for a moment then walked over to the stove and handed me his hefty coal hammer, "See if you can straighten it with that," he suggested and, with a last reluctant look at the cosy cabin, I sloshed back to the loco where Sam was, of course, back in the cab where he had been joined by our guard, come to report the load and let us know he was ready to go. I squeezed back in-between and the guard came with me. I crept under the coupling and buffers with water and muck dripping everywhere and we took it in turns to hold the offending hose while the other belted the bent lug. It was not easy in that wet and narrow space. After some minutes of this we tried the hoses together again – admittedly without much hope - but - the hoses came together, not very square but they were together! I wriggled out and shouted up to Sam to "make a brake" but he soon looked over the side and shook his head sadly. I returned to our guard still in-between – and now welting away at the two joined lugs. "We're getting a brake!" came Sam's shout as I prepared to creep back into that damp and dingy gap. "I think you've done it!" I said to the guard and he left the hoses and crept out, saying, "I wouldn't want to be the bloke who has to unfasten them!" – prophetic and fateful words, for that 'bloke' was standing next to him in the streaming 'four-foot'! We adjourned to the cab where Sam happily pointed to the vacuum gauge and the two needles gradually creeping up the glass until they stopped precisely on the regulation 21 inches required to take the train brakes off. We thanked the guard who squelched his way back along the train to his hopefully dry and cosy van at the other end of the train, whistled a fanfare at the box although the 'boards' were still off, and at last lifted the heavy 'Plasmors' away over the junction and towards the climb to Finsbury Park and the main line at 05.50, just catching the guard's green light as we went into the right hander at the bottom of the climb.

But the Fates had not finished with us that night by a considerable margin. D1533 slipped on the wet rails as Sam got us away and he was unable to give her the full power needed to lift 800 tons up the curved Canonbury bank to Finsbury Park. But we still would have made it – if Finsbury Park No.3 box hadn't stopped us dead on the bank just beyond the main-line underpass. "We're not going to get away from here" said Sam with conviction – I had just stripped off my streaming waterproof and I slowly pulled it on again as that signal came off in front of us and Sam tried valiantly to move D1533 and 800 tons of dry cement away on that wet uphill rail; but we stood no chance, and I was soon down in the streaming ballast trudging across in the apparently eternal rain, to the telephone at the junction signals with the down main-line goods roads where I told the 'bobby' in 'No.3' that we would never start our train on that bank, and resisting the temptation to ask why on earth he'd let us through to stop there with such a load anyway. "I'll get an engine round behind you" said 'bobby' and I returned to the cab where more time passed and I dripped on the cab floor until a 'Sulzer 2' came down the bank on the up Carriage road, giving us a cheeky 'toot' as it ran by to the rear of our train via No.1 box. Some minutes later, hanging, streaming, out of the cab, I heard the 'Sulzer's' 'crow' from the back of the train, out of sight beyond the fly-over, and as I answered the call from my side and gave Sam 'right', he dropped the air brake off and gingerly opened up. With our

rear assistance we soon rolled through Finsbury Park and were given the main line. Sam opened the controller fully after Wood Green and our 2570 horses – twin 'Cromptons' would employ, nominally, over 3000 - galloped and rumbled gamely away up the bank, thundering and whining through Potters Bar tunnel, as I once more got out of my waterproofs and draped them with Sam's on the backs of our seats, the screw brake wheel and other cab protuberances. And it was as I finally sat down that my eye was caught by an alien object on the floor at the back of the cab. I laughed and Sam looked across at me as though he wondered if the night's events had become too much; I pointed to the intruder and Sam looked and laughed too, "How's that bobby going to break his coal up now?" he wondered, for the Dalston signalman's coal hammer still lay where I'd dropped it on our cab floor.

We just managed our maximum permitted speed, 75m.p.h., after Hatfield and through Welwyn Garden City when we suddenly realised that it had stopped raining. But this unfortunate night hadn't finished with us yet, and as we ran onto Welwyn Viaduct with the first signs of an amazingly Homeric rosy-fingered dawn showing on the horizon off to our right across the long vista of still dark east Hertfordshire, Sam suddenly exclaimed, "Now what!" And, looking across I saw that Sam's face glowed blue in the reflection of the blue fault light which had just flashed up in front of him. The engine still rumbled healthily, the traction engines still whined below, but something was apparently wrong somewhere. I opened the engine-room door to the deafening clatter of the big Sulzer 12LDA, working hard but apparently in good order, took one step inside then back again, faced by a great torrent of black oil splashing down onto the walkway from a point somewhere up in the engine-room roof. I closed the door quickly and told Sam who immediately shut off, "Lube oil pipe's fractured," he diagnosed straight away keeping a keen eye ahead as we dashed through the Welwyn tunnels, still signalled main line after the two road bottle neck, and with power off we careered on, powered by the sheer momentum of 800 tons of cement travelling at some 70m.p.h., and the slightly favourable gradient. So, as Sam had said, 'now what'? Sam never swore and he greeted bad language with a lift of the eyebrows; needless to say his eyebrows were lifted on a pretty regular basis when he was in the crew

The great Welwyn Viaduct completed for the original G.N.R. in 1850, limited to one track each way; from which I saw a glorious sunrise just as D1533 failed on us on 7th of November 1965. (Colour-Rail)

room at 'the Cross', and on that night I will admit that on several occasions I had been the cause of Sam's elevated eyebrows; indeed I feel sure that I lifted them several times as we ran through Stevenage and we agreed that as we were still rolling steadily, we'd hope to make it into Hitchin without attracting the signalmen as any attempt to turn us in slow road at Wymondley might rob us of our momentum before we could reach the station – and Hitchin loco. And so it thankfully turned out.

We coasted by Hitchin South box, a puzzled signalman leaning out as we slowed into the station, and Sam braking gently to bring us to a smooth stand on the main line adjacent to the down platform end and Hitchin Yard box at about 07.15, the engine still steadily ticking over in healthy Sulzer fashion.

I got down and crossed to the down platform and the station foreman who relayed our predicament to the box and also to the diesel loco depot which then stood

beyond the down yard, today occupied by the engineers and their variety of track maintenance machines. We were blocking the down main line which would soon be busy with the first of the day's East Coast expresses, and it wasn't long before we were joined by a gang of fitters who, without much surprise to us, declared D1533 a failure; my notes say, 'cooling pump and fan u/s' – no mention of the flood of lube oil which we had fully expected to seize the engine before we reached Hitchin, and, in fact the engine still ran, for my notes also say 'engine to Hitchin depot' – after it was uncoupled by a Hitchin shunter. I watched with bated breath from the four-foot as he got between, and wondered if I should go up into the cab and pick up the Dalston signalman's coal hammer; but Sam stood with me and his eyebrows raised only momentarily as the shunter, practiced and professional, applied his own hammer and invective, and quickly knocked apart those offending brake hoses.

Hitchin approaches from the south today, from Benslow Bridge. In the 1960s Hitchin South box stood south of the bridge; a spur in the present car park accommodated a DMU which ran a shuttle service to Peterborough. The white stone pyramid on the up side marks the site of 34D, Hitchin steam shed, today's single track up yard, until recently reception for the road-stone and departure point for scrap metal. (Author)

1970s Hitchin with a 'Brush-4' heading a down express, Benslow Bridge beyond. In 1965 I arrived here with driver Sam Gardner and 800 tons of cement after an eventful night with D1533 which refused to go any further. (Paul Hepworth)

This 'Brush-4' on the up main passes the spot on the adjacent down main where sister D1533 came to a stand with the block-cement on the morning of 8th November 1965. The Yard Box beyond presides over the down yard and diesel depot hidden behind the approaching train. (Paul Hepworth)

From the end of Hitchin down platform today; the Yard Box is long gone, it stood directly behind the twenty-first century drivers' safety check mirror which here reflects the up platform. Just 50 years earlier we detached D1533 on the down main here and ran down to reverse into Hitchin diesel depot. (Author)

Hitchin down yard in 2017. In 1965 the line-up of yellow engineers' track machines would have consisted of a mix of 34G 'Type-1' and 'Type-2' diesel locomotives to which we added a sick 'Type-4' on that November morning. The goods yard occupied the bare plot between the down slow and the loco yard. (Author)

Sam and I still breathed short breaths as Sam eased D1533 away from our troublesome trucks, dropped back onto the down slow, pulled forward and then back again into the loco yard and the direction of the shed foreman, all the time expecting that steady Sulzer 'tickety tock' to stop with a final horrid screech of ceased bearings; but we made it with the engine still turning over dutifully as Sam at last pressed 'engine stop'. We 'screwed her down', had a last look into the hot and swamped engine room, collected our damp waterproofs and other gear, took D1533's key to the foreman and then headed back to the station, now 'home passenger' back to King's Cross.

As we had gingerly entered Hitchin loco yard with D1533, two nose-coupled 1,000h.p. 'Choppers', 'English Electric Type-1s' (20) waited to come out, and as soon as we were in clear they left to pick up our very late 'Presflos' and work them north. It was the first time I'd seen these 'Type-1's, for although ten were allocated to 34G, Finsbury Park TMD, they worked exclusively from Hitchin – 34G's northern outpost – and I never saw one in London; I believe they worked only to Peterborough. At first sight I was reminded of the Hornsey 'Paxman's, as they had but one cab situated at one end of a long bonnet; but the 'English Electric' '1's were, and, indeed, still are, a very different beast to the 'Paxman's, for while just one 'Paxman' has been preserved, around 50 'EE-1's (20s) are still running, not only on heritage railways, but also in main-line service; most refurbished for Direct Rail Services or maintained for hire by Harry Needle Rail Services; they are used to top and tail nuclear flask trains, to power Autumn railhead treatment trains, and recently hauled London Underground's new 'S-stock' trains from the 'Bombardier' works in Derby, to LUL's West Ruislip depot in West London.

As the first diesels to be delivered under the 1955 Railway Modernisation Plan, the 'EE-1s' were surprisingly successful, the first – D8000 (20050) – emerging from English Electric's Vulcan Foundry in 1957, while the last - D8328 (20228) - brought the total to 228 in 1968. Today D8000 is preserved at the National Railway Museum in York in original handsome B.R. dark green, while the penultimate member of the class, 20227, is still in main line service, one of several used on the LUL stock movements.

So, in the early morning of Monday, the 8th of November 1965, in the bright Hitchin sunshine, such a contrast to the preceding filthy night, driver Sam Gardner and I watched two of these stalwart 1,000 horse-power locomotives brighten our unfortunate night as they lifted our 800 tons of block cement effortlessly away from Hitchin on the down main line, the staccato syncopation of their full-throttle exhausts confirming them as 'Choppers' indeed! In April 1966 all ten 34G 'Choppers' would be transferred *en bloc* to Immingham on Humberside.

'Type-1' 'English Electric' 1,000h.p. Bo-Bo, TOPS '20'. D8027 is brand-new at Hitchin in 1960 adjacent to the still busy steam shed on the up side. The 10 34G 'Choppers' stayed at Hitchin after initial substitution for the North British 'Type-2's on suburban passenger trains. (RCTS)

On that November 1965 morning we went back to 'The Cross' on the 08.20 up passenger, riding in the back cab of the 'Brush-2' train engine. We were back in the S.O.P. by 09.15, some eleven hours after signing on.

After this exceptional Sunday night I returned to the routine of the 'shed duty gang', the regular diet of 'relief' and 'as required' turns although with a fair mixture of 'station pilot', 'e.c.s.', suburban passenger, 'engine movements' and 'runround' jobs. A notable event which occurred on the night of Wednesday, 15th December 1965 was at the time just another relief job although even then we realised that DP2 was very different to the 'Deltics' which she outwardly resembled. That night I was with a top-link driver - they sometimes stooped to a shift 'on the shed' – Brian Elston, and we relieved DP2, also taking a break from her usual top-link duties, on an arriving parcels train at about 01.45. We took her to the loco and thought no more of it; but of course DP2, apart from being an English Electric demonstration locomotive – 'Diesel Prototype 2' – was to come to a violent end some 19 months after my short trip with her when she was in collision, ironically from my point of view, with a derailed Cliffe to Uddingston cement train at Thirsk, and was so badly damaged that her final duties were to provide spare parts for later 'English Electric' 'Type-4' (TOPS 50) locomotives which had been developed from DP2 herself and which were just then, in 1967, coming into service for the still to be electrified West Coast route beyond Crewe to Preston and Glasgow. DP2, while looking every inch a 'Deltic' at first glance, was powered by just one conventional English Electric 16CSVT engine, giving 2,700h.p. The 16CSVT was eventually fitted to the new 'Type-4s' – which were revamped to look nothing like the earlier 'English Electric' locos, but put me in mind of a chunky 'Brush-2'! The 16CSVT engine was an uprated version of the 2,000h.p. 16SVT fitted to the original 'E.E.4s' (40) which were the first B.R. 'big' diesels in 1958 and which we were familiar with at King's Cross, although the East Coast allocation worked from Gateshead. All this, of course, was in the future in December 1965, and I was completely unaware of the dubious honour attached to my brief journey with DP2 on that Wednesday night.

A last notable 1965 diagram was 'No.5 Runround' worked on the 28th December. It was notable for the succession of farcical coincidences which occurred. I was with a young driver, Dave Daveney, (who I still, meet with several others, now not so young, at the King's Cross staff socials at Hatfield). 'Number 5 Runround' was evidently another remnant from by-gone days, for there were no runround jobs that I remember numbered 1 to 4, nor any from 6 onwards; in fact the only other runround diagram celebrated with a title was the 'Provender', already mentioned; other runrounds, often as required, were just that – 'runrounds'.

We signed on at 11.45 and at this 'dead' time between Christmas and New Year we didn't expect to be all that busy and thought that our first task would consist of a walk to the goods yard to find our motive power. And while this would most certainly happen, it would not be quite in the direct way we expected. We were immediately instructed to catch the 12.03 to Hornsey and find a '350' in Ferme Park. Well, usually this would have been a perfectly reasonable quest, there were always pilots both working and stabled in Ferme Park; but at this holiday time Ferme Park was strangely deserted when we got there, both down and up sides, and the only working, or, at least, ticking over, pilot contained two bored Hornsey men who wondered hopefully but vainly if we were their relief. We went to the yard foreman's office and 'phoned home'. The King's Cross 'inside' foreman told us to come back and walk over to the goods yard where he was sure there was a spare pilot! So we crossed to Hornsey station and eventually 'rode the cushions' back into 'The Cross' then took our belated walk into another strangely deserted goods yard, King's Cross, at about 14.00 and had a 'mash' and a bite in the shunters' bunk before reporting to a bored goods yard foreman who directed us over to the far, 'Top-shed', side of the yard, and there, sure enough, we found a lonely line-up of no less than five '350' pilots, all on their Christmas holidays. "No wonder there aren't any in Ferme Park!" said Dave. We climbed into the nearest loco, D3714, and Dave fitted the big brass 'spoon' which served as starter and master-controller on a '350', leaned on it, and waited for the 'English Electric 6KT' to turn and rumble into life – not a murmur; all of Dave's efforts resulted in total silence, not a sign of life. "Battery's flat" was our unanimous and learned verdict and we turned our attention to the next in line, D3722, which started with a satisfying roar after the usual initial succession of doubtful knocks and whines of protest. So, the next job was to move D3714 forward to a crossover with D3722 until we could run round her. "Better put the hook on while I go and tell them what we're doing," decided Dave, then paused, gazing at D3722 in disbelief; the loco stood nose to the north which meant that the big fuel gauge mounted just in front of the cab was towards us - the needle indicating almost empty! We decided not to start another engine and Dave went off to the foreman's office while I waited for D3722 to make her air then unscrewed her and buffered up to D3714 which would have to be moved anyway – unless we started again at the other end of the line-up! Dave returned with instructions for us to tow D3714 to Clarence Yard and have D3722 refuelled. "Yeh, but will we get to Clarence Yard?" I wondered. Dave shook his head, "Foreman says we will," he said with a grin, "so we will!" The omnipotent loco foreman!

I walked ahead and set the road as Dave dropped D3722's brake off and opened the controller. D3722 heaved and roared mightily, her exhaust shooting high and black clag into the air as Dave gave her more throttle, using up our precious fuel oil, but D3714 didn't budge; Dave shut off. I walked back and Dave joined me, we checked the screw brake on D3714 and it was most certainly off; not only was D3714's battery flat but her brakes were locked on. There was one more thing we could try before giving up; with the two locos closely buffered up after the attempt to move I got in-between again and coupled the vacuum brake hoses, Dave 'made a brake', eased D3722's vacuum train brake off – and with a hiss of releasing brakes D3714 creaked forward against the coupling chain – we were in business!

Well, we eased our way out under the arches, propelling D3714 into the exit road of the goods yard where still nothing else moved. I phoned 'Goods and Mineral' box to ask for the road to Clarence Yard then boarded D3714 in accordance with the rule that engines hauled dead must have a 'rider'. The bobby gave us the exit board and a wave as we made our way out of the goods yard, through Copenhagen tunnel, up Holloway Bank to Finsbury Park, both listening closely to the song of D3722's engine, expecting it to fade every yard; but we rolled into Finsbury Park down goods without mishap, then, given the dolly into Clarence Yard, Dave gave D3714 a final push into the yard at just about 17.00 hours, just about three hours since we'd arrived in the goods yard after our pointless trip to Ferme Park. We phoned the Clarence Yard foreman and by the time we'd shunted D3714 into the appointed road, uncoupled and screwed her down, a fitter had come out of the depot to see to D3722's refuelling - loco men didn't do refuelling! – and I set the road

into the appropriate fuelling road where Dave placed the engine; the fitter put the hose in – and a minute later stepped smartly back from the fountain of diesel fuel which exploded from D3722's filler cap. "Gauge stuck" said the fitter as he wiped himself down and looked up at the offending fuel gauge; we got down and looked in horror at a gauge which now stood on the 'full' mark, not really knowing whether to laugh or scream.

We phoned the King's Cross foreman again and eventually took D3722 back to the goods yard and back into the pilot line-up on the west side where we'd found her some four hours earlier, arriving at about 18.30. So we'd taken just about a whole shift by the time we arrived back at the S.O.P. to do two almost fruitless round trips, one 'on the cushions' and one which, well, did achieve something, we took one dead 'pilot' to the T.M.D. for a battery change.

Two accidents in our area of the East Coast Main Line provided a remarkable opening to 1966. On the evening of Wednesday, 12th of January a 'Brush-2' was hurrying the 17.27 departure from King's Cross, an evening 'Cambridge Buffet Express', down the main through Hatfield at about 70m.p.h. when a broken rail derailed the rear bogie of the sixth (TSO) of the usual seven coach formation just north of the station; the coach swung across the down slow and stopped with its rear end foul of the adjacent Luton branch line, fortunately remaining upright, as also did the last (BSO) coach which also swung across the down slow, losing its leading bogie which also ended up on the Luton line. It seems that casualties were slight, probably and mercifully because the vehicles remained upright. I spent most of the first part of January with Sam on 'reliefs' and 'as requireds' and during that week, ending 15th of January we were starting an 'as required' turn at the bracing time of 03.00 each morning, in time to cover the arrivals of the first up sleepers and mails, and therefore knew nothing of the derailment until we arrived on the Thursday morning by which time normal running had evidently been restored as my notes do not mention the incident, and relief of the arrivals carried on as normal during the early hours. The second 'disaster' occurred in February and we shall come to it in due course.

On the 17th of January my seniority took me into 'Number 6 (Suburban) Link', and I went out to the Finsbury Park S.O.P. where, as related above, I'd spent eight weeks in Hornsey 'No.4-link' during the summer of 1965.

CHAPTER 8

KING'S CROSS 6 (FINSBURY PARK) LINK

n steam days, the 1960s 'King's Cross 6 link' had been known as the 'Met-link' and its crews had worked the 'N2' 'Met' 0-6-2T locomotives on the inner-suburban services between King's Cross and Hatfield or Hertford. In the mid-1960s 'King's Cross 6 link' still worked these inner-suburban services but, as I have outlined already, with a strange mixture of power during those days of slow evolution from steam to diesel power. The off-peak services were worked by single-manned diesel multiple units, while the morning and evening peak hours consisted of steam-age suburban compartment stock, the remaining ancient articulated 'quad-art' sets and five or

six coach 'blockenders', hauled by 'Type-2' diesel locomotives, giving employment to 'Hornsey 4-link' and 'King's Cross 6-link' 'second men'. King's Cross second-man duties at Finsbury Park consisted in working these morning and evening peak-time passenger jobs and also, on night shifts, in accompanying drivers on DMUs after 22.00 when double manning on all forms of power was compulsory throughout the railway system.

Many of the regular 'King's Cross 6-Link' drivers were 'stop-link' drivers, which meant they were veteran drivers who for various reasons had elected not to go forward in their natural progression into the main line

'Brush-2' D5673 between New Barnet and Greenwood (Hadley Wood) with an empty – according to the '3' indicator – and ancient quad-art set 'strengthened' with a parcels GUV in October 1961; modern sets cannot be 'strengthened'. (RCTS)

links, but to stay in the suburban links. These 'stop-link men' were all, of course, ex-steam men, had probably prepared and perhaps fired Ivatt 'Atlantics' and certainly fired and most likely driven Gresley 'Pacifics', before, for whatever reason, they decided to climb the links no further. Most were quite alright to work with but a few were inclined to be real 'grumpy old men', and one or two, perhaps understandably, were downright contemptuous of a man who sat on the other side of the cab and did virtually nothing instead of wielding a shovel over a roasting fire and balancing the boiler water level as they had in their youth on steam engines. These 'old'uns' had perhaps been obliged to 'stop' themselves for family or health reasons, and I think some really hankered after a turn of speed 'down the main'; I recall one of these veterans bemoaning the old days and bitterly seeing his present position as "a glorified tram driver."

'First generation' diesel multiple units came to King's Cross suburban services in 1958 although they first saw service with British Railways in the Yorkshire West Riding in 1954 and were the outcome of enquiries started in 1951 by a body set up by the Railway Executive entitled the Lightweight Trains Committee. The committee had visited Ireland and the Continent where DMUs were already established and reported in favour of DMUs for British Railways in 1952, therefore orders for DMUs were in hand with several manufacturers before the 1955 Modernisation Plan. King's Cross's allocation in the mid-1960s were two and three-car Cravens of Sheffield units with BUT engines.

I remember several 'characters' from the old 'stop' drivers out at 'The Park' in '6-Link'; one taciturn old steam man, Bill, who still dressed, as many did, in full blue overalls and 'civvy' cap, and who had a habit of saying, "All right, we'll go" every time he got two buzzes from the guard to start a night-time DMU from a station; and big, happy, old 'Sam' Harding who's initial was W. on the roster, goodness knows how he became 'Sam', but he was a pleasure to work with and I was always pleased to see his name next to mine on the roster, especially if it was one of our peak-time inner-suburban diagrams with a 'Type-2'.

So our '6-link' 'second-man' shifts tended to be anything but full day jobs and when we did get a day shift it often meant hours spent in that sombre 'waiting room' or its immediate vicinity on what were ambitiously entitled 'Ferry' diagrams, which involved our riding in the south end cab of a DMU as the unit was propelled, driven from the north end, into Western Sidings, a roomy covered carriage shed which stood south of Finsbury Park on the down side, between the main lines and the down Canonburies, about opposite where our block cement train had been stopped, and here the DMUs were stabled and maintained. There was little of this 'ferry' work during the day so, again, 'ferry' turns offered little action until units started to arrive for stabling in the evening; but we could be most sure that if we left the station for a walk out into the salubrious surroundings of Finsbury Park, we would have an irate foreman-timekeeper waiting for us when we returned.

I was in '6-link' for about six months and although I tend to complain about our Finsbury Park S.O.P. I was out and about much more than I had been in 'Hornsey-4', often on the morning and evening peak suburban trains, mixed, of course, with the eternal empty coach trips between King's Cross and the various carriage sidings. I also became better acquainted with the King's Cross junior drivers who worked alongside the veteran 'stop' men on their own seniority succession through the links, and, when with them, I was often 'put in the seat', regularly driving our 'Sulzers' and 'Brushes' on trains rather than just ferrying light engines between the station and the 'Passenger Loco' with occasional trips out to Clarence Yard.

On Sunday morning the 20th February 1966 Wrestlers Bridge, just north of Hatfield station and ironically close to the site of the January 'Cambridge Buffet Express' derailment, collapsed, completely blocking the East Coast Main Line. The bridge had apparently been 'under surveillance' for some time as the easterly arch, spanning the up slow, was known to have subsided from true by about five inches and some longitudinal cracks had occurred in it. On that Sunday morning the engineers actually had possession of the main lines under the bridge and had removed the up fast track and ballast in order to add a layer of sand 'blanketing' and so improve maintenance of the up main at this point – nothing to do with the condition of the bridge and its 'surveillance' which was totally ignored! The east arch collapsed and fell into their excavation on the up main. Fortunately there was no traffic in the vicinity at the time and all trains were immediately diverted via the Hertford loop. I had been 'rest day' off on Saturday 19th and didn't sign on until 21.30 on Sunday night for '331 Diagram', a busy, all empty coach transfers job, with King's Cross driver Sid Webb and 'Brush-2' D5606; a job only affected by the bridge fall when we were unable to relieve and take over an engine from a Peterborough crew in the middle of the roster as they were delayed in coming up via the Hertford diversion; we retained D5606 and had her refuelled in Hornsey depot. The up slow roads were reopened during Tuesday 22nd and normal working resumed for Wednesday 23rd. For the rest of that week I was rostered on '481 diagram', a busy, night DMU second-manning job which consisted in two late suburban return trips from Finsbury Park; 20.11 to Hatfield and e.c.s. on to Welwyn Garden City, returning all stations to Finsbury Park and relief, then 22.11 all stations to Potters Bar and e.c.s. on to Hatfield, arrive 23.05, whence we returned after a break with the 00.35 staff train, all stations back to King's Cross, finishing off with the 03.15 staff, King's Cross as far as Finsbury Park where we were finally relieved. This was a typical week of DMU nights in King's Cross 6 'Suburban' link although on the Monday and Tuesday nights of that 'Wrestlers Bridge' week we were terminated at Hatfield with the 20.11 because of the bridge collapse. My roster for that week decreed that I work every night, Monday to Friday; Monday to Thursday with gruff old 'stop' driver Harry Gutteridge who took his rest-day on Friday when 481 diagram was worked by Stan Harrison, a young King's Cross '6-link' driver. Stan gave me a rare chance to drive a DMU when he 'put me in the seat' for the e.c.s. Potters Bar to Hatfield stretch.

These first DMUs had mechanical transmission and there was a bit more to driving them than just dropping the brake off with the left hand and opening the controller with the right which were the basic moves made in getting a diesel- electric locomotive on the move. Firstly, power control was operated on a DMU with the left hand, while the right hand not only applied the brake but also had to change gear! Power controller and gear change controls were identical stubby silver levers each surmounted with a black knob and moving in notched quadrants, while the brakes – operating on the nowadays universal 'pneumatic' or 'compressed air brake' system instead of the old vacuum system which required a vacuum to be created in the brake pipe throughout the train while running – were

applied by a long detachable silver handle which preparing and disposing drivers slotted into and out of its own domed quadrant next to the gear-change lever. On moving away the right hand pushed off the brake and selected first gear as the left notched open the controller, which was closed and opened again as each subsequent gear was selected; it was as near as could be to driving a road vehicle, and gear changes were decided by keeping half an eye on the rev-counter, the other half on the road ahead of course; the biggest difference to car driving for me being the disconcerting fact that you couldn't hear the engines; I'd never realized before that hearing the engine was an important if sub-conscious part of car driving! Synchronization of these actions on a first generation DMU took considerable concentration – to a first-timer anyway, and when the time to slow down and/or stop arrived, more concentration was needed in operating the brake, that long lever being hauled inwards, while an initial or partial application could be maintained by using the 'lap' position, a (for me, elusive!) notch in the brake quadrant beneath the lever in which one's thumb could be lodged (and locked!) until a greater or lesser application was required. Well, like so many things, all of this, obviously, soon became second nature to a regular DMU driver; but my own DMU driving hours were woefully short and I never did get the hang of that 'lap' position.

On Monday, 28th March 1966 it was decreed that the flat week's working hours for locomotive crews be reduced to 40 hours. In 2017 this may not sound so generous, 40 hours is a long working week nowadays; but the 1966 reduction improved on the previous legislation of 1947, which had reduced the standard week's hours down to 44. For me, at the time, this was fine but as a single man still living in the parental home and so contented in the job it didn't mean as much as it did to the married men. On a practical daily level it meant new rosters effective from Sunday, 17th April, which for me was the start of a week of nights after a rest day Saturday. The shifts were surely shorter and my records show this, but I cannot recall noticing much difference at the time. The jobs of course remained the same in King's Cross 6, Finsbury Park, 'suburban', link; nights on DMUs, day shifts on 'ferry', peak time inner suburban and empty coach jobs, never getting further than Welwyn Garden City or Hertford but for me, never boring, and, in the main, contented.

This introduction of shorter hours and new diagrams surely helped towards the speeding up of the slow, plodding and inefficient transition from steam to diesel and electric power and it was quickly followed by another radical, innovative and, in retrospect, inevitable, move to modernisation; single manning, the result of the controversial Manning Agreement between railway management – i.e. the government – and ASLEF, the locomens' union, - thrashed out in the "corridors of power" during 1965 - which decided that, very often, only a driver was needed in the cab at the front of even a locomotive hauled train.

At King's Cross this innovation arrived with the new rosters of April 1966, but we didn't notice the implications until the end of May when train heating finished for the summer. But during June we 'second men' began to find ourselves rostered for a new kind of diagram, known simply as 'Second Man Duties'. The new rule required all light engine movements still to be double-manned but many passenger trains, suburban and long distance, were now to be driver only. Well, it had to happen, they could not go on paying men to sit on a comfortable seat and ride round in a locomotive cab for hours on end doing little more than 'keep a sharp look out' – the unwritten 'rule 1'. To some these new duties were welcome, they were an extension of the shed duty jobs, sit in the rest room and make the occasional light-engine trip from the station to the 'Passenger Loco' or vice versa. But many second-men of my seniority, just starting to get 'on the road' regularly, and realising the implications behind single manning – i.e. to get rid of the second men – didn't like it at all. Instead of our rostered running jobs, 'second man duties' confined us to the station precincts, it was like being back in the 'shed gang'. 'Second man duties' consisted in joining drivers on light-engines and to accompany them to and from their trains around the station and local depots and sidings.

My introduction to 'second man duties' occurred on Monday, 13th of June. I was taken off 330 empty coaches diagram - and accompanying light engine manoeuvres – to work an 07.30 'second man duties' turn. My only job was given to me at about 13.00 and I went into King's Cross on the 13.09 to second-man a loco back to Finsbury Park carriage sidings. Unable to find said loco or driver anywhere in the station I reported to the King's Cross 'inside foreman' who told me I was too late, the job was done! Well, as this was in the over-manned terminus, this wasn't surprising. I was then sent back north of King's Cross to find a driver in Holloway Carriage Sidings – where I was told I was not required! My short notes do not say how I got to and from Holloway which was a considerable distance by road, beyond the tunnels from King's Cross, and far too far from Finsbury Park to walk. In any event after somehow making my way back to Finsbury Park S.O.P. I went home, somewhat dissatisfied with 'second-man duties'.

I was rostered to work this 07.30 second man roster all week, rest day Friday. On Tuesday I was given my only job on that shift just before eleven. I walked to Finsbury Park Carriage Sidings where I met Ray Brooks, a sharp mannered, stocky young King's Cross driver who I will soon get to know very well when I get into '4A-link'. On that Tuesday he had charge of the prototype 'Baby Deltic', D5900, and had just left his empty coaches in the sidings; I rode with him through Finsbury Park station to Clarence Yard TMD where I earned my keep by phoning the depot foreman and setting the road into the appointed bay in the works as Ray slowly followed me through the yard with the braying D5900. Ray then returned to the 'Cross', I to Finsbury Park S.O.P. and, soon afterwards - I went home!

So these latest 'second man duties' diagrams, brought in at this time as the latest attempt at 'rationalisation' in the painfully slow transition from steam to modern traction, brought little improvement in the efficiency of train working. We 'second men' were still on the pay-roll, still being paid whether we rode on an engine from King's Cross station to King's Cross depot or whether we rode on an engine from King's Cross station to Newcastle station. The only way the idea would have worked would have been to make all second-men redundant, pay us all off in one fell swoop; and there were no doubt many in the higher management echelons who would have put such a plan into practice had they been able. But no trades union would have allowed such a move and ASLEF stood firmly in the way of such legislation, while, indeed, our drivers, especially those in 'No.2 Leeds' link and 'No.1 Top' (Newcastle) link, were against such an idea; I remember seeing one veteran 'No.-1' link man back onto his Newcastle train soon after my return to King's Cross in July 1966, and how vociferous he was against the idea of driving nearly 300 miles on his own, "nobody to talk to, nobody to moan at, nobody to keep a sharp look out, supposing we fail, supposing *I* fail, nobody to make the tea, etc. etc." Nowadays, of course, 'driver only' is everyday practice, although the journey times, at 125 or so miles per hour, while calling for constant concentration, are much shorter. But in the mid '60s, taking their mates away from these veteran steam men, although they no longer be hard-working fireman, did not go down at all well. The 'firemen', now 'second-men', were now, really, on diesel locomotives, assistant drivers, although the fact was never recognised, as the majority of us did a bit of driving once the drivers got to know us, and especially when we were rostered with a regular mate, although foremen and inspectors turned a blind eye because there certainly was no official licence for us to drive.

On Tuesday, 14th June 1966, I changed turns for the rest of the week with a colleague who liked the idea of 'second man duties' and I spent Wednesday and Thursday on a double manned early morning suburban passenger and empty coach diagram with 'Brush 2's; I was rest day Friday while on Saturday I was kept busy with young King's Cross driver Ron Cardy and 'Sulzer-2' D5052, working empty fish vans and various empty coaching stock between Finsbury Park 'Macfish' sidings, Ferme Park, King's Cross and most of the area carriage sidings. I worked that Sunday, again on empty stock trips, with Finsbury Park driver Charlie Owers, half the shift with D5651 which we swapped for D5059 in Hornsey loco at about 12.30 when we also managed a good, civilised meal break in the fondly remembered Hornsey loco rest room, before taking D5059 and a train of coaches into King's Cross from Hornsey carriage sidings to finish the shift.

The next week I heard that I would be moving into 'No 7 link' on Monday, 4th July as I started a week of afternoons, working '339 diagram' with driver Les Hammons. The opening moves of '339 diagram' provided a variation on the usual empty coaches/suburban passenger theme; we walked to Finsbury Park carriage sidings where our 'Brush 2' waited, stabled, but already coupled to our train of empty coaches, which we took over the 'Widened Lines' to Moorgate. When our coaches departed as an evening suburban passenger service we duly dropped down the platform and into the spur, then came out onto the next set of coaches to arrive; but instead of working these as a passenger train we took them empty back over the Widened Lines, up through platform 16, well into Gasworks tunnel whence we reversed into a suburban platform - 13 booked - to become the 17.48 passenger to Welwyn Garden City. We ran light engine from Welwyn Garden City to Hornsey sidings where we picked up 3A72 e.c.s. and worked into King's Cross; in 'The Cross' we swapped our 'Brush' for a King's Cross crew's 'Sulzer-2', already standing on a train of empties which we took back to Hornsey, finally leaving the 'Sulzer' on Hornsey shed and booking off. As ever, how the complexities of these movements, in pre-computer days, when most trains still consisted of locomotive and coaches, were worked out, defeats me, as also, in the case of '339 diagram', does the reason for not taking the coaches for the 17.48 directly into King's Cross – or else working the passenger train from Moorgate? Perhaps it came into Moorgate as an evening passenger train? A perusal of the appropriate 1966 working timetable would, no doubt, solve this problem.

For my last week in 'No.6 Finsbury Park Link' I swapped out of an 07.00 'second-man duties' diagram called 'Extra Cover', for 332 diagram, starting at 05.45. While there was nothing really remarkable about the diagram, the driver would turn out to be truly remarkable. I had recently become aware of him on occasion in our Finsbury Park rest room where we signed on and off, where we second men so often waited for a job to turn up, and where '6-link' drivers on single-manned DMU turns often took their breaks, generally chatting, swapping jokes, relating experiences, complaining about rosters and signalmen and sundry other aspects of the job. When several crews met in this way, usually during the evening peak, the rest room would liven up considerably and among this motley gathering suddenly appeared, I think he had just come up into '6-link', a tall, dark, dapper, driver always smartly dressed but never in uniform, sporting a prominent Roman nose and a matching prominent voice, brash, amusing, sometimes even arrogant, and yet always engaging, a voice and personality which often dominated the conversation in the room. And it was this driver, driver Roy Head, who I joined for the first time at Finsbury Park at 05.45 on the morning of Monday, 27th June 1966 to work my last turn in '6-link'. As we signed on I wondered how I would get on with this vivacious character.

332 diagram opened with a ride on the 06.00 local from Finsbury Park to Hornsey, then a walk across to the depot where, on that Monday morning, we prepared

D5612. Despite his extrovert bluster in the company of his peers, driver Roy was a pleasure to work with; his conversation easy, friendly and considerate; before we left the depot he produced a packet of chocolate biscuits, perhaps not quite the right snack for 6 o'clock in the morning, but, as I was to find out during the months to come, snacks were a regular accompaniment to a shift with Roy Head. My reason for spending so much time on the introduction of driver Head will be made clear at the time of my last link change towards the end of October 1966.

We took D5612 light to Potters Bar where we crossed to the up side and picked up one of the two empty coach sets which were stabled in Potters Bar up siding each night after working a down evening peak service. I told Roy that my sister and friends caught the 08.11 to Moorgate and he promptly decided that I'd better 'chauffeur' them and put me 'in the seat'. The road went over, 'dolly' came off and we duly dropped down into the station to pick up sister, travelling companions, and sundry other commuters, leaving the old home town promptly at 08.11, calling at Hadley Wood and Oakleigh Park then non-stop to Finsbury Park and all stations to Moorgate, arriving 08.45. On release we made the usual Moorgate movements; light into the spur and take the coaches of the next arrival out to Finsbury Park carriage sidings where we were booked to arrive at 09.35 and where we remained as pilot; sorting coach sets ready for the evening peak departures, and assisting the carriage fitters in brake testing until relieved by a pair of our own men at about 13.00 when we went back to the S.O.P., signed off and went home.

I worked King's Cross '332' diagram with Roy and various 'Type-2s' on Tuesday, and Friday, with rest day for both of us on the Wednesday. On Saturday we worked '331' diagram with a start at 05.16 and after preparing D5671 on Hornsey shed we ran light into King's Cross and took the inevitable train of empties round to Hornsey carriage sidings via Bounds Green, and then doubled the circle by running light to Waterworks sidings – via Ferme Park fly-over. Waterworks stood exactly opposite Hornsey sidings on the down side. We were booked to shunt the 'odd stock' at Waterworks, but actually worked a train of empties over the fly-over and into Bounds Green sidings where a pair of Hornsey men eventually found and relieved us to finish the shift, the week, and, for me, my time in King's Cross 6 Link.

CHAPTER 9

KING'S CROSS 7 LINK

With King's Cross link promotion moving upwards from number 8, the shed link, progressively to number 1, the 'top', 'Newcastle Lodge', link, to move from 6 to 7 looks like a retrograde move; but this apparent backward progression for King's Cross second-men was yet another reflection of the slow transition away from steam practices; 6 was essentially a DMU link, successor to the steam days' 'Met-link' but located out at Finsbury Park to be convenient to Western Sidings DMU stabling point; we second men were allocated there primarily to cover the remaining loco hauled, peak time, suburban trains and DMU night-time 'second-manning'. For some arcane roster office reason it was more convenient to send us from 8 link into 'suburban' 6 at Finsbury Park, and then into 7 – which was familiarly known as the 'run-round' link – although the remaining 'run-round' jobs were now mixed into the great leaven of the constant empty coach movements and loco-hauled peak-time inner-suburban trains which made up a good part of both 6 and 7 links. In steam days there had been a full and busy inter-yard 'run-round' link, but by the mid-60s diagrammed 'run-rounds' were drastically reduced while the name had remained with 7 link.

I was to have two regular mates in 7 link, as alike as chalk and cheese! The first, in July 1966, was Len Henderson, a softly spoken, amiable and most likeable man, probably a little older than most of his 7-link peers, perhaps, as myself, a late starter on 'the loco'. We started together immediately on Monday the 4th, on a civilized day shift, 262 diagram, signing on at 10.20 and working empty coaches all day; we relieved D5066's crew in the station at 10.35 and prepared D5057 on Hornsey shed at 14.25 for the second half after a decent break in Hornsey's familiar crew room. We finished on a trip from Finsbury Park carriage sidings at 17.30 with the last set of empties for Moorgate which in turn formed the last Moorgate commuter departure of the day. We followed the passenger light-engine, gently back over the 'Widened Lines' and up through the 'Hotel curve' and platform 16 into Gasworks whence we reversed into the station and were relieved by a set of our own men around 18.30, a full and busy day. From the start Len shared the driving and was always prepared to guide and advise in a most patient and professional manner; with Len, 'second-manning' was truly driver-training.

We worked 262 diagram for the rest of the week with Saturday rest day, and met again at 13.00 on Sunday, 10th July to relieve the early crew on D5602 and work 260 diagram, the afternoon station pilot. Apart from the occasional trip out to Holloway or Clarence Yard the 'station shunt' was, as detailed above, confined to shunting stock around the station platforms and the 'Milk Yard'. Rostered station pilot diagrams belonged to 7-link so I saw a lot of 'No.1' and 'No.2' shunt while I was in 7, but the constant shunts and cross-station movements, and ins-and-outs of 'Gasworks' never palled.

Week commencing Monday, 11th July, with a rest day on Thursday, found us on another 'pilot' diagram which graced the mix of duties composing No-7 link, and which, in retrospect, now holds a place in railway history alongside Hornsey '368A diagram'; the empty car-sleeper trip from Holloway 'cattle dock' and the 'Palace Gates shunt' described above. King's Cross '692 diagram' was officially known, for reasons lost in the mists of King's Cross time, as 'Number 7 shunt', but was more familiarly known as the 'Ashburton Grove Shunt', and often known by still more familiar and colourful names, especially in the heat of Summer, for reasons which I soon discovered in mid-July 1966.

The idyllically named Ashburton Grove sidings served the not so idyllic Islington Dust Yard, situated south of Finsbury Park, off the 'down Canonbury' lines from Dalston just before they ran under the main lines to reach Finsbury Park No.2 box by Clarence Yard and the TMD, then on to the station, near the point where our block cement train stalled the previous November. All this area on the downside, with East Goods Yard, was part of the great 1870s Finsbury Park development. From the 'Canonbury', Ashburton Grove sidings paralleled the main lines as they headed down Holloway Bank into King's Cross, albeit at a lower level, separated by a fairly steep and short grassy embankment, the significance of which will be revealed in three months' time!

Looking towards the ECML fly-over; a 'Brush-2' is running under on the down Canonbury goods towards 'No.2 box' and Finsbury Park down side; the down passenger lines run right of Ashburton Grove Box; Ashburton Grove sidings on the left; the pilot stands just inside. The grassy bank behind the pilot gave access to my vantage point from which I watched 'Flying Scotsman' climb Holloway Bank on October 22nd 1966. (Paul Hepworth)

Looking away from the ECML fly-over; Ashburton Grove box and sidings on the right; the bogies have gone and the future site of The Emirates Arsenal stadium is winding down in this 1970s picture. In the distance is 'Finsbury Park No.1' box with the just discernible complication of cross-overs and connections between up and down roads beyond which is the way to Canonbury, Dalston, Broad Street and points south-west. (Paul Hepworth)

Ashburton Grove box only looked after access into and out of the sidings. Things never changed here from the 1870s Finsbury Park expansion right up to its 1970s demise and it retained its simple original G.N. track diagram throughout, a working railway museum piece sadly unsaved. (Paul Hepworth)

'Finsbury Park No.1' box; 'Outpost of the Empire'; the two visible roads are down Canonburies, coming from Dalston, Broad Street and 'The South'. The up Canonburies run further left and the connections and run-rounds between them lie behind the camera. (Paul Hepworth)

Ashburton Grove sidings ran into a huge and lowering, grey building known as 'The Vestry' - an early name for parish committees which met in a church vestry, in this case Islington. 'The Vestry' accepted North London's household waste, delivered from council refuse lorries at the south end onto a long conveyor belt which conducted the refuse into the interior of the great building itself where some kind of sorting process finally delivered it to the railway from the north end, demonstrably in much the same condition as when it entered from the road, but tidier! This 'tidy' waste was loaded from the 'vestry' into the waiting rail wagons which occupied two roads inside the 'vestry'. Many of the wagons were remaining examples of a class of big, Gresley-designed, 50-ton bogie wagons built in the 1930s for the LNER's ICI sulphate traffic into their Haverton Hill plant on Teesside. At Ashburton Grove the pilot propelled the empties into the two 'vestry' roads for loading then moved them out loaded, eventually putting them together to form a full train, fondly known

as the 'Ashburton Pullman', which conveyed the waste via the down Canonbury, through Finsbury Park and so onto the down slow road as far as Welwyn Garden City. From Welwyn the 'Pullman' turned onto the Dunstable branch, recently closed to passenger traffic in 1965, but still open for the 'Pullman' to make its stately way to Blackbridge Sidings landfill tip at the end of a short branch which turned north from the branch just before the old Wheathampstead station. Blackbridge tip and sidings finally closed in 1971.

The 'Ashburton Pullmans' were worked by Hatfield, then by Hornsey crews when Hatfield closed. It was worked latterly by two 'Paxman Type 1s' – and two would definitely be needed on such a load with gradients at each end of the trip; from Canonbury, up the climb which had defeated 'Brush 4' D1533 and driver Sam and me in the previous November, and at the end of the journey in order to access Blackbridge Sidings.

In the twenty-first century, for Ashburton Grove read 'Emirates Stadium', for Arsenal Football Club's vast and shiny new home now covers most of the old 17 acre refuse recycling site. Being strictly neutral where football is concerned I can surely offend nobody by pointing out that Arsenal's ground stands on a rubbish tip! 'The Emirates' was opened in 2006 following the initial proposal that Arsenal F.C. would build their new stadium here in 1999, followed by planning consent in 2002. Financial delays meant that building did not begin in earnest until 2004 and Arsenal took quite a gamble in the project when a brand new replacement, 'state of the art', 'Household Refuse and Recycling Centre' opened in Hornsey Road, somewhat east of the Ashburton Grove site, in October of that year at Arsenal F.C.'s expense. 'The Emirates' was not opened until 2006 but it would seem now that the gamble has paid off. A deal made at the start of the project meant that for a sponsorship sum of £100million from the United Arab Emirates, Arsenal F.C. must call the stadium 'The Emirates Stadium' for 15 years. The total cost of the new stadium was £430million.

During that hot summer 1966 week we signed on at 13.30 before making our way out by the 13.40 passenger to Finsbury Park and then walking to Ashburton Grove to mobilise '350' D3724 and work the 'Ashburton Shunt', dropping those big empty bogies into the vestry and hauling them out loaded full tilt uphill, one eye ahead on the sidings exit board – which must not be passed when it was 'on'! – the other constantly trained back on the shunters' signals, watching for them to stop the 'go ahead' and quickly revert to 'come towards' to drop back into the next road - before we reached that exit board! - our responsibility, not theirs – when the throttle must be slammed shut, a brief steadying touch on the long brake lever as the 'spoon' key was pushed hard through its quadrant, brake off, and roll *gently* back into the next road, bogies and buffers clanging and clashing in protest at such violent treatment.

We were rostered to shunt Ashburton Grove from 14.30 on the afternoon shift and were then booked to move on via the 'Canonbury' to Clarence Yard sidings with empties if required. From there we ran back through to No.1 box for access to Highbury Vale yard, south of the up 'Canonbury', to shunt coal wagons as required. At some point during these perambulations we took a break, preferring to do this when we'd moved on from Ashburton Grove as it was healthier to eat among the coal wagons rather than the odorous refuse wagons and their wriggly and furry inhabitants, surely the fattest maggots and rats in North London!

We finally stabled D3724 in Finsbury Park carriage sidings each evening at about 19.30 for later collection by the '7-link' 'MacFish shunt' diagram crew who took vans dropped off by the up fish trains from Aberdeen and Grimsby across to the 'MacFish' depot on Finsbury Park down side by the circuitous 'Canonbury' route via No1box, a job which I would soon be rostered for.

On Monday the 18th July we signed on at 07.00 after a Sunday off, then worked five days, all with 'Brush 2' D5610 on the early shift 'No1 Shunt' with Saturday rest day and the start of two weeks' annual leave for me, spent, inevitably, in the north-east, County Durham, my mother's home which I had grown to like so much - and there were different railways to investigate around Tyne and Teeside.

Looking back, it seems ironic that my holiday coincided with the first transfers in what would become by early October the complete removal of the 'Sulzer-2s' from the King's Cross area. D5057-D5060 were moved across to Willesden during week ending 6th of August; but nearly all of the class went to Scotland, following in the tracks of the memorably unreliable North British Locomotive Company 'Type-2s' which the Sulzers had replaced in London in 1960; now, in 1966 they replaced them again; but this 1966 replacement assisted in the final demise of steam in Scotland. The famous and still extant D5061, together with sisters D5062/4/5/6/8/9/71/2 and D5095 went to Edinburgh Haymarket for much the same work which they'd done from King's Cross; empty coaches and suburban passenger trains, although the latter notably included workings through to Carlisle on the now long lost and lamented 'Waverley' route, following in the mighty steam footsteps of Haymarket and Carlisle Canal Gresley 'A3' 'Pacifics', and becoming the last locomotives to work that hilly route across the border, albeit on much lighter loadings. The rest of the 'Sulzer-2's went to Glasgow Eastfield which had tolerated the 'North British' enigmas for some five years.

The exodus of the 'English Electric Type-1s' and the 'Sulzer-2s' were King's Cross area's first tangible contribution to the BRB's 'National Traction Plan' where, initially, "regions were expected to offer up surplus locomotives for reallocation." (David Clough P.140) King's Cross apparently decided that the 25 'Sulzer-2's came into this category – while the 10 'English Electric 2s', 'Baby Deltics', were retained, perhaps to keep all 'Deltic' engined locomotives together for ease of maintenance. Another BRB observation, David Clough points out, was that "substantially fewer locomotives were being diagrammed than were available," and this, in retrospect, explains why during 1966 'Type 4s' on suburban and empty stock workings became commonplace and were obviously used more intensively between their main line workings. It is apparent, again looking back, that King's Cross/Clarence Yard TMD now intended to power their share of the ECML with 'Brush' Type-4' (47) and 'Type-2' (31) locomotives, together, of course, with eight of the 21 English Electric 'Type-5' 'Deltics' (55); and the 10 'English Electric' Type-2 'Baby Deltics' (23).

A considerable amount of transfer and exchange occurred within both 'Brush-2' and 'Brush-4' allocations during 1965/6 and new 'Type-4s' were still being delivered; but my figures show that the total allocation of

'Brush-2s' and '4s' during 1965 was about 40-50 of each – plus the 25 'Sulzer-2s'; while in early 1967, after the loss of the 25 'Sulzers', approximate figures were 60 and 50 'Brush-2s' and '4s' respectively, These figures are necessarily approximate as it was difficult to keep an accurate track of the 'ins and outs' at the time and interpretation today is not easy but they suggest that the King's Cross area's contribution to the National Traction Plan saved 15 engines in the area when the 'English Electric-1s' are included.

On Monday the 8th of August 1966 I returned to a week of nights to find that I was with dear old Pat Quigley who had changed turns with Len. The diagram was 693, and proved, coincidentally, to be the 'MacFish shunt' which utilised the day-time Ashburton Grove '350', stabled each evening, as mentioned above, in Finsbury Park carriage sidings. We rode out to Finsbury Park on the 22.40 passenger, walked into the carriage sidings to find that D3724 was still on the 'Ashburton

512 'Brush/Sulzer' 'Type 4' diesel-electrics were built between 1963 and 1967. They could be found on every kind of train, passenger and freight, throughout the British railway system. The first 32 were allocated to 34G and D1513 was new but employed on menial duties in June 1963 when she was caught heading a string of empty wagons down the main just north of Potters Bar. On a wet and eventful November night in 1965 sister D1533 also brought an unusual 'Type-4' load 'over the top' at Potters Bar. (RCTS)

263 'Brush/Mirlees' 'Type-2's were built between 1957 and 1962 and could be seen working throughout the railway system. The first 20 went to Dick Hardy's Stratford shed; the G.N. line received its first 'Brush-2's in late 1959 actually allocated to Hornsey, as was D5592 seen just two months old and already typically working into King's Cross with empty coaches in April 1960. (RCTS)

Out of the 22 'English Electric' 'Deltics' built in 1961 eight were usually allocated to 34G, the others were shared between 64B Haymarket (Edinburgh) and 52A Gateshead. King's Cross (34G) 'Deltics' were named after race-horses in true Gresley 'Pacific' fashion; here 'Meld' is caught manoeuvering between the station and the 'Passenger Loco'. via Gasworks Tunnel. (RCTS)

The ten 'English Electric' 'Baby Deltics' were kept on at 34G after the 'National Traction Plan' and continued to stable at Hitchin who always kept them clean. The first of the family, D5900, awaits release from King's Cross suburban platform 14. (Colour-Rail)

Grove/MacFish' diagram. We 'wound her up' and waited through the night for the arrival of the express fish trains from Aberdeen and Grimsby into Finsbury Park up side, when we detached the 'MacFish' vans, marshalled strategically at the rear of each train, ran them up the Canonbury to Finsbury Park No.1 box, ran round, crossed into No.3 box's control on the down Canonbury and so into the 'MacFish' yard on Finsbury Park downside, where shunter and 'MacFish' night staff guided us at their convenience, uncoupled us, and had the box send us into Ferme Park downside where we took to the fly-over, and were so returned by No.5 box to our berth in the carriage sidings to await the arrival of the second fast fish. The first fish arrived soon after midnight and we were back in the sidings after our circular trip by 01.00. The second fish arrived about 01.30 when we detached and repeated the trip. In the 'MacFish' yard we shunted and sorted as required and

then went from Ferme Park fly-over, up the Canonbury to Highbury Vale sidings, where we stabled D3724 for collection by the early turn 'Ashburton Grove' crew. There is no record of how we went from Highbury Vale back to Finsbury Park so I feel sure no provision was made for such irrelevancies on the diagram; 'immobilise for Ashburton Grove shunt' being the last diagrammed instruction, so I presume we walked and then found a staff train or light engine back into 'The Cross'; we certainly had several of the small hours, wet or dry, in which to resolve our return to civilisation.

On Monday, 15th August I was back with Len when we had two 06.30 starts on 259 diagram, 'No.2 Shunt', and were a bit peeved when the loco turned out on both days to be '350' D3711 which we had to collect from Hornsey depot on the Monday morning, there being only 'No.1 Shunt' during Sunday night. But we expected a bit of comfort on the station pilot!

On Wednesday we worked 255 suburban and coaches diagram which was booked to be single manned but I certainly didn't argue when I was told to work it, and we were both surprised when we walked across to the 'Passenger Loco' for our engine, to be presented with a brand new 'Type-4' 'Big Brush', D1989 of Gateshead.

"All I've got spare!" said the outside foreman.

"We'll take it!" said Len.

"You'll have to!" said the outside foreman, as if we objected!

We prepared the big 'Type 4' and took her off the shed to work the 08.30 'all stations to Hertford North', super power indeed for six lightly loaded suburban coaches, a much lighter load even than we'd had behind D1535 on the Cambridge job back in March last, and this time I'd get a little 'go'! Len, of course, claimed first go and took us carefully through Gasworks and Copenhagen tunnels, finding that with almost twice as many horses as usual hauling such a light load, a much tighter rein was needed, and we climbed up to 'the Park' on little more than half throttle instead of the usual 'Type 2' full power blast up Holloway bank. I was reminded of that wet night last November when I assisted driver Sam with sister engine D1533 on the cement train, but things were reversed now in that we had little more than 200 tons of passenger coaches to lift between stations with brief bursts of power, instead of 800 tons of block cement which had needed a full power slog all the way out from Finsbury Park. At Hertford we ran round and I made a quick brew in the porters' room before taking the driver's seat for our 09.30 return to King's Cross.

"Now be careful," advised 'Father Len' through his pipe as we waited 'right away', "remember you've got a lot of power in that lever – don't go mad – and brake easy." And it was indeed a new experience to feel that big engine walk away from each station as soon as the controller was opened a couple of notches; a temptation to give her a little bit more as we rumbled through the one and a half miles of Ponsbourne Tunnel out in the Hertfordshire wilds between Bayford and Cuffley, a temptation quickly checked by low growls from behind Len's pipe which glowed a warning red across the cab. We didn't call at Hornsey or Harringey on this return trip and the road from Wood Green to Hornsey is wonderfully straight and the temptation to pull that long silver lever back beyond the halfway notch loomed again – and was severely censured again! However

all went well and we rolled gently into 'The Cross' at 10.18 – 'right time'! We were relieved by a pair of 'King's Cross 7' colleagues; I don't know where they had to take D1989 but they were suitably surprised at such extravagance.

We had time to go up to the room for our break; food and our second brew. At 11.15 we relieved in turn and came down a peg when we found ourselves aboard the laggardly D5648, the black-sheep of 34G's 'Brush-2's; for no matter how the TMD tinkered and persuaded her, she just did not produce the 'sparkle' of her sisters on passenger trains, notably the 'Cambridge Buffet's; but we took our empty coaches only as far as Holloway sidings then we moved her on light-engine to Finsbury Park sidings where we left her secure for whoever was unlucky enough to work with her that evening. We were on Finsbury Park platform by 13.00 and went home with 'rest day' the next day, Thursday.

We were booked 255 diagram again on Friday 19th August but this time Len worked it on his own as booked and I was put onto 680 diagram, 'The Provender Runround' with pleasant young Peter Page. We walked over to the goods yard, found and mobilised D3693 and were kept busy working trips around the local yards until we stabled our '350' in Ferme Park downside at 14.10.

I spent that weekend on the early turn 'No.2 station pilot', on Saturday with Len and on Sunday with driver Brian Kevaney, on both days feeling every joint in the station yard as D3711 was still No.2 shunt engine. At 09.00 on the Sunday morning we took a train of empties round to Hornsey carriage sidings and arrived on Hornsey loco round about noon when we left D3711 for a refuel, an exam and a rest, leaving King's Cross station Sunday shunt duties to 'No.1 station pilot'.

On Monday I started a week of afternoons with various drivers, Len being on 10 days leave; Monday and Tuesday found me on 'No.1 shunt' but this time in the comfort of D5672. I was on '279' empty coaches diagram with driver Ron Markham and D5055 on Wednesday, and D5622 on Friday, and 'rest day' Thursday, then a couple of second manning and relief jobs with Sunday off and back with Len for an 04.00 start on '264' diagram with D5605 on Tuesday, 30th August. We took the 05.00 parcels to Welwyn Garden City, then came up passenger, most stations to Broad Street, empties to Western Sidings and a final relief in 'the Cross' at 11.15. We worked '264' with D5605 on Thursday and Friday, with rest day on Wednesday, while on Saturday I started at 03.15 to finish the week during the small hours second-manning a variety of 'Type 2s' and '4s' between the station and the 'Passenger Loco'.

Week commencing the 5th of September 1966 brought in new rosters, probably as part of that slow, still ongoing change from steam to diesel working and, in theory anyway, better to accommodate single manning. But a big effect of these changes on 7-link was a change of rostered mate, so that for me it was "farewell" to jovial driver Len Henderson, and "hello" to driver Ken Major. Ken and Len were as different as their initial letters; Len was an amiable family man, contented, jovial, patient, while Ken, younger, unmarried, often dour, discontented and unamused. To be fair Ken wasn't without a sense of humour, but a laugh did not come readily to him; where Len was always ready to laugh and joke, Ken would be more likely to complain, mainly about the job which his conversation usually revolved around; conversation often didn't flow easily with Ken – although he was easy enough to get on with in his own serious way, shared the driving, usually putting me 'in the seat' when we were 'light engine'.

But between leaving Len and joining Ken I worked a notable shift on Sunday night the 4th of September. I was listed to sign on at 22.45 and join '1-link' driver Fred Hart to work to Doncaster on the 23.45 departure for Newcastle. This was a conventional passenger train, 1A80, and followed ten minutes after the elite, sleepers only, 'Night Scotsman', for Edinburgh, and no doubt included several of the ubiquitous parcels vans, once so very much a part of the railway scene. There were some six sleeping car trains from King's Cross at this time; to Edinburgh, one with a portion for Newcastle via Sunderland, detached at Darlington; to Aberdeen, including one mixed train, coaches and sleepers; and even the 01.10 to Leeds. With the sleepers and the overnight freights and the intermediate passenger trains such as our 1A80, the ECML in those days was as busy by night as it was by day. We were first stop Grantham, then Newark, Retford, Doncaster, where we were relieved by homeward bound Gateshead men who called at York and Darlington on their way to Newcastle

We walked over to the 'Passenger Loco' and were allocated D1972, a 'Type-4' 'Brush' almost as new as D1989 which we had on 17th August on the inner suburban

working mentioned above. D1972 belonged to 64B, Haymarket, Edinburgh, so wouldn't get back home tonight. Our load was of course a good deal heavier than the inner suburban rake handled by D1989 on my previous trip, but nowhere near the 800 tons of cement behind D1533 on that wet November night last year.

We left eight minutes down, for reasons unrecorded, on this fine September night and Fred took us expertly and effortlessly away through the tunnels and up Holloway Bank, an everyday task for him, a new experience for me as we roared through Finsbury Park and tackled the climb to Potters Bar in a style which I had never experienced before. We whirled through the old home town, top of the bank, with Fred easing the controller back to the 'notches', and I reluctantly left my seat and the rapidly unrolling moonlit view ahead to go back and make a 'brew' on the 'Baby Belling' cooker; all locomotives of 'Type-2' and above had one of these little luxuries, another modern technological advance, in this case an advance on frying your eggs and bacon on the shovel; they were particularly advantageous on long distance jobs when station and yard facilities could not be accessed. Fortunately on D1972 our 'baby' was at our end of the engine so that I only needed to step through the engine room door to reach it; but when the cooker was at the other end a long walk past the cacophony of diesel engine and generator was necessary, especially hazardous on the way back through the narrow walkway with a hot loaded tea can! I stepped back into the cab with the tea just as we ran down into the old Stevenage station to be surprised by the brief blaze of flying platform lights as we hurtled on into the dark Hertfordshire countryside.

Unusually, we didn't stop at Peterborough, but rolled slowly through on the steep curve which has long since been ironed out so that today's HSTs and 91s tear through the recently extended station on the through roads at full 125m.p.h. We paused at Grantham and Newark and Retford, all quiet in the middle of the night, but with busy night staff to see parcels and the few passengers on and off and then to see us quickly away and on into the sleeping countryside.

We went back from Doncaster 'on the cushions' on one of the up sleepers which we must have caught quite quickly as I have an arrival time back at 'The Cross' at 05.45.

I had never worked with Ken Major before our first rostered turn together on the Monday night when we started a week with D3312 and each other on '693' diagram, the 'MacFish shunt', working the two night fish-van trips from Finsbury Park up-side to MacFish down sidings via Canonbury as described above. And so, from the brief but exciting night express driving experience, I returned, on the Monday night, to the opposite end of the scale, to the jolts and bumps suffered for a week of nights on the 'bar-stool' of a '350' pilot on the MacFish shunt.

We had the weekend off then things settled back into the '7 Link' routine with Ken; empty coaches and sub-urban peak hour trips, run-rounds, station pilots, and station second-man duties when Ken worked a DMU diagram.

But after just six more weeks it was 'all change' again when, quite suddenly as I recall, a new link was created. It was designed to combine a few jobs from '4-link', the 'Cambridge', with a few from my current '7-link', and was called '4A-link'.

So on Sunday, 16th of October 1966 I worked a last '7-link' turn with Ken, starting at 07.50 and taking 3A71 empties out to Hornsey with D5676 which we took back light engine to the 'Passenger Loco' by 10.00. This gave us one of those long, comfortable breaks in the room before we went out to Finsbury Park on the 12.10 local. There we found and prepared D5609 in the carriage sidings whence we took 3A38 empties into 'the Cross' where they became 1A38 – the 14.00 Edinburgh, 'The Heart of Midlothian'. When 1A38 departed we took D5609 over to the 'Passenger Loco' and I finished my time in '7 link'.

CHAPTER 10

KING'S CROSS 4A LINK

King's Cross '4A Link' was known initially, according to my notes, as the 'Cambridge Spare Link'; but this title is deleted and replaced by 'Outer Suburban Relief' and, indeed, we saw little rostered Cambridge work for some time. A big advantage of '4A' link was that it was only five weeks long so that one could plan the rest of life from the near future, often difficult in some links which took months to complete; the 'shed duty' '8-link' was a voyage through the Universe, surely nobody ever completed it! Looking over my '4A' records, this five week repetition isn't now so apparent and can be illustrated more by the weekly rostered hours than from the actual diagrams worked; but even these appear to be very approximate, sometimes; early

mornings, i.e. before 07.00 start, afternoons, two weeks of days, i.e. after 07.00 start, followed by nights seemed to be the first run; but there were frequent roster changes during the 'rationalisation' of 1967, and again, I can only think that all this change was part of the constant attempt to create a modern railway system, and in order to do this there was still, over a decade since the passing of the 1955 Modernisation Plan, and after the last five years of Dr. Beeching's line closures, much of the old, now inefficient, steam practice to get away from.

A more personal advantage of '4A-link' was sheer good fortune, my name appeared next to that of driver Roy Head, introduced and mentioned earlier when I was in 'No.6-link' out at Finsbury Park. So popular was Roy

In 4A link I visited Cambridge frequently, often with the 'Cambridge Buffet Express'. Here D5681 brings empty 'Buffet' stock into the north end of Cambridge in June 1964. The train is about to run into the space now occupied by the new island platform, 7 and 8, while the buildings beyond served the goods yard which I worked into with night freights. (Colour-Rail)

that two of my '4A' colleagues immediately asked me to swap places – which I would not! And indeed Roy and I would become just that little bit more than workmates, especially after my leaving in 1968 when Roy became unwell – but, all in its turn!

My first week with Roy in '4A-link' started at 05.00 on Monday, 17th of October and was focused around a suburban morning peak return trip from Finsbury Park to Hertford; but in order to make this trip the inevitable empty coach manoeuvres had to be made first. We went out to Finsbury Park on the 05.20 local and walked to the carriage sidings where we relieved a night crew on D5642, which was our loco for the whole week, rest day Friday. We took a rake of suburban coaches through Finsbury Park station and up the 'Canonbury' to 'No.1' box where we ran round, and returned to Finsbury Park downside to make the 07.06 departure all stations to Hertford where we were due to arrive at 07.49 – we were one minute early on both Tuesday and Thursday mornings! Departure time for Broad Street was at 08.17 which we duly observed each morning, but right time arrival at Broad Street could not be achieved due to hold-ups every morning on the North London junctions around Dalston; we were all of 18 minutes down on the Monday morning but within five on Thursday. From Broad Street we ambled back light-engine up the down 'Canonbury' bank to Finsbury Park and then on to Bounds Green sidings, taking the best part of an hour. We left D5642 'immobilised' at Bounds Green and took 'the cushions' back to King's Cross from Wood Green.

On Saturday, 22nd of October 1966, there being no loco hauled commuter trains, Roy was rostered on a DMU diagram while I was allocated the 06.00 Ashburton Grove shunt; not, one would think, the most popular diagram for a Saturday morning; but, in the event, a most fortuitous posting. I was with driver Ray Brooks who I'd second-manned on D5900 back in June. Ray and Roy had been firemen together, sharing much the same seniority, and it seems they'd become quite pally over the years in that indefinable way which can grow between workmates, the way which would grow between Roy and myself; we always sat with 'Brooksy' and his mate in the room when breaks or shed duty jobs brought us into the room together, which seemed to happen quite regularly at this time; this was remarkable in that the great variety of shifts which occurred in our job meant that at times you could meet the same faces regularly

for some time and then not see them again for months. During this time a strange love-hate relationship sprang up between me and 'Brooksy' whose abrupt, straight-faced manner invited a kind of defensive repartee from me, and this resulted in an almost inevitable slanging match between us whenever we met, no harm or real unfriendliness in it, and Roy, with Ray's mate assisting, were often instrumental in getting us going, upon which they, with others in the room, would sit back and enjoy the banter.

On that Saturday morning I set out with 'Brooksy' on the 06.15 to Finsbury Park and we made our way, companionably enough - so different, again, in that indefinable 'workmate way', as a working team than when in the company of the rest room - to Ashburton Grove where we reported our arrival to the shunters who were at breakfast in their 'bunk'; so we found and woke up D3311 stabled among the rubbish wagons, then had an early 'brew' while we waited for some action which didn't really happen, in fact we wondered why there was an 'Ashburton shunt' on a Saturday at all. I think we swapped and tidied a few wagons but by about 07.45 we were standing idle on the road nearest the main line, which pleased me no end and I reminded Ray of a topic which I must surely have broached on the way out to Finsbury Park for a special train was leaving 'The Cross' at 08.05 this morning and it had been foremost on my mind since waking in the early hours and when signing on at six. 'Flying Scotsman' was working 'The Elizabethan', a special train named after the legendary non-stop to Edinburgh which had run throughout the last years of steam power, hauled by a 'Blue'n', as King's Cross loco men knew the 'A4' streamlined Gresley 'Pacifics'; they were known in the enthusiast world by the more popular name of 'Streaks', but not to the men who worked with them. This 1966 'Elizabethan' was not, of course, running non-stop to Edinburgh, in fact it was only going as far as Newcastle and 'A3' 'Pacific' 4472 'Flying Scotsman' was working only as far as York, where the most bizarre locomotive changeover, even for the last of steam days, would take place, when the train would be worked forward by Southern Railway, rebuilt 'Merchant Navy' class 'Pacific' 35026 'Lamport and Holt Line'. These legendary Southern engines still worked the last steam hauled main line in England between Waterloo and Weymouth, which at this time had some nine months left before the inevitable diesels took over;

35026 was used for several northern 'last steam' excursions during 1966, but York to Newcastle was certainly the rarest appearance.

Brooksy said, in his usual pseudo-belligerent way, that I could go up to the main line to see the 'Scotsman' if I liked, but "I've seen and fired enough of those things, I don't wanna see any more of THEM!" So I got down and climbed up the grassy bank to stand next to the up goods roads, looking across the full width of the last lap of the East Coast Main Line; across the up slow and main lines, then the complimentary down roads, to Clarence Yard and the TMD beyond. Here, in front of the site now occupied by Arsenal F.C.'s huge 'Emirates' stadium, I had a grandstand view down Holloway Bank with Copenhagen tunnel just out of sight round the distant left-hand curve and overbridge, and it wasn't long

On the inaugural run to York after its 1990s restoration, 'Flying Scotsman' approaches Wood Green (Alexandra Palace) on 4th July 1999, a few miles north of my Holloway vantage point a full 33 years earlier. (Author)

before a billow of smoke from Copenhagen's hidden portal preceded the long gone vision of a spotless 'A3' 'Pacific' tackling Holloway Bank once more, exhaust a vertical and volcanic visual accompaniment to the familiar rhythm of the syncopated Gresley 3-cylinder beat, increasing in volume as she approached, a fine sight and sound which I remembered so well from years now gone, but usually as the train topped the long climb to Potters Bar, the long climb which really started right here, straight out of King's Cross onto Holloway Bank where I was fortunate to be this morning. 'Flying Scotsman' was in LNER apple green at this time and made a powerful sight with her two matching tenders, the first proudly announcing the long gone 'L N E R' in bold cream letters, the second, added to give her a greater range between water refills, sporting her second LNER number '4 4 7 2'.

I stood transfixed as this visual and vocal spectacle approached; then the spell was shattered by a voice close in my ear which suddenly said, "Blimey, he ain't half 'ammerin' her!" It was Ray, of course, trying mightily to suppress an uncontrollable grin of delight on his chubby face as he watched that fine steam locomotive which he had himself fired many a time, thunder past, once more charging her way northwards. We watched the train pass in companionable silence and listened to her 'getting down to it' beyond Finsbury Park before I turned to point out to him that he'd been unable to resist coming to watch the engine he'd "seen too much of," and we scrambled back down to our humble '350', chiding each other good naturedly, while 'Flying Scotsman' took 'The Elizabethan' on to York, achieving 90m.p.h. down Stoke bank towards Grantham, the East Coast racing ground where she'd topped 100m.p.h. in her heyday, and where her streamlined younger cousin, 'Mallard' had achieved the world steam speed record of around 126m.p.h southbound in July 1938.

At York, Saturday, 22nd October 1966 – when the through roads were still extant - the most unusual meeting of 'Flying Scotsman' and 'Lamport and Holt Line' working the 'Elizabethan' from London to Newcastle. (RCTS)

At York 'Flying Scotsman' was duly relieved by the Southern 'Merchant' which, to the amazement of northern enthusiasts, took 'The Elizabethan' on to Newcastle, brand new territory for her, where she arrived at 13.12, two minutes before time. 'Lamport and Holt Line' was turned and watered and left Newcastle on the return leg at 13.46, one minute down; but she was one minute early into York and 'Flying Scotsman' left on the last leg at 15.22, two minutes down; she was right time through Grantham and after another dash down Stoke Bank was one minute up through Peterborough and no less than six minutes early passing Hitchin, arriving back into King's Cross before her booked time of 19.14 – an altogether successful round trip which I was so pleased to witness going down from an ideal spot on Holloway Bank.

'Flying Scotsman' was not originally booked to work this train; in fact the train was initially advertised to run on the 8th of October, starting from Peterborough, then the official southern limit for ECML steam, and to run through to Edinburgh powered by two of the last few 'Blue'n's' to remain in BR service in Scotland. The plan was for Gresley streamlined 'A4' 60034 'Lord Farringdon', for many years a King's Cross 'Blue'n' - recently withdrawn from Ferryhill, Aberdeen, shed, after those last few 'Indian Summer' years which the survivors of these fine engines spent on the celebrated '3-hour' Glasgow-Aberdeen expresses - was promised to work to York and then 'The Elizabethan' would go forward behind Peppercorn 'A2' 'Pacific' 60530 'Sayajirao', officially serving out her last few months from Tay Bridge, Dundee, shed. But then the train's organisers, the Altrinchamian Society, requested a start from King's Cross and the Eastern authorities agreed to this after pointing out that time and pathing constraints meant that a London start must see a termination at Newcastle. Complications immediately cropped up. The two promised 'Pacifics' were withdrawn and declared 'unavailable', while, in view of the alterations to the itinerary the date of the tour was put forward to the 23rd of October. 'Sayajirao's sister, 60532 'Blue Peter', then still at work from Ferryhill, was requested as a replacement for 'Sayajirao', but the Scottish Region could not (or would not) release her. It was then that the great Alan Peglar was approached and 'Flying Scotsman', which he had owned for some three years and ran regularly on excursions as one of the first preserved main line locos,

was engaged to work 'The Elizabethan' from King's Cross to Doncaster, from where two more lately redundant Aberdeen 'A4's would work; 60024 'Kingfisher', to Newcastle, then 60019 'Bittern' returning from Newcastle to Peterborough whence 'Flying Scotsman' would run the last leg back to King's Cross. British Rail, Eastern Region, initially assured the Altrinchamians that, although now officially withdrawn, the two 'A4's were in store and would be available to work 'The Elizabethan' – which, as the day approached, they were not! 35026 appears to have been widely available for special trains north of the Thames at this time and thus provided the most unusual colleague to 'Flying Scotsman' on the Altrinchamians' 'Elizabethan' on the day; but 'Lamport and Holt Line's last blaze of glory on foreign soil ended in March 1967 when she was withdrawn, while the last steam hauled Weymouth to Waterloo service ran in July of that year. While 35026 made a most rare, noteworthy and competent substitute for 'The Elizabethan's northern leg, one cannot help but wonder about a connection between the sudden, and repeated, non-availability of the promised and expected Eastern 'Pacifics' and the known reluctance for British Rail authorities to host steam hauled trains.

Alan Peglar had, mercifully, purchased 'Flying Scotsman' in 1963 after her last run in British Rail service from King's Cross to Doncaster with the 13.15 Leeds on the 14th of January in that year, thus saving the one and only example of a class of 78 of the finest, most elegant and most successful steam locomotives ever designed and constructed - anywhere. (Well now, this is a brash and subjective statement, I know, and I can hear the howls of dissent rising from many (I hope) reader enthusiasts. But it is an opinion shared by many other enthusiasts.) Alan Peglar organized and ran many specials with 'Scotsman' – as did her several owners over the 50 and more years since his so fortunate rescue. At the time that I witnessed the departure of 'Flying Scotsman' with the 1966 'Elizabethan', it was little more than a year since she had returned to service after her first overhaul in preservation at Darlington, Doncaster no longer having the steam facilities. That overhaul took about six months, and it is a strange irony that just fifty years after this 'Elizabethan' run, 'Flying Scotsman' has just completed her inaugural run from King's Cross to York after an overhaul which has taken some 10 years in all, an overhaul which should have taken, at most, five years, and which should have seen her back on the road after the grand unveiling ceremony which I was pleased to attend at NRM York on the evening of 27th May 2011, almost five years ago now (March 2016). However, still more faults including cracks in 'Flying Scotsman's frames were found during 2006, resulting in another complete strip-down and a price tag of four million pounds. But at last perseverance and determination have warmed 'Flying Scotsman' back into steam, and it's almost worth seeing her wearing those hideous but essential 'blinkers' just so long as she's still with us.

The mysterious sounding and tongue twisting Altrinchamian Railway Excursion Society who ran the 1966 'Elizabethan' have a noteworthy history. Tim Littler, 15 years old in 1966, a pupil of Altrincham Grammar School who had taken charge of the school Railway Society in January 1963, organised 'The Elizabethan' which was his third rail tour that year. He ran his first coach excursion from Altrincham to Crewe Works in February 1963 – at the age of 12! More rail tours followed. Tim became managing director of the family wine firm, Whitwams, in 1975 and formed GW Travel Ltd. in 1989 where 'GW' did not denote a railway but rather Tim's ancestor Gerald Whitwham who started the wine business just about 200 years before in 1788. GW Travel specialised in steam hauled rail tours in Eastern Europe and in 1996 ran the first private Trans-Siberian Express Tour using no less than 72 steam locomotives to cover 13,000 kilometres in 28 days. In 2007 the 'Golden Eagle Trans-Siberian Express' was a specially constructed train for the Trans-Siberian tours, the first privately owned train in Russia. In 2012 GW Travel became 'Golden Eagle Luxury Trains Ltd.' which is their title today when they run the Trans-Siberian tours and many others in far Eastern Europe and on into Asia; to Teheran, to Tashkent and Mongolia and many other

After completion of a controversial ten year overhaul in January 2016, a magnificent 'Flying Scotsman' visited 'Locomotion', the National Railway Museum, Shildon, in July, elegantly hauling humble brake van trains. (Author)

remote destinations including far north into the Arctic Circle – and all by rail!

Back in October 1966, after that remarkable end to my first week in '4A' gang, life went on in similar style to life in '7' gang; empty coaches, peak suburban passenger, 'run-round', station pilot, shed-duty and engine movement jobs around the station and the 'Passenger Loco'. But the second week saw us rostered to work '287 diagram', the first rostered Cambridge working to come into the link. '287 diagram' crew signed on at 19.20, walked to the goods yard and worked 4 or 5J21, fitted or semi-fitted freight, to Cambridge with a 'Brush-2', calling to detach or pick up in Hitchin down yard as required. The King's Cross crew were booked to be relieved by Cambridge men in the sprawling Cambridge goods yard situated east of the passenger station across a complication of through running tracks. 4J21 was then worked forward to Ely and Whitemoor, but in actual practice this relief rarely happened and we kept the J21 engine for the return trip. '287' was sometimes booked to be single-manned; but what the criteria for single-manning '287 diagram' were I do not now know; suffice to say for now that this was the case on week commencing 24th October 1966 when Roy was learning the road to Cambridge, and for that week I was allocated to '278 diagram', empty coaches, with driver Stan Harrison and a 'Brush-2', signing on precisely at 19.48, making a return empties trip from 'The Cross' to Hornsey carriage sidings, then running light engine to Ferme Park up yard to take a fitted goods, 4B10, into King's Cross goods yard. Well, 4B10 didn't run at all during that week, although we were never informed in advance and after dutifully turning up to collect it our last move each morning was to run from Ferme Park into Hornsey depot at about 02.00 when we made our way by staff train back to The Cross - not the most economical of diagrams, but typical of the times. It will be seen later that during the summer of 1967 we were very glad that 4B10 *did* run as it provided a way of getting back to London from Hitchin at the end of a Cambridge goods diagram.

I accompanied a variety of drivers during the following weeks as Roy continued his road learning in preparation for our new '4A-link' Cambridge duties. In fact we didn't meet again until early on Sunday, 13th of November when we signed on at 05.50 for a most unusual diagram, listed simply as 'No.9 Engineers'. To find the train with this singular name we travelled out to New Southgate on the 06.10 from King's Cross, passing 'No.9 Engineers' standing just south of New Southgate station on the down main line which was in the engineers' possession, closed to other traffic. A big old 'Sulzer 4' of the type which had given me such trouble on my very first shift nearly two years ago stood on the north end of the train and proved to be D188, a long way from her Gateshead home; however our loco was at the other end of the train, and to have a loco each end of a train in these days, long before 'topping and tailing' became an everyday occurrence, was unusual. After exchanging greetings with the crew of D188, we were joined by one of the engineers who explained what we were to do as we walked back along the short train, the make-up of which I unfortunately have no note but which must surely have included an engineers' 'dynamometer' test coach, to the south end where we were met by a welcome and now rare sight, a 'Sulzer-2', the familiar and, for me, much missed, Sulzer 6LDA engine 'tickety-tocking' gamely. All 25 of our 'Sulzer 2s' had by now been transferred, for the main part to Scotland, and the example which we were to work with today was D5005 of the earliest, 1958, Midland, batch; these had spent their first three or four years on loan to the Southern at Hither Green, working both passenger and freight turns on the Kent coast line prior to that route's electrification. On this November 1966 Sunday D5005 came across to us for this special working from the Midland Region. My notes tell me that we had to "work (the) experimental special train between New Southgate & Harringay at varying speeds over (a) determined test section of down main line at Wood Green." And this we did, ferrying backwards and forwards, taking a run up from the appointed starting place just south of New Southgate station, accelerating through Wood Green Tunnel, then over the test section along the straight stretch from Wood Green (Alexandra Palace today) station at the appointed speed, given us by an engineer before each run, through Hornsey station, to the end of the 'determined test section' just north of Harringay station, between Ferme Park yards; D188 powered us back mightily on the northbound trips while we did our best southbound.

Unfortunately my notes tell me little more about these unusual tests and I can find no mention of them in any reference sources; whether the use of 'Type 4' versus

'Type 2' locomotives, both Sulzer powered, remembering that our '2' D5005 was hired in for the day, is a clue; whether it was acceleration and/or braking, or similar, I don't know, I would love to find out, even now.

We were relieved at New Southgate somewhere around noon, although I haven't, again unfortunately, recorded the actual hand-over time.

On Monday Roy went back to his road learning while I started a week of nights on 'No.2' station pilot with a variety of King's Cross drivers on a variety of King's Cross 'Brush-2s', with a long weekend; Saturday and Monday rest days and Sunday off.

There followed a week of early mornings, around 04.00 start, which, commencing on Tuesday, 22nd of November after the Monday rest day, was notable for the drivers I worked with; on Tuesday and Wednesday '264 diagram' included a return trip to Welwyn Garden City, parcels outward, and return with a commuter train from Hatfield to Broad Street; on Tuesday I accompanied driver Noel Thurston, practical joker extraordinary, on D5671, while on Wednesday I was with Charlie Kilford, a huge young driver, a gentle giant of a man known as "Pussycat" for the huge Cheshire-cat grin which so often wreathed his round jovial face; poor Charlie was lost to us along with his second man, a young man of close seniority to myself who had actually changed his rostered diagram that night, when a loose-coupled goods became too much for the brakes on a 'Brush-2' as they approached Hatfield on 23rd March 1968; the train was switched into a siding, demolished the stops and finally collided with an overbridge abutment.

On the Thursday and Saturday of that week in November 1966 I worked respectively '251' and '252 diagrams', empty coaches, with my last '7-link' mate, Len Henderson; we worked two returns trips from King's Cross to Hornsey carriage sidings on the Thursday, changing 'horses' with a convenient break between trips; 'Brush' D5644 then a much maligned 'Baby Deltic', D5903. On the Friday on the same diagram with the much maligned Ray Brooks, we had D5589 then D5900, this last a strange coincidence as this was the engine on which I met Ray, back in July 1965; and also, the month before that, D5900 was the loco in which I rode in the back-cab from Hitchin to Peterborough with Horace Fairy when D5588 let us down. The Saturday 252 diagram with Len saw us making e.c.s. trips to Hornsey,

Holloway and Bounds Green where we left D5602 and returned to The Cross 'on the cushions'.

On Sunday, 27th November I signed on at 12.30 to meet Roy on a Sunday engineers' 'relayer' diagram, that Sunday's 'No.3,' a more conventional 'relayer' than the speed trials with D5005 two weeks earlier, in fact a typical weekend engineers' loose-coupled rail and ballast train which attended the gang of shovel and crow-bar wielding men employed on rail relaying and heavy maintenance tasks, so different to today's virtually completely mechanised, self-propelled, relaying and ballasting trains in their distinctive Network Rail engineering yellow. We took the 12.50 to Finsbury Park and walked north to relieve the early turn King's Cross men on D5589 at the head of a substantial ballast train. The early turn crew had brought the train to the site and when the job was finished we were booked to take the train to Hitchin 'stock yard', now long gone but then situated on the up side just south of Hitchin station and known more officially as the 'Engineers' Yard'. In the event, after sitting for some two hours, slowly easing up a wagon-length at a time so that the gangers could unload, we were told that our destination was Ferme Park down yard, so, after running round at Canonbury, Finsbury Park No.1 box, we had a very much shorter trip to our stabling point than anticipated and left D5589 in the 'Passenger Loco' by 16.00 and went up to the rest room 'as required'.

D5589, incidentally, was one of 14 'Brush-2s' which came to King's Cross in the summer of 1966 from Immingham, from Sheffield Darnall, a couple from Stratford, and D5679 poached from March in part replacement for the 'Sulzer-2s' sent away under the National Traction Plan. How the balance was maintained at Immingham and Darnall I do not know; I think Immingham were allocated 'Brush 4s'.

After a quick brew in the room we were sent off by the 16.40 to Hornsey to collect and prepare York's nearly new D1994 and bring her into 'The Cross' to go home on the 18.30 York parcels departure. After Roy emerged from the depths of D1994's engine room liberally sprayed with luckily still cool coolant from a fractured radiator he declared her a failure (among other, more descriptive, things) and the foreman found us a big old 'whistler', 'English Electric 4' (40) D393, one of Gateshead's, which must have worked up on a Ferme Park freight arrival.

'English Electric' 'Type-4' D206 heads north through Welwyn North on 15th May 1959. I saw D200 brand new the year before from Brookmans Park booking office, my first job. At this time Welwyn North boasted a goods yard and shed on the down side, now, inevitably, the station car park. (RCTS)

I took a liking to these pioneers of the BR big diesel loco types, unusually successful for early diesels, some 200 were built, the ECML allocation eventually replaced on top link work by the 'Deltics', although I remember being especially conscious of their length for some arcane reason when setting back onto a train from Gasworks Tunnel, although they were the same length as the 'Deltics' - I think the recessed cab door on the 'EE-4's took my eye off the long straight line of the body; these 'Type-4's and '5s' were, at 69'6", just under 13' feet longer than our everyday 'Brush 2s' – which were a whole 6' feet longer than a little old 'Sulzer-2' equivalent! Therefore it was surely much easier to charge round the station front, in and out of Gasworks, on the station pilots, with a 'Type-2' than it would have been with a '4' – I recall one occasion seeing a 'Brush-4', 63'7", deployed as station pilot, surely not for long! On this occasion, with D393, however, we whistled our way up the goods road from Hornsey and through Finsbury Park, and were at the right end to run straight onto the waiting parcels vans in the 'Milk Yard' where we were relieved by a '2-link' crew at 18.05. We returned dutifully to the room, had an extra brew and were not called again until we were told to go home at about 19.30.

The next week I worked with Roy on a rather strange afternoon coaches diagram, 273, rest day Friday, which involved an e.c.s. trip, 3E03, with a 'Baby Deltic' to Holloway Carriage Sidings where we stayed for some two hours before working 3N24 – the Pullman coaches to form the evening 'Yorkshire Pullman' – unusually stabled in Holloway - back into 'The Cross' at 17.00 when our 'Baby Deltic' was taken over by Hitchin men, no doubt to work a late evening outer suburban train after the Pullman's departure. We then spent some three more hours in the room before walking to the goods yard where we found a stabled 'Brush-2' which we prepared and attached to fitted freight, 4E55. We left King's Cross Goods at 20.55 and took our 'fast goods' - as far as Finsbury Park No.2 box! Here our 'Brush' was detached and we took it via Finsbury Park station into Clarence Yard depot where we left it and made our way back to King's Cross to sign off. 4E55, presumably, was picked up and worked forward by another loco and crew – I noted on the Tuesday night that it was an 'Ipswich freight', in which case – as we were booked to be relieved by Hornsey men at Finsbury Park, although we actually went light-engine into Clarence Yard each night – perhaps a Hornsey crew took 4E55 across to Temple Mills from where it would wend its way to Ipswich - a most mysterious diagram and in a retrospect of 50 years I wish I had made more of this strange working in my notes.

The next week found me booked as 08.00 'As Required' with various drivers and relief jobs, rest day Thursday, while Roy, now road learned and signed, went to Cambridge on DMUs until Friday when he was also rostered 'As Required' and we set out on another unusual job, somehow making our way to Camden Goods to collect one of our first 'Brush-4's, D1504, returned ex-works from Crewe, to bring back to Clarence Yard. We came back via the North London to Dalston, thence Canonbury and my notes make no mention of a pilot-man who we must surely have had over the Midland's bit as far as Dalston Junction. The trip from "Camden Goods 09.20 LE" took 25 minutes to the time we dropped back into Clarence Yard where we stabled D1504 ready for her return to East Coast mainline work and made our way back into The Cross for some light relief work.

Our shifts ran close to those of Ray Brooks at this time and during our long stays in the room during the week on 273 diagram we all met fairly frequently, and the banter and pseudo-animosity between Ray and myself reached new heights. As I arrived for the first shift of a week of nights, as I thought with Roy, on Sunday, 11th of December I wasn't so much surprised to see Roy and Ray standing talking together, as to see them standing in the doorway between the signing-on lobby and the rest room. I called a greeting and wondered why they watched me so closely as I went to sign on; I picked up the pen, prepared to sign and suddenly stopped as I saw that my name on the signing-on sheet was next to 'R. Brooks' and not, as it should have been, as I thought, next to 'R. Head'; I looked across at the delighted duo of drivers standing in the rest-room doorway who immediately collapsed into gales of laughter, "We've changed turns," hooted Roy, "for the week," snarled Ray, trying

mightily to maintain his most forbidding demeanour. I looked from treacherous Roy to revengeful Ray in some dismay, then turned my back on them and signed on, resigned to my fate for the forthcoming week.

That Sunday night's diagram was '285', and consisted of just one job – all night on 'No.1 shunt', the station pilot. Brooksy frog-marched me out of the room to the great delight of all present, we went down into the station, located our charge, D5673, and let the late turn men go home. "Oh no you don't!" roared Ray as I made to sit down in the right hand seat. "You're gonna earn your keep this week, matey!" I stopped in some surprise. "That's your seat," he indicated the driver's seat, "all night!" I dutifully moved across the cab to take up my allotted place, thinking that if this was Brooksy's idea of punishment I could take lots more. "After you've gone back up the room and made the tea!"

Sunday nights were quiet nights on the station pilots, in fact 'No.2 shunt' retired to the 'Passenger Loco' for refueling and exam after midnight, leaving 'No1' to cope alone until the early hours and the arrival of the first sleepers and mails when they both went to work in earnest, splitting and dividing sleeping cars from passenger coaches and mail and parcels vans and forming the trains of empties which would be worked out to the various carriage sidings. That particular Monday morning I found Ray 'in the seat' when I got back with another brew just before the first overnight came in; he drove for the rest, the busiest part, of the shift, which, although he probably didn't realise it, was nearer to the 'punishment' he claimed to visit upon me. We were relieved by the Monday early 'shunt' crew at about 07.15 after what was really, of course, a quite convivial night.

We would have the weekend off after this week of nights and on the Monday to Thursday nights we worked '265' diagram which was one of those 'back to face' shifts which gave us a run out to Hatfield and back with a morning suburban passenger trip at the very end of the job. We signed on at midnight, prepared a 'Brush-2' on the 'Passenger Loco' and took 3E30 empties out of 'The Cross' just as far as Holloway sidings, then on light engine to Ferme Park down side to wait for what was really a 'run-round' trip, 7E59 loose-coupled transfer, over the fly-over then up the goods road and across into King's Cross Goods Yard – whence we returned light, down-road, up the bank, back to Holloway sidings where we had a long break before taking 3C18 parcels vans back into 'The Cross'. 3C18 vans were duly loaded and worked away north as 1C18 at 06.00, releasing us to run out across the station yard into Gasworks tunnel and then drop back into the suburban onto our 06.25 passenger departure calling all stations except Harringay and Hornsey to Hatfield. We came back with an up commuter trip leaving at 07.34 from Hatfield's up bay, ran fast from Oakleigh Park to Finsbury Park and were relieved in King's Cross by Hornsey men on arrival at 08.09.

We finished the week on Friday night with another stint on 'No.1 shunt', this time with D5651, a good deal busier than the Sunday night job, but, worked between us, I left Ray peacefully at 07.30 on Saturday morning after a most amicable 'punishment week'.

After a week of early morning (03.50 start) coaches and suburban diagrams, worked with a variety of drivers, I was rostered another Saturday rest day so that, with Christmas Day falling on a Sunday, I had two consecutive days off over the Christmas holiday, something which happened only occasionally with the exigencies of providing a 24 hours round-the-clock service. I finished 1966 with a varied week of afternoons; after starting on Monday, Boxing Day, with a holiday special empty coaches job, '6X diagram', consisting of two return trips from King's Cross to Hornsey Carriage Sidings with young driver Andy McCarthy and D5652, I went to Cambridge on Tuesday with the 'midday' 'Cambridge Buffet Express', departing at 11.35 with '4-link' driver Ken D'Ath on D5587, a recent re-shed from Immingham. We came back at 13.40 from Cambridge, arriving back into King's Cross at 15.04 – two minutes early! After this flourish we finished quietly, taking D5587 light to Bounds Green sidings to collect the inevitable train of empty coaches, 3A56, which we sat behind in 'The Cross' until relief at 18.30. Wednesday was the rostered rest day; then on Thursday and Friday I suffered the Ashburton Grove shunt with young drivers Tony Blaxill and Stan Harrison respectively, and the current 'pilot', D3710.

To finish the week – and the year - I went to Cambridge again on the Saturday 'midday Buffet', departing at 12.25. I signed on at 11.30 and prepared D5675 on the 'Passenger Loco' with jovial Maurice (Morry) Holman who put me straight 'in the seat'. Well, I'd driven local trains to Welwyn Garden City and Hertford on the inner suburban lines by now, but this New Year's Eve 1966 was the first time I'd take a train through Finsbury Park without stopping, throttle wide, then ease through Wood Green, then full power again up the long climb through New Barnet, Greenwood, Hadley Wood and Potters Bar tunnels, shut off after Potters Bar as the gradient eased and we approached the sharp curve through Hatfield – since very much rebuilt and straightened out – after which a last brief gallop before shutting off for the turn in, main to slow, on the approach to Welwyn Garden City.

I was still new to the road after Hitchin, over the Cambridge branch and tended to be over-cautious, especially in my down-hill approach to Royston station where too early brake application would result in a time-losing crawl into the platform, while entering too fast would result in in an abrupt, jolting stop, or worse, a most inconvenient over-run taking some of the train out of the platform altogether. Experience later improved things here, but on that last day of 1966 with no signal checks we arrived four minutes late into Cambridge.

For a while we 'second men' were not officially sanctioned to drive and would get no official driver-training until seniority brought us to the top of the links and we were 'taken off' to become drivers, these early days surely prepared us for that momentous 'official' time; no driver, of course, would allow a 'second' to drive if he doubted his competence, every driver was responsible for the safe running of train and engine and his whole career, and perhaps more, could be destroyed by an incompetent 'second man'. But most drivers through the links gave the 'second man' a turn 'in the seat' and this was especially so with 'regular mates' when a working bond usually grew up between driver and 'second' – although this was not always a happy pairing and I knew of one top-link couple who travelled to Newcastle and back together for a long time without speaking to each other, apart from words which were absolutely necessary for working the job, surely a most unhappy situation.

Perhaps the nearest the diesel 'second man' position came to that of the steam fireman was in that the 'second man', as well as learning the skills of driving - and I understand that many steam drivers often let their regular fireman have a go at the regulator while they kept their hand in with the shovel -, also learned the road, although, of course, no new or promoted driver was

New 'Deltic' D9005 brings the up 'Tees-Tyne Pullman' out of Hadley South tunnel in the 1960s. There were but two lines between Potters Bar and New Barnet until the mid-1950s, notice the ancient eastern and modern western tunnel portals. The trackmen stand on the approximate site of lonely Greenwood signal box just north of where the lines quadrupled again. (RCTS)

expected to sign to say he knew a route before he had completed the allocated road learning time. And I cannot but think that those long years as fireman, then in the diesel days as 'second man', did much towards 'knowing the road', for during my years as a second man I can recall only one 'Signal Passed at Danger' incident and this involved an unfortunate King's Cross 'Top-Link' driver who agreed to take his engine from Newcastle Central station onto Gateshead shed due to a shortage of Gateshead shed staff; somewhere on that short journey, after working all the way down from London, he passed a stop signal, fortunately without mishap.

I accepted Morry's option to drive back on that last 'Cambridge Buffet Express' of 1966 when all went well until we climbed away from Royston when an ominous blue light suddenly sprang up on the display in front of me – 'Engine Fault' – and D5675 became noticeably hesitant, and while still pulling, was obviously not developing full power. Morry went back into the engine-room but could find nothing amiss so we rolled into Hitchin, where no engine-change was forthcoming and we were told to carry on if we could. We continued, slow speed - throttle wide open - UP through Potters Bar! - and finally staggered into King's Cross 20 minutes late, where we were relieved by men instructed to take D5675 directly to Clarence Yard TMD.

After this somewhat inauspicious end to 1966 we signed off and went home to greet 1967.

Work in King's Cross '4A' link carried on in early 1967 to much the same broad pattern which it had followed since its inception in October 1966, and with much the same duties as 'No7' link; empty coach workings combined with peak time suburban passenger runs, run-round jobs and station pilots; but then, as rosters changed quite frequently, the promised Cambridge branch diagrams gradually came into the link so that we did indeed become the 'Cambridge Spare Link' as was apparently, originally intended; '287' was a night freight diagram, mentioned earlier, '4J21' Cambridge and Whitemoor 'fitted' goods, starting from King's Cross goods yard after 19.00; '273 diagram' involved an early morning (03.00-04.00 start) trip delivering newspapers to all main stations to Hitchin, then, initially, 'home passenger'; but from September 1967, as '276 diagram', this ride home was changed so that we went to Royston and worked a morning commuter service back to King's Cross, while '294 diagram' was an afternoon shift, starting prompt at 15.07, and included a return passenger run to Royston, 2B65, as all stopping Cambridge branch services were designated; '258 diagram' was another Cambridge night goods job, signing on at 19.15 and starting with a ride to Enfield Chase on the 19.30 local and a walk off the down platform south end to 'Enfield Old Sidings' where waited 7J62, empty loose-coupled coal wagons which we worked as far as Cambridge. 7J62 was often powered by a 'Baby Deltic',

most unlikely power for working a loose-coupled train, and the only reason for the roster powers to allocate such a beast for such a train was, we decided, sheer sadism!

Although I have mentioned four jobs in a five week roster we rarely worked one of these jobs for a full week and, indeed, those five weeks could become a very mixed bag, which, for me, increased the interest; the greater the variety, the greater the job satisfaction.

The most consistent of these rostered Cambridge branch diagrams was the early morning newspaper round which, as '273 diagram' before September 1967, we signed on for at the deathly hour of 04.00, prepared a 'Brush 2' in the 'Passenger Loco' – keeping a sharp look out for plastic bag water bombs which some 'mates', variously engaged in engine movements or their own preparation duties, liked to lob over the top of other locos under preparation - and took her over to platform 1 to pick up 3B64, 05.00 departure newspapers. 3B64 stopped at Finsbury Park then most stations to Hitchin; we shunted a van off at New Barnet and another at

We were surprised at the provision of 'Baby Deltics' for our 7J62 night coal empties to Cambridge, but here *two*, D5902 and D5909, power a down loose-coupled goods just north of Potters Bar in July 1968. (Colour-Rail)

Welwyn Garden City, and were booked to finish in Hitchin down platform at 07.31. When the Hitchin news was unloaded, we pulled forward, propelled the empty vans into the down yard, uncoupled and moved into the adjacent shed yard where we stabled the engine, usually well before 07.30, and made a mad dash out of the depot gate into Nightingale Road which we raced across, bags akimbo, dodging the already busy Hitchin morning road traffic, then along Station Approach and into the station booking hall, joining Hitchin commuters streaming through the underpass to the up platform, usually just in time to catch an early 'suburban' passenger departure, leaving the commuters to compete for their places in the coaches while we climbed into the rear cab of the locomotive on the front in order to get back to 'the Cross' as quickly as possible; not that we were finished then but it gave us more time in the rest room before we did our last job, the inevitable empty coach run out to Bounds Green after relieving one of our crews in the station on another 'Brush-2' at about 09.30. From Bounds Green we ran back light to the 'Passenger Loco' where we secured the engine, put the bill in and went home.

From the September 1967 roster changes '273 diagram' became '276' which we signed on for at the earlier but equally unearthly hour of 02.50, leaving 'The Cross' with 3B64 at 03.50 and running from Finsbury Park straight to Hatfield; the Barnet news probably went over to road transport at this time. With the Barnet and Welwyn Garden detachments taken out of '276 diagram' and the earlier start, we were booked to arrive at Hitchin at 05.30, a full two hours earlier than on '273', and our dash for the ride from Hitchin to King's Cross 'on the cushions' was no more. We still stabled the engine off 3B64 in Hitchin loco, but instead of the charge across Hitchin's early morning traffic to the station and the ride home, we then reported to the Hitchin foreman who allocated us another engine, usually a 'Baby Deltic', which we took light-engine to Baldock sidings where we picked up coaches and continued north to Royston, there to run round and drop into the up platform to become the 08.35 suburban passenger departure for King's Cross, calling at Stevenage, Welwyn Garden City and Hatfield, booked to run into 'The Cross' at 09.45 when we were relieved by King's Cross men and signed off.

This job, starting as it did at a time when most folk are fast asleep, presented a different aspect at different times of the year. We were usually ready to go in good time and had our first 'brew' before we left the 'Passenger Loco', and on dark winter mornings the first job on starting up was 'cab heaters on', then we would thaw out in the warm cab after our often frosty walkround outside; tea and biscuits and a few minutes of relaxed camaraderie, not saying very much in those 'wee small hours', Roy usually pointing out once again, how different it used to be preparing steam, how we'd 'never had it so good'; then it was time to drop down onto the exit stops with memories of my eventful first shift as second man on that spot, one of us got down to the phone to let the 'bobby' know what we were, then following the 'dollies' in and out of Gasworks tunnel – twice in order to get across to platform 1 on the 'arrival side' – we'd drop back onto 3B64; coupled up by the shunter we 'made a brake', had the regulation word with the guard who took the driver's name, told us how many vehicles and how many tons we had behind and how many stops we were to make, then we were ready to deliver the news as soon as we got the road. We went through the same routine in summer-time, of course, but in dawn or daylight and a comfortable outside temperature there wasn't the same snug comfort of climbing into that warm oasis of the cab after the bite of cold and sometimes pouring wet in the dark shed yard.

'294 'afternoons' diagram' covered much the same territory as 'early turn' '276' but started at the much more civilized and precise time of 15.07; we found our 'Brush-2' somewhere in the station precincts and relieved a pair of our own King's Cross men, then, as usual, followed the 'dollies' into Gasworks, across the station yard and onto the front of our 2B65 outer-suburban passenger train, the 16.21 departure calling at Finsbury Park, Potters Bar and all stations to Royston, the pattern still followed by the semi-fast outer-suburban EMUs today. We arrived at Royston at 17.46 and had plenty of time to run round and have a brew and a bite before starting back with a similar return working at 18.39, arriving back in 'the Cross' at 19.59. When our coaches were taken away, probably to Finsbury Park sidings, we followed the 'dollies' out into the yard, were 'stood off' out of the way in the 'dead end' spur between the west and east tunnel mouths or the 'Milk Yard', and took the opportunity to have a last 'brew' before picking up 3E85, the inevitable empty coaches which we were booked to take out to Holloway Carriage Sidings at 21.34; there we stabled them and carried on light-engine to Hornsey loco where, in diagram jargon, we 'immobilised' the engine and went 'home pass', or, in lay terms, left the engine on Hornsey depot as directed by the foreman and made our various ways home.

'258 diagram', the second Cambridge night goods job with a start from 'Enfield Old' sidings, was rostered into '4A' link during the summer of 1967, probably with the roster changes of the 9th of June, although I worked it with Roy for the first time on a warm Wednesday evening, the 9th of August, travelling passenger to Enfield Chase station on the 19.30 Hertford local from King's Cross, and I still remember how we looked at each other in disbelief as we approached Enfield Chase station and saw 7J62 waiting in the down sidings, our train of empty coal wagons - behind D5904 – a 'Baby Deltic' – on loose-coupled wagons!

I had called at Grange Park and Enfield Chase stations many times with local passenger trains by this time, but had never taken much notice of these sidings on the downside between the stations. They were the remains of a complex of tracks which had multiplied since the GNR first reached Enfield's western outskirts in 1871 with a branch line from Wood Green; even then with the intention of providing a relief loop to the GNR's increasingly busy and congested main line, although the line beyond Enfield was not started until 1906, and the original station, situated west of the present Enfield Chase, was the branch terminus until 1910. Legislation to take the line beyond Enfield was granted in 1898, but housing development meant that the line could not be taken forward from the existing station and necessitated the building of a completely new station sited east of the existing terminus. The new station was opened in 1910 with new carriage sidings, soon to be known as 'Orchard Sidings', built to the south of the station between the new down road and the original goods sidings next to the old up or departure road from the original station. In 1923 Enfield became 'Enfield Chase', to distinguish it - a little late - from the GER's Enfield Town station which had served the centre of Enfield since 1848. In 1962 a new coal concentration depot in similar fashion to that at Palace Gates was built on the site of the original station, utilising the remaining Enfield sidings, which became known as 'Enfield Old', from where, in the evenings of the late 1960s, 7J62 coal empties departed for Cambridge. This kept the empties out of the way of the main line, and I would think they were eventually taken forward

from Cambridge to March, Whitemoor Yard, as indeed was '287 diagram's 4/5J21 fast freight. From Whitemoor coal empties would be taken west to join the East Coast Main Line at Peterborough where the Great Northern's London bound coal trains from the Notts, Yorks and Durham coalfields had assembled for the final run up the ECML slow road to Ferme Park yard for the last 120 years. But in 1967 London's coal was now stock-piled in concentration depots such as at 'Enfield Old', freeing the main line from the congestion of this essential traffic but also robbing Ferme Park Yard of a considerable quantity of traffic, and this 'robbery' would escalate during the last years of the 1960s as rail freight declined generally and the fully-fitted 'block-train' became the 'freightliner' of today's railway, and the constant clash and clatter of over a century of 24/7 shunting in Ferme Park marshalling yards gradually approached a haunting silence as the slow and long sought after railway modernisation at last became a reality.

In 1967 the north end of the 'Old' sidings stood opposite Enfield Chase signalbox and on that first trip with 7J62 we established a routine for working the outward leg of '258 diagram'; we were due away at a precise 20.06; on arrival at Enfield Roy went straight to the train to let the Hornsey men go about their business while I crossed the main-line tracks to the 'box on the more essential mission of making our first 'brew'. Enfield Chase signal box was a 25-lever frame box, built with the branch extension in 1910, at the same time as similar boxes at Grange Park and Cuffley on the branch's initial extension north of Enfield. The entry door was, typically, at the top of a long flight of steps; Enfield's at the north end. I always recall Enfield box more vividly than any of the others I frequently visited in order to convey a message to the 'bobby' or when a phone wouldn't do – or didn't work, or to observe the sacred train protection 'rule 55' if retained too long at a stop signal, or, most importantly, as at the outset of '258 diagram', to make a 'brew'. As in all shunters' bunks, all signal boxes always had a coal-fired iron kettle, sometimes of immense Victorian Great Northern Railway proportions, permanently on the boil. Enfield box's 'kitchen' was at the south end and necessitated a walk across the whole length of the box to reach that vital kettle; stepping through the door, the first impression I recall was the vast sea of highly polished brown linoleum which occupied most of the midst of the box with the lever-frame, block instrument shelves and bells and all the tools of the signalman's trade ranged along the east, left-hand, side, and the nightly admonishment from the duty 'bobby' (signalman) to, "walk along by the frame, mate!" – to walk on that buffed and shining lino was little short of a capital offence!

As I made the tea the 'bobby' would ring 7J62 out to Gordon Hill, get us the road and set the turn-out from the 'Old Sidings' onto the down main, then pull the 'dolly' off, and as soon as I emerged on the verandah at the top of the steps Roy would open up and get 7J62 under way, which was fine for me if we had a 'Baby Deltic', as I then had plenty of time to trip - never literally thank goodness - down the steps, cross the thankfully empty up and down running roads and clamber aboard, one hand on the side-rail, the other clutching the wildly swinging tea can as the blue clag fired vertically skywards from

the loco's exhaust to be matched inside the cab by Roy's blue vocabulary as he persuaded the reluctant 'E.E.-2' to get hold of those troublesome trucks. If we had a 'Brush' I did indeed need to nip about because she got away in much more sprightly fashion than a 'Baby Deltic' and I sometimes scrambled aboard at the turn-out with Roy asking me where I'd been and threatening dire recrimination if I spilled 'just one drop' of that precious 'brew'.

But then we were away and I'd lean out and acknowledge the guard's signal, summer flag or winter lamp, from his brake van at the rear as we blasted through the station, and then I'd serve tea with snacks, balancing against the erratic motion, with the 'Baby Deltic' moaning mournfully but now rolling steadily, or else with the 'Brush's' 12SVT whistling cheerfully, as we trundled through Gordon Hill and Cuffley, in 1910 no more than a hamlet but for some time the terminus of the

Actually Welwyn Garden City box on the main line, but the picture is typical of most suburban boxes and is reminiscent of Enfield box on the Hertford loop where I used to make the tea before setting out for Cambridge with 7J62. I was always ordered to walk along by the frame to avoid spoiling the high shine of the lino. (Paul Hepworth)

short branch extension, now one of the busiest stations on the Hertford line; then through the dark 2684 yard (2454metres) length of Ponsbourne Tunnel, the longest tunnel on the GN, which needed its own brick works to be built near Cuffley in 1910, and, together with the construction of Horns Hill and Hertford viaducts, and the intervention of the Great War, meant that Hertford North station was not opened until 1924, although a single track was laid through to Langley Junction in 1918 to carry military traffic only.

I had never travelled beyond Hertford North until '258 diagram' gave us 7J62 and after the short 384 yard Molewood Tunnel, we rolled out onto the remote northern end of the Hertford Loop, through Stapleford, now long closed, and Watton-at-Stone, stations, still known as the 'New Line', which in 1918 turned the 'Hertford Branch' into the 'Hertford Loop', running through to the East Coast Main Line at Langley Junction, Stevenage. The loop is often useful today as a relief to the main line when accident or engineering work closed the main line or as a diversionary route for freight or special trains, or else, notably in the late 1960s, for any through trains starting on 'the loop'.

The Hertford Loop joins the East Coast down slow road just south of Stevenage station at Langley Junction and we would then proceed to Hitchin with 7J62 and usually our planned 'path' took us straight through the station and across onto the Cambridge branch without a stop at about 21.00. Sometimes, however, we would be held for a main-line train to come through Hitchin and we then wondered about the whereabouts of our '4A link' colleagues working 4/5J21 which left King's Cross Goods at 20.30 (in 1967) and usually arrived at Hitchin after 21.00, often to pause on the down slow north of the station in order to detach vans and shunt them into Hitchin down yard, then propelling back to reach the branch crossover, blocking the branch junction in the process. Although there was over half an hour between the booked departure times of the two trains, 'J21' from King's Cross goods and 'J62' from 'Enfield Old', it was always possible that 'J21' would get a good run down the main and get onto the branch before 'J62' – always a point of conjecture when we arrived at Hitchin, either with 'J21' or 'J62'. In any event we often met the other crew at Cambridge where 'J21' was due to arrive at 22.50, after 'J62' at 22.17. Although we were booked to be relieved by Cambridge men working forward to

March on '287 diagram', we almost always detached from 'J21' and retained the loco for the return trip; on '258 diagram' we were actually booked to detach and retain the engine off 'J62' – those Eastern men didn't want 'Baby Deltics' on their patch!

While both '258' and '287 diagrams' had nominally rostered return workings we could never be sure on either job how we would actually work back. '7B18' was an unfitted train of sand wagons which was often rostered as the return working on '287 diagram' – 'J21' down. We trundled the sand up through Royston to the main line at Hitchin, then ran slow road to Stevenage and Langley Junction where we took to the Hertford Loop over which Roy would hustle the heavy loose-coupled sand wagons in pitch black on moonless nights, at a hair-raising clatter, until we eased up through Grange Park station and rolled past the unusually quiet Bounds Green sidings, through Wood Green (Alexandra Palace) station to drop into a temporary concentration siding on the up side, provided at that time for a North London building development project just south of Wood Green station. Having delivered the sand the guard unhooked us then pinned down the wagon brakes while we ran round, then he unhooked his brake van which we hauled clear of the wagons until we could run round it in turn, couple to its south end, and take it, complete with guard, either to Ferme Park up yard or else King's Cross Goods as directed by the controlling powers on the telephone. We were then booked to take our loco to Clarence Yard depot, but, if the powers could be persuaded, went through to the 'Passenger Loco', much more convenient for going home at 02.00 or sometimes even 03.00. On some nights '7B18' didn't run and on those occasions we usually ran light engine all the way back to Clarence Yard or, again, into 'the Cross' if we could wangle it; when this happened we could hustle along, greens all the way up the main, and sometimes be back by 01.00.

The return working on '258 diagram' was often, but not always, another heavy class 7 loose-coupled train, '7B56' ballast wagons destined for Hitchin 'stock yard' which lay on the up side just south of Hitchin station as mentioned earlier. The 'stock yard' was full of wagon loads of, and stacks of all materials and equipment necessary to the maintenance of the running track, from the actual rails and sleepers down to the very fish-plates, nuts and bolts which tied one to the other, and, also, the ballast which lay between rails and sleepers; and it was this last commodity which we took from Cambridge to the 'stock yard' during the night as 7B56 – often with a most unsuited 'Baby Deltic'. Arrived in the 'stock yard' we would sometimes have to do a bit of shunting and sorting with our guard - great fun with a 'Baby Deltic'! - before we could place the ballast wagons, and then the 'boxes' directed us over to the down side and into Hitchin loco, from where, the diagram told us, we were 'Home as required' – which, interpreted, meant "you're on your own from here, lads"; for the Hitchin night foreman could only rarely be persuaded to find an engine to ferry up to London, and in the '60s at around midnight or later, north of Welwyn Garden City, there were no staff trains nor passenger trains until the next day's timetable started; so ingenuity – or perhaps 'engineuity' - was called for; on three occasions we hitched a lift on '4B10' fast freight which was stopped at Hitchin; the first occasion, Wednesday night the 9th of August 1967, provided, for me, a new and memorable experience. We had come light engine from Cambridge with D5907 – '7B56' didn't run - which we left in Hitchin loco, duly reported to the foreman who said "nothing to go to London, but, 4B10's detaching on the up side then right-away Ferme Park."

We dashed out into the yard – it seems we were always dashing about at Hitchin – and sure enough, could see wagons standing over on the up side. So here was an ideal way of travelling 'home as required' if we could get across to it. We made a mad, ankle-threatening dash across the complex of lines at the loco-yard throat, then across the down running lines, mercifully unoccupied, 'health and safety' a thing of the future, with shouts to the guard who was just climbing back into his brake and we climbed up after him onto the open verandah, no time to charge the long length of the train to the loco, they'd got the road! The guard told us to go inside while he gave right away to the loco with his lamp and we set off with the first jarring lurch as he came back inside and told us they'd set some wagons off in the Cambridge branch sidings; then, amidst the already deafening clatter, motioned us to the long side benches each side of the van and took up his own place on the short bench at the south, train, 'guard's office', end of the van. In August, of course, the brake stove was not burning, but I recall the inside of the long-wheelbase van as clean, warm and comfortable, an impression

soon to be dashed, for the 'Brush-2' on the front soon got down to it, and both Roy, obviously experienced in this mode of transport, and our host told me to stretch out along the bench; I had sat conventionally, feet on the floor, but by Stevenage discovered why it was indeed essential to stretch flat out when riding in a guard's brake van at the back of a fast freight train; steady enough at first but as we approached the top permitted fitted freight speed of 75 m.p.h. it would not have been possible to sit upright; I have never experienced such a ride; the constant violent side-to-side motion and rumbling rattle of the four sparsely sprung wagon-wheels on a vehicle which, long-wheelbase version though it be, was never intended to travel at such speeds, all experienced in a total darkness occasionally penetrated by the brief flash of passing station lights, can only be experienced to be believed; and such was the railway goods-guards' regular working environment! A diesel's cab was luxury indeed compared to a brake van, a point I would remember the next time I poured the tea as we set out with '4J21' or '7J62', or especially, when we rocked back over the branch at the front of '7B18' sand or '7B56' ballast.

We caught '4B10' on two other occasions, but were able to make our way to the front of the train and ride in the relative comfort of the rear cab of the engine. 4B10, incidentally, was the goods which we were rostered to pick up in Ferme Park up yard back in October 1966 during '278 diagram'. I have no note of whether this engine change still occurred when we rode back on '4B10' in the summer of 1967, but it certainly made getting home at the end of '258 diagram' easier.

If we were unable to go up on '4B10' and nothing else turned up we were obliged to wait in Hitchin's crew room until one of the first up mails called at 03.04; but there were often other ways of getting back to London, such as during the mixed week ending Friday the 15th of September 1967 when on Monday, the 11th September we worked 258 diagram with D5904 and went home from Hitchin in the back cab of the '4B10' loco; we were 'rest day' Tuesday, '258 diagram', with D5650 on Wednesday when we met '287' men at Cambridge and were able to leave D5650 at Cambridge and travel home in the back cab of their 'Brush 2' on 7B18, with a fortunate ending in the 'Passenger Loco' on the Thursday we worked '287 diagram' ourselves, '4J21' down with D5590, and this time working '7B18' back to Wood Green, van to Ferme Park and D5590 stabled, not quite so conveniently, on Hornsey depot. The week ended on the Friday with us booked to work '7J62' down on '258 diagram' but we actually worked a mix of both diagrams! We went down to Cambridge with D5902 on '7J62' and were duly joined there by '287' crew with D5650. At the week's end neither of our return workings was running so we had our break and a joint 'brew' in Cambridge crew room and, with two locos to go – hopefully - to London, awaited orders with much speculation. The Cambridge night foreman soon appeared and asked us to couple our locos, pick up and work a class '8' special goods to Hitchin 'stock yard' – '7B56' in disguise really, although this class '8' freight consisted of a long string of flats loaded with rail sleepers, considerably heavier than the usual '7B56' ballast. We couldn't couple a 'Baby Deltic' with a 'Brush' 'in multiple', i.e. so that both engines actually became one power unit, controlled from the leading cab, but must work 'in tandem'. i.e. double-headed in the time-honoured steam fashion, each loco working independently. We figured that D5650, with her positive 'Brush' get-away, would be best in front and Roy would match her and overcome D5902's reluctance to the best of his expert ability. And so, we second-men hooked these two incompatible locomotives together, and coupled up to the sleeper train at about 23.30. We were soon given the road, synchronised with short toots on the horns when both drivers simultaneously dropped the engine brakes off and opened their controllers; D5650 moved us away, surely initially taking the full weight of the train including D5902 as we moved out onto the up main while Roy did his best to juggle and persuade D5902 to pull her weight, which he managed after several unavoidable jolts before we joined the 'Great Northern' line at Trumpington Junction – I recalled our trip home in the brake-van of '4B10' last month and thought of our guard tonight who had just assured us of his presence with his lamp as we wound out of the goods yard – but on that earlier occasion we had travelled at over 70m.p.h. while on that clear September night we made a slow and steady progress to Hitchin, both locos hauling the heavy train in something like harmony, and the guard was most likely soon settled in his van.

We rolled into Hitchin 'stock yard' at about 01.00 and, with the guard none the worse for his shaky ride, had to split and shunt the train as none of the available roads offered the necessary capacity to take the complete train. We uncoupled D5902 and stood off while D5650 powered these short shunts, then hooked the couple together again in order to get across to the loco in one move; we dropped into the depot and uncoupled again at 02.15, having already ascertained on the phone that both engines must stay at Hitchin. We had the inevitable 'brew' and chat and went 'home as required', on the cushions, on the 03.04 mails.

I spent Saturday night the 16th with Roy 'as required' at 20.00 with a mixture of relief, loco preparation and cover for 'engine movements' in the 'Passenger Loco'. We were off that Sunday and I started a belated two weeks annual leave on Monday, 18th September – in the North-East of course.

I returned on Monday the 2nd of October 1967 to a week of days, signing on at 09.37 for '269 empty coaches diagram' with Wednesday rest day. I worked Monday, Tuesday and Thursday with one of the very few drivers I'd rather not have been with, let's call him Vic, and was pleased to meet Roy on the same job, which took all day but never took us beyond Holloway carriage sidings, on Friday.

That week finished with a Saturday job which appeared for the first of several occasions on the '4A' link roster, '267 diagram', the 13.30 'Cambridge Buffet Express' with the 15.40 return from Cambridge. We did this 'Buffet' job after signing on at 10.50 and initially relieving a main line arrival which took us onto the 'Passenger Loco' at about 12.30 where we stayed to prepare our own engine and, since the motive power policy change of the previous year when we lost all the 'Sulzer-2s', it very often *was* a 'Sulzer-4' (47); indeed these universal 'Type-4' machines had started to appear frequently, even on empty coach diagrams so I had gained more experience of them since my first drive from Hertford with Len and D1989 last year, although I had never taken one away from King's Cross and down the main, non-stop through Finsbury Park. On Saturday, 7th October 1967 we had the second of the class, four year old D1501, and my request to drive the outward trip was met with an indifferent shrug of Roy's shoulders. So far I had shared driving on station-pilots, runround trips, empty coaches and suburban passenger jobs. With Roy who did what was usually decided by which seat Roy sat in at the outset, or who got on the engine first, who sat down first, or, on day jobs, who'd been out the night before!

So we got the road, got 'right away' at dead on 15.40. I dropped the loco brake off, pulled the controller back to notch 4, heard that immediate angry 'big Sulzer' diesel clatter, the whine of the traction motors, felt the pull of those extra 1280 horses as we eased into Gasworks, then opened again through Belle Isle and into Copenhagen tunnels, briefly with full-power as we climbed Holloway Bank and roared through 'The Park' at 60 plus, eyes and concentration riveted ahead, the big 2,580 horse-power 'Type-4' bounding along in completely different fashion to the 'Type-2's which I was accustomed to, rated at just under half the power; the difference would take a little getting used to and I was ordered to shut off completely through Wood Green and admonished to, "take it easy, take it easy" as we climbed easily through Barnet and Hadley Wood, cruised over the top at Potters Bar, rolled round Hatfield's curve, eased, then braked carefully to cross to the slow road so to stop promptly in Welwyn Garden City number 3 down platform. We called at Hitchin and after negotiating the Cambridge line under constant cautions from Roy, I brought us carefully into Royston, and with a perhaps too respectful rounding of the sharp left-hander to join the Great Eastern main line at Trumpington Junction so that we ran into Cambridge just two minutes down on that particular Saturday; then I uncoupled, we ran round, I coupled up, then went along Platform 3 to the porters' room to wash the grease off and make the tea.

On return to the loco Roy put me in charge of the biscuits before taking his place 'in the seat' and telling me to carefully watch some "real driving", to which I pointed out that he only had to roll her downhill into London, the hard work had been done; and so we went on, although it will be seen later that our conversations weren't all banter.

The next day was Sunday and, as happened more frequently at this time, I was given a Sunday main line job, '226 diagram', a return to Grantham, with 'top-link' driver Harry Hayward, outward with an eleven month old 'Brush-4' D1106, working '1A48' home to York, a 'slow' express train, calling at Hitchin, Huntingdon and Peterborough. We were relieved

at Grantham by Doncaster men who would call at Newark and Retford before they arrived at their home station. From Doncaster, York men would take '1A48' home to its York destination, calling at Selby which at that time was served by the ECML. Nowadays the town is by-passed by the 'Selby Diversion' line which was laid in in 1983 to avoid possible subsidence as a result of National Coal Board mining developments in the late 1970s. The NCB paid for this diversion line, this at a time when many coal mines were already closing; many miners were transferred to the Selby Coalfield from other, closing pits in the 1980s, and coal was successfully mined from five pits; the coal from them all was carried underground to be brought to the surface through one central drift mine at Gascoigne Wood. The Selby coalfield closed in 2004. Selby is currently served by regular 'Northern' DMU rail services to York and Leeds, and eastwards to Hull.

We were booked to arrive at Grantham at 18.39 on that Sunday night and didn't leave on the return working until 20.06, with '1A49', whose provenance I have not recorded, probably also from York as it was powered by 'Brush-4' D1108, nine month old sister to D1106 which we'd worked on the outward leg. There were 12 '11xx' series Type 4s, D1100-D1111, which made up the very last batch of these most successful, nation-wide top-link locomotives. About 50, now known as class '47', are still in secondary main line service, used on charter passenger services and by the smaller freight companies, while many more still run on 'heritage railways'. Together with D1990-D1999, the last 22 were allocated to York in 1966/7 to replace the very last steam locomotives there. D1111, the last 'Brush Type 4', emerged from 'BR Crewe' works in February 1967, just one month after D1108 which I worked home on from Grantham on that night of Sunday, 8th of October 1967.

In the event D1108 rolled into Grantham 24 minutes late, worked by home-coming Grantham men; we called at Peterborough and Hitchin and although I neither recall nor record any further delays, we actually arrived into King's Cross at 22.25 instead of our booked 22.00. On this occasion I had the main-line privilege of being relieved in the station by a shed-duty crew instead of the usual light-engine trip to another train or the 'Passenger Loco'; progress was being made – soon to be sadly curtailed.

With rest day on Tuesday I worked the next week with Roy on '294 diagram', the afternoon Royston return passenger job with a 'Brush-2' as detailed earlier. That Saturday Roy was on a DMU diagram and I was made 14.00 'As Required' which, upon signing on, I discovered had become mysteriously 'S/O Special Motors' with driver Ron Wilson. We took a 'Deltic', D9017 'The Durham Light Infantry', from the 'Passenger Loco' out to Clarence Yard TMD, but only to swap for 'Type-4' D1994, another member of York's last batch of 'Brush 4s', which we prepared and took across to the up 'Canonbury' and so to Dalston to pick up a train of new Ford motor-cars, a heavy enough load brought from Dagenham by Stratford men with nothing more than 'Brush-2' D5644 which we replaced – in that same spot where I'd picked up the block-cement train with driver Sam on that wet and fateful night back in November 1965!

But the rails were dry this time, Ron got the long train of 'Fords' nicely away at about 16.10 and we climbed steadily to Finsbury Park then onto the down slow road, 'over the top' at Potters Bar then through to Welwyn Garden City where we had a long stand before we were allowed through the double track section across Welwyn Viaduct, through Welwyn North station, the two Welwyn tunnels, back on to the slow road at Woolmer Green and, after the two track section after Huntingdon, eventually taking two hours to get to Peterborough where we were directed through the station on yellows, and in one of those 'snap-shot' memories, I recall looking back as we crossed into the brightly lit down platform road, today's number 4, to

The impressive Welwyn Viaduct which I crossed many times during my 1960s time at King's Cross. The viaduct narrows the ECML to two tracks here. In this photo taken a little earlier, a handsome Gresley 'V2' 2-6-2 takes a short down parcels train across the viaduct. (Colour-Rail)

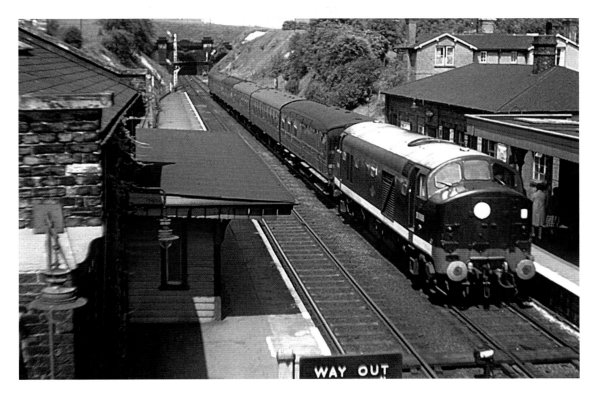

In the 'bottle-neck' two road Welwyn North station looking north towards the tunnels. 'Baby Deltic' D5905 calls with a train from the Cambridge line in May 1961; the access to the still extant goods yard trails in from the down line just beyond the still soot stained gantry. (Colour-Rail)

Woolmer Green up side. A 'Brush-4' comes up the main into the 2-line Welwyn bottle-neck at Woolmer Green with an ECML express; the down slow turns out from the main on the left – the man on the ground seems to be perilously oblivious of the approaching train! (Paul Hepworth)

see that long line of double-decked motor cars – the enemy! – snaking in behind us from the main line; and so we were brought to a stand opposite New England shed from where two Peterborough men crossed the main lines and came aboard to relieve us. We walked back to Peterborough station - recently (2013-5) much enlarged with new up and down island platforms at a cost of £2.5million - and went home 'on the cushions', leaving Peterborough at 20.35 and arriving back in 'The Cross' at 21.50.

I had a day off on Sunday, 15th October then started the best part of a week of early mornings, 04.15 sign on for '255 empty coaches diagram' with trips to Holloway and Hornsey which I worked with a different driver each day until Friday when I signed on with Roy, who presumably had been on DMU jobs, at 02.50 for the aforementioned '276 diagram'; newspapers to Hitchin, on this occasion with D5606, and then the loco swap and 'Baby Deltic' – D5909 this morning – light engine to Baldock, then e.c.s. to Royston to make the 2B65 passenger run back into King's Cross. This one-off '276 diagram' working at the end of a week shows how haphazard the '4A-link' jobs actually were; by no means the five weekly repeats which the broad template of the link suggests to me in a retrospect of 50 years.

The weeks following produced a mix of empty coach and station shunt diagrams until, on Thursday and Friday, 15/16th November, after Monday to Wednesday on '288 empty coaches diagram' with Roy, we worked '287 diagram', '4J21' fitted freight from King's Cross Goods to Cambridge Goods. We went down with D5615 and on arrival in Cambridge yard were surprised actually to be relieved by a Cambridge crew as booked but never practiced. We were then booked to relieve another Cambridge crew and work the sand train, '7B18', to Wood Green, as was often the case, but, in practice, usually with the retained engine off '4J21'.

The Cambridge men prepared to take D5615 and '4J21' on to Whitemoor, and, with no sign of '7B56' on this west side of the big yard, we reported to the yard foreman in the old goods yard buildings. The foreman directed us to walk across immediately to a train which we soon found on the east side of the sprawling goods yard, waiting behind two 'Brush-2s'; the leading engine was D5646 and her indicator panel showed the unusual code of '8Z00', her companion was D5640 and they were coupled in multiple, thereby forming one 2,940

horse-power unit. Behind the locomotive(s) stretched a very long train of flat wagons loaded with an impossibly continuous length of railway rail. Waiting for relief in the front cab of this outfit were two men from March shed who were pleased to see us, told us all was well with the locos, how the unusual load rolled round corners well enough; we all wondered why they couldn't have worked home with '4J21', then they set out to make their way home, no doubt using a similar 'enginuity' to that which we often used to get back south but which we did not need to apply that night. We were joined by our guard who confirmed that we did indeed head a train of continuous welded track, took Roy's name, gave us the tonnage, then walked back along the long train to his brake.

I had time to make a 'brew' before we were given the road at 23.10 and Roy eased us gingerly out onto the up main; I looked back to confirm the guard's lamp signal and watched in awe as those flat bogie wagons snaked slowly out behind us, the long welded lengths of rail flexing with the curves of the running rails. Roy took us slowly onto Great Northern tracks at Trumpington, gently easing the controller and concentrating on the feel of this unusual load; it kept him unusually quiet, and, recognizing the signs, I kept my own dutiful silence as we rumbled steadily through the pitch black countryside; but by the time we rolled through Royston, Roy had got the measure of the load and was back in full flow, commenting on this unusual but fortunate job, wondering about the amazing flexibility of the rails we carried, what time we could expect to arrive at Langley, would they send us light up to 'The Cross' from Hitchin, etc, etc? We had 'greens' all the way and Roy took us steadily through the lights of Baldock station then 'got hold of them', braking gently after Letchworth, preparing to lead our flexible load carefully and expertly onto the ECML up slow road, through Hitchin, and so to our unusual destination, the long siding just south of Langley Junction where the connecting line to the 'New Line' and the Hertford Loop line leaves the up slow road; at that time old Stevenage station stood about a mile north of the present station which was built in 1973 conveniently close to Stevenage New Town. Presumably Hitchin 'stock yard' did not have one clear road long enough to accommodate 8Z00 and we eased into Langley Junction siding at about 01.05. The siding is still there today and now serves a Lafarge Aggregates concentration depot which receives a Sundays only self-discharging aggregates train, '6M33', 'DB-Schenker' 66-hauled, originating from Lafarge's huge Mount Sorrel quarry, north of Leicester and travelling via Stamford to Peterborough then onwards to Langley each Sunday.

On that Autumn 1967 night our guard uncoupled us then secured the train and came with us, light-engines, to Hornsey loco, arriving at 02.15, when we uncoupled the pair of 'Brush 2's, stabled them, then found a staff train which took us into 'The Cross' by 02.50.

The next night, Friday the 17th of November, found us on 287 again with D5614 on 4J21, and things were back to 'normal' when we were told to detach and retain D5614 and work 7B18 sand to Wood Green, then 'EBV' to King's Cross Goods and LE to Clarence Yard TMD. We eased out of Cambridge at 23.45 and arrived at Wood Green at 02.00, then we took guard and brake to the goods yard as directed but then, after Roy's 'engineuity' on the yard foreman's phone, we took D5614 into the 'Passenger Loco' and signed off at 03.35; then with Saturday as rest day and booked off on Sunday we were off for a full weekend.

The next week's roster put us on a mix of early mornings, starting at 05.20 on '256 diagram' on Monday, Tuesday and Friday; a return suburban run to Hertford, then an empty coach trip to Western Sidings and finishing with a run light engine to Hornsey depot. The loco on each occasion was a 34G 'Brush 4', D1761 on Monday and D1775 on both Tuesday and Friday mornings, and these 'Type-4' locos were now rostered regularly on peak suburban passenger and empty coach jobs between their main line passenger workings; looking back to steam days this was equivalent to utilising a 'Pacific' on these humble local duties, but was more feasible with diesel locomotives and realised in the National Traction Plan. On the Wednesday and Thursday we were listed as 06.00 'As required' and I spent Wednesday with Dave Foster working '668 run-round diagram' on '350' D3712, feeling every rail joint between the Goods Yard and Ferme Park several times on a busy mixture of shunting and trip working, while on Thursday I worked a shed duty relief job with '4-link' driver Ken D'Ath, relieving and preparing and including the first ride on a 'Deltic' for some time when we took D9003 'Meld' to the 'Passenger Loco'; but it was also the last occasion when I recorded an individual 'Deltic' number on reliefs.

We were back on nights for the next week. To work two weeks of nights in such close proximity was unusual, but this apparently became the usual pattern after roster changes in early September 1967. However, after the opening Sunday night, November 26th, with 'engine movements' from 22.00 until 06.00 in the 'Passenger Loco', and two nights of varied empty coach diagrams, on Wednesday night we worked '258 diagram', and we were pleased to see a 'Brush 2', D5606, at the head of '7J62' coal empties as we ran into Enfield Chase station on the 19.30 from 'The Cross'. It turned out to be an *almost* 'text book' working when we worked '7B56' back to Hitchin; but we were away from Cambridge by 23.00 - freights could run early providing they did not inconvenience other services – and took D5606 onto Hitchin shed at ten minutes after midnight. We knew that the crew off '4J21' were still at Cambridge when we left and 'engineuity' on this occasion discovered that they were coming back light engine, and weren't far away, so we arranged for Hitchin South box to check them on the approach to the station so that we could hitch a lift 'home as required' in their back cab.

Thursday night worked out exactly to the book when we secured D5605 in Hitchin loco at 00.35 and no amount of 'engineuity' could find us an early ride back to London, so we were obliged to wait and have a 'brew' in the salubrious surroundings of Hitchin depot's rest room, very sparsely inhabited in relation to the constant bustle and comings and goings of the night-time King's Cross room. We went up on the 03.14 mails.

And so we approached the end of 1967 and the completion of my last full year with the Motive Power Department. December started with Roy on a week of various early morning empty coach diagrams; on Sunday afternoon the 10th I went to Peterborough on a parcels train with jolly Jack Crate in charge of Immingham 'Brush-4' D1554 which we took to New England depot and swapped for King's Cross D1521 to take back a passenger train, all stations to Hatfield then Finsbury Park and 'The Cross'. With a rest day on Wednesday I spent the next week on the evening 'No. 2 Shunt' with a variety of 'Brush-2's in the pleasing company of driver Les Coulson, a cheerful and dapper middle-aged bachelor, never without his big 'bulldog' pipe which must surely have 'wowed' the many 'nice young ladies' he allegedly knew, and of whose innocent conquests he never tired of regaling us.

The week before Christmas saw me with Roy on a mixture of shed relief and empty coach jobs and, with a rostered long weekend, we were actually off from Saturday, 23rd to Tuesday, 26th December, an unusually long Christmas leave for loco staff. On Wednesday and Thursday, 27th and 28th we worked '294 diagram' with D5606 and D5604 respectively on the afternoon return to Royston, while on the Friday we signed on at 13.05 to work a stopping return to Cambridge with an impatient 'big-Brush' D1866, raring to go on each hop between stations with such a light load.

I finished the week with driver Ken Drinkwater, a fellow '4A-linker', on a shed duty relief diagram, while I finished the year on the 31st December with a one way trip to Grantham in the company of '2-link' driver Wally Blazey and Gateshead's D1993 on 1A52. We were relieved by a homeward bound 'Geordie' crew who wished us "Happy New Year", as they set out to call at York and Darlington and were pleased to be heading for their Newcastle homes in time for their so important 'Hogmanay', as were we.

In Grantham crew room we discovered two of our own men waiting to work our 'Deltic'-hauled train back to 'The Cross' and the second-man was D.C. 'Electric' Smith of my own link and seniority. His driver agreed for me to ride with them and Wally said that I was "welcome to that row" and went into the train 'on the cushions'. So I saw 1967 out in the cab of a 'Deltic', the only time I rode in a 'Deltic' hauling a train; Dave's driver complained more about our chatter than the 'Deltic' howl, but I was home just in time to join the 'Potters Barbarians' and welcome 1968 in appropriately.

On Monday night the 1st of January I started 1968 with Roy and 'Baby Deltic' D5906 on '258 diagram'; '7J62' coal empties from Enfield Old at 20.06 to Cambridge Goods where we arrived at about 22.00. We unhooked and stood D5906 off while we went in search of a 'brew' and confirmation of our booked return working, '7B56', the engineers' train; but we weren't surprised to be told that it wasn't running tonight. We had our break and I took us back, leaving just after 23.00, light-engine over the pitch black branch to Hitchin where we stabled D5906 at 00.10. We were then 'home passenger' by the first 'mails', no 'engenious' working found.

We were rest night Tuesday, empty coaches Wednesday and Thursday and worked '258 diagram' again, with D5906 again, on Friday night, although on this night the yard staff directed us to '7B56' already awaiting us in the yard. We attached D5906 and this night were soon joined by our '287 diagram' colleagues with their 'Brush-2' on '4J21'. We had a joint break and 'brew', then, as the sand, '7B18', wasn't running, we were given the 'o.k.' to couple the 'Brush' in front of the 'EE', and so work 7B56 to Hitchin 'in tandem', another piece of 'enginuity'. Arriveing at Hitchin 'stock yard' we quickly uncoupled D5906 and took her onto Hitchin loco where Roy stabled her while I rushed the key into the foreman, then we sprinted back through the deserted station, off the up platform – the 'Hitchin charge' again! – and so back to the 'stock yard' to hitch a lift back to London with '287' crew.

The next week was early mornings with Roy, rest-day Friday, with a mix of local jobs and a mix of weather which showed that it was as contrary 'pre-global warming', 50 years ago, as it is today. It snowed heavily on Tuesday the 9th of January although I apparently had no trouble in getting in, but our Tuesday 06.20 '282 diagram' empty coaches diagram was cancelled and our only job was to go out to Finsbury Park to dig out D5588, completely buried in Clarence Yard sidings; but she answered the starter willingly enough and we ran her into 'The Cross' where we were relieved by a pair of homeward bound Cambridge men. On Wednesday we were on a regular '4A'-link turn, 05.20 on for '256 diagram', initially taking 90 minutes to get D5597 light engine to Hertford to work the 07.48 up passenger to King's Cross. We left at 07.55, seven down, were told to call all stations and therefore didn't think arrival into King's Cross York Road 18 minutes late too bad. At York Road we were relieved and the train went on to Moorgate. We were directed to the main station where we relieved on D1104 waiting to take empties to Holloway sidings. With the whole of the East Coast disrupted by the heavy snow, stock was all over the place and upon arrival at Holloway we were immediately required to make our way back into 'The Cross' to collect more empty coaches, this time bound for a very crowded Hornsey Carriage Sidings. We left King's Cross with 3A03 coaches soon after 12 and finally reversed them into Hornsey sidings at 14.45, then we ran into Hornsey loco where we stabled D1104 at 15.05, a long day's work.

The snow was quickly washed away by heavy rain later in the week, and, after a temperature of -5 during the night of Wednesday the 10th we worked '256 diagram' again on a wet and warming Thursday morning, when, the power of D1868 was to no avail against adverse signals; we were three minutes late away from Hertford and eight down running into 'The Cross'. Saturday, 13th finished the week with an 04.00 shed duty relief morning, remarkable only for being quite warm for January. Some things never change!

We went back to nights the next week and worked '287 diagram' - for me, for the last time - on Monday, Tuesday and Wednesday nights. The down Cambridge/ Whitemoor goods was 5J21, semi-fitted, all this week, and on Monday, 15th our return trip found us reversing the working order of the 5th when we put our D5627 in front of '258 diagram's D5902 on '7B56' as the sand, 7B18, was not running again – and this time *we* waited in Hitchin 'stock yard' while they took D5902 onto Hitchin shed. On the Tuesday we saw nothing of the '258 crew' and ran D5593 light-engine from Cambridge to Clarence Yard, while on the Wednesday we stole their train when they were delayed going down with '7J62', and we worked their rostered '7B56' to Hitchin 'stock yard' with D5650, our '5J21' engine, then ran light-engine to King's Cross 75. There was considerable banter, later, about this last move, the '258' men ran very late light-engine back to Hitchin depot after us and had to catch the 03.14 mails home; but as we pointed out, me and Roy to Ken Drinkwater and his mate, all's fair in getting home from the wilds of Cambridge goods yard, and that week certainly showed the variation in demand of the freight services.

The next week was a full week of '269 empty coaches diagram', broken up with a Wednesday off rest-day and completed with '267 diagram', '4A's rostered Saturday 13.30 'Cambridge Buffet Express' which I worked with Roy for the last time, carefully reining in the 2,580 horses which D1532 made available on this relatively light train. During the next week we worked '4A link's' '294 diagram' the afternoon Royston return diagram - again, for me, for the last time. The week ended, on Saturday, 3rd of February with a 15.00 relief 'shed duty' job for me while Roy went off to Cambridge on an afternoon DMU diagram. But my seniority now regularly attracted weekend spare jobs in higher links and at 17.45 I was directed to join driver 'Jack' Warner on '185 diagram', a one way

trip as far as Grantham with '1N96' for Leeds, calling at Huntingdon and Peterborough. We had 'Brush-4' D1972 and arrived at Grantham 'right time' at 20.13, to be met by a worried loco foreman to tell us that he had no relief for us, and to beg us to work forward to Doncaster. My driver looked at me with raised, enquiring eye-brows – and on we went!

We'd hardly left Grantham when Jack declared his need to visit the other little luxury fitted inside the engine room of main line locos, a need he'd intended to attend to upon arrival at Grantham; D1972's toilet was fitted at her furthest end from us and with no little surprise I found myself sliding into the driver's seat, quickly taking over the 'dead man's treddle' as Jack stepped away with a grin. "If you get a yellow shut off, and you know what to do, but brake gently!" said he and I found myself sitting alone in the cab of a 'Brush-4' running effortlessly through the night at 75 m.p.h. The road was straight, the night fine and moonlit, the colour lights unmistakable, and – green! When Jack came back we were still bowling comfortably along at about 78 and he told me to ease the controller a little, "I don't suppose you want to come out of there now," he said and stood at my shoulder directing me into Newark and Retford and through the final slow-road crossover on the approach to Doncaster; "let her roll", as the station, then the platform, came up at a frighteningly fast rate but I remembered previous practice and managed a not too bad stop – although I got an old-fashioned look from our Doncaster relief when they had to walk a bit to where the cab door finally halted, a little after our booked time of 21.20. "My mate thought we were right away Newcastle!" said Jack. "Oh aye," was the laconic Yorkshire reply, two words which could be easily translated into "Mad Cockneys!"

What the result would have been if Doncaster had no relief, I do not know, the driver knew the road to Leeds and I know what my answer would have been! In the event we went home 'on the cushions' on the 23.18 up mails.

And so Doncaster was to be the furthest duty North I would achieve in my short career as a second-man, diesel locomotives; and I was fortunate enough to drive a 'Brush-4' during a good stretch of that night journey.

CHAPTER 11

THE END OF A BEGINNING

Monday, 5th of February started a week of early mornings and also the last full month of my curtailed career. I worked that first of the last weeks with Roy on empty coach diagrams Monday to Wednesday, then two days on '276 diagram', the 04.50 'newspaper round' with the engine swap in Hitchin depot, 'Brush-2' to 'Baby Deltic', and the passenger run from Royston to King's Cross. We were rest day on Saturday the 10th.

During these last three weeks I had several last trips to Royston and Cambridge, the last a Royston return on Tuesday, 27th with 'Brush-2' D5605 in the company of driver Eric Haddon who I had worked with once or twice before and who was a Potters Bar neighbour.

My last job with Roy was on Friday, 1st of March 1968 when we worked, perhaps appropriately, a simple shed duty, 'As required', turn. I don't think we said a lot as we shuttled between the 'Passenger Loco' and Clarence Yard; Roy had already persuaded me once to revoke my notice and it was finally up to me.

On Saturday the 2nd of March I toured 'The Cross' on the station pilot for the last time, working 'Number 1 Shunt' from 07.00 until 15.00 with driver Jimmy Wilson – I didn't record the loco number, a sure sign of the times!

I worked my very last shift on Sunday, 3rd March 1968. My last loco was, fittingly, 'Brush Type-2' D5627 and I accompanied cheerful young driver Wally Christoff. We went out to Wood Green then walked to Bounds Green carriage sidings where we found D5627, relieved a Hornsey driver then remained in the sidings, steam-heat testing stabled weekend coaching stock, keeping some warmth in them between duties. We stabled D5627 at about 13.00 and I went 'home passenger' for the last time, reluctantly leaving the rest and roster rooms which I had come to know so well during the brief time in which I had become acquainted with them.

And so a somewhat low-key ending to the beginning of the career which I had wanted so much for so long, but which seemed to offer little future prospect for my seniority in the late 1960s.

It must have been during early February 1968 that I reversed my 1964 application for transfer from the clerical grades, as I note that I was called for interview with the Area Station Manager, Welwyn Garden City on the 16th of February. This decision was the outcome of much speculation and agonising about future prospects which had occupied me during the last several months. Although, looking back now, single-manning had made little immediate difference to our job, there was much rumour of more extensive use of this inevitable method of working. Also, about this time, the few crews which still worked from Hatfield were brought into King's Cross; the Hatfield to Dunstable branch had closed in 1965 and the 'Ashburton Pullman' refuse trains were now worked through to Blackbridge by Hornsey men - and a new word started to be heard in the loco vocabulary – 'redundancy'. And it was in this increasingly uncertain atmosphere that I initially gave notice on Monday, 20th November 1967, then, after a long talk with Roy, I withdrew the notice on Wednesday the 22nd. I worked with Roy on that Friday morning the 24th on '256 diagram', and, at 05.30 on a cold November morning, little was said until we sat in the cab of 'Type-4' D1775 and had our first 'brew' before leaving the 'Passenger Loco' to run light-engine to Hertford when Roy looked across from 'the chair' and said with a grin, "Feel better now?" And, as Roy took us, light engine, through the King's Cross tunnels with that big 'Sulzer' engine ticking away contentedly behind us - I certainly did.

But the doubts and uncertainties persisted into the New Year until I finally plunged again and asked for the clerical-grades transfer which was granted during February, and so on Monday, 4th March 1968 I started a week's 'refresher' as a booking clerk – known in the burgeoning new age of the 1970s as a 'clerical officer' - at Hatfield station.

Some months after taking up my new position I passed through King's Cross station after a visit to London and met '2-Link' driver Jim Hawker who I had made my first snowy acquaintance with (P.30) at the outset of my diesel days. Jim told me that Roy had been taken ill. I immediately went to see him, not far away, in hospital at New Southgate. He was pleased to see me and I was very pleased to find him fully recovered and ready to leave. However Roy was unable to return to driving and saw out his final railway service in the time-keepers' office on platform 10 (today's 8) in King's Cross station, actually situated beneath the first floor loco signing-on point and rest room which we had both known so well. In the time office Roy prepared and oversaw the time sheets, rosters and signing-on procedure for all the station platform staff; he soon settled down and never seemed to regret leaving his long career in locomotives, steam and diesel. I kept in touch with him over the ensuing years, especially after my return to King's Cross as a 'clerical officer' in the Travel Centre in 1987. I occasionally visited him at his home in Pentonville Road where he lived with his wife Kathy and their daughter, and we also occasionally met for meals.

I left railway service completely in 1970, and after three years in the Post Office International Telegram Service in the City of London which involved the 24/7 shift working which I just had to have, took an opportunity to return to full time education and so realise another late ambition when I was accepted for a two year course at Coleg Harlech in North Wales. This was followed by three years at the then North London Polytechnic (now Royal Holloway University) for a B.A. History degree topped off with a post-graduate diploma in librarianship in 1979. After a spell as a chartered librarian in Barking and Dagenham Libraries, where, now married, we lived at that time, I returned restlessly, perhaps inevitably, to the irresistible lure of British Rail booking offices in 1984 and after 'graduation' from the offices of the Hertford loop and a year at busy Stevenage I finally reached the lofty heights of King's Cross Travel Centre in 1987. I saw Roy regularly at this time as I went to and from the Travel Centre until Roy retired in 1998 and I followed with early retirement in 1999. Our acquaintance continued into the new millennium but then unfortunately dropped to the 'note on a Christmas card' level.

CHAPTER 12

ROY HEAD, PHILOSOPHER AND ENGINE DRIVER

Roy Head was my rostered driver for little more than 16 months; looking back it seems as though it was a lot longer and I will always count those few short months as the most contented in my varied working life. Roy, then in his early 30s, was probably one of the youngest drivers in '4A Link' and I, at 27, was certainly the oldest second-man of my seniority, having just scraped into the job at 25 years old in late 1964. How much this relatively close proximity in age benefited our partnership is difficult to say; but we soon discovered that we had joint interests in so far as we both looked beyond the workaday problems of everyday life, and the job, which, naturally, made up the main topics of most railway workmate conversation. We realised these joint interests as we spent waiting time, often an hour or so, sometimes several hours, in yards and sidings and stations, and had time to sit and talk, especially in the 'wee small' morning hours on night shifts, when many crews took the opportunity to 'get their heads down'. But in the companionable warmth of a diesel locomotive cab, we found that clear nights found us looking out at and discussing stars, planets and the Universe which led on to discussion of such topics as 'God', philosophers, philosophy and similar scholarly topics in which we both read widely. And, yes, these really often were our serious topics of discussion as we waited to make the next move, and often when we were on the move; arguing about the meaning of 'essence' or 'forms' as we wheeled the clattering goods wagons through the dark Hertfordshire night behind a howling 'Baby Deltic' or whistling 'Brush-2'. But never, by an obviously conscious but never spoken agreement, never did we hold such conversations in the rest room where we joined in the general banter and argument; criticism of the way the job was going, silly management decisions, the job, the railway in general - and steam days, which all drivers, of course, remembered with differing degrees of nostalgia, love and hate, notably the recent confused overlap of joint steam and diesel operation when at last the long

1950s deliberations which produced the Modernisation Plan and Dr. Beeching's report bore results. New diesel locos, at first gradually, then in a great hurry, joined the earlier diesel shunters, until steam was finally phased out to bring us into the years of my own brief experience, recounted here, when the operation of diesel locomotives which had been pressed into service, often unproved, still had a long way to go before the benefits of new and more efficient operating methods would be fully experienced. And of course Roy had much to say on this topic both in the room with his peers and during our hours together working on the locos. I heard about his early firing days; on the goods yard pilots, the now closed branches from Finsbury Park, notably for Roy, the Alexandra Palace Branch, then later, firing Sir Nigel Gresley's fine 'Pacifics'; then his steam driving jobs, again from pilots until occasional Cambridge jobs with 'B1's and 'B17's until the diesels replaced them; but I usually had to ask for such information and I now wish that I had asked more. Roy did not seem to look back on steam days in the same nostalgic way as many of his peers, notably Jack Crate who would eulogise at length in his fine Oxbridge tones about 'the old days', and while Jack was always immaculately dressed in steam overalls - another surprise that such a dapper character didn't wear 'the greens' as our current uniform suits were known - Roy never wore uniform at all and, indeed, came to work looking as though he was set for a turn in the office where, indeed, he finished his railway service.

And so, with this mix of conversation Roy and I were never bored with each other's company and in waiting times could be as likely to discuss the latest roster changes as the theories of Baruch Spinoza. And I now feel sure that, for my own part it was these interests and an increasingly insatiable urge for knowledge as much as anything to do with the way the job was going which drove me out of a finally achieved vocation and, eventually, back to full time education, and, therefore, a chance to take up another, academic, vocation. Roy, like so many with ability in pre-war generations, was not really given this chance and while my own voluntary move made sure that I never became an official engine driver, in Roy's case his health assured that he never drove electrics - in one case there were regrets while in the other I don't think there was regret. Roy could always be contented with whatever life dished up to him.

Roy died on the 23rd of February 2009. We had lost touch and I did not know he was ill during the preceding year and I was rendered immobile and speechless when his name was read out in the B.T. Pensioners Federation's AGM obituaries at Hatfield that March. He was buried on the 2nd of March 2009 in the Catholic section of the huge St. Pancras and Islington Cemetery which is actually situated in East Finchley, North London. With strange and ironic coincidence it was in August of that year that I was invited to a day on the Colne Valley Railway in Essex and found myself totally unexpectedly at the controls of a 'Brush-2' again, ex-Immingham D5683, now 31255 and arrayed in EWS maroon and gold livery obtained after withdrawal and preservation in 1999; a most memorable day.

At later AGMs it was also a great shock to see the names of Jack Crate, Ken D'Ath and of course many other familiar names which have now left us, but at the BTPF and King's Cross staff reunions it is always good to meet many who were my 'young drivers' in the 1960s and who later became the pioneers of East Coast electrification, initially seeing in the King's Cross inner-suburban electrification with the first of the second generation EMUs, the 313s, in 1976.

CHAPTER 13

THE NEW RAILWAY – PART 2

Two years after the King's Cross inner-suburban electrification, the more senior drivers saw the main-line replacement of 'Deltics' by the first 125m.p.h. 'push-pull' 'train sets', the 'High Speed Train', consisting of a fixed rake of Mark 3 coaches powered by 2000+h.p. diesel locomotive power cars – one at each end! So with the innovative new 'push-pull' HSTs on the main line, the ageing DMUs on the outer suburban trains replaced by 312 EMUs in February 1978 when electrification reached Royston, and the 1976 313s

on the inner suburban services, there was, from the late 1970s, no longer a need for a replacement locomotive or a 'run round' at the completion of a journey, while the eternal empty coaching stock movements between the station and the many carriage sidings were virtually eliminated. All carriage sidings were closed by the early 1980s except for Bounds Green which became the site for a brand new Traction Maintenance Depot, initially for the HSTs, and replaced Finsbury Park, Clarence Yard TMD which closed in 1983; the 313 and 312 EMUs were

ECML power, diesel and electric. HST and 'Electra' locomotives stand ready in King's Cross during the 'nationalised' East Coast Railway franchise. The HSTs were new in 1978 but in 2018 are still in ECML front-line service. 43308 stands in platform 6 at the head of the colourful East Midlands Mark-3 set on long-term loan to the ECML, while '91' 91109 of 1988 is in 5. (Author)

ECML electric power. Ten years after the introduction of the HST the ECML was electrified and 32 new locomotives, class 91, were built by BREL and GEC. In this Sunday morning view of King's Cross in GNER days the utility of modern units is demonstrated as every ECML departure from 08.30 to Noon is ready to go, locomotive attached. (Author)

accommodated in another new depot built from 1973 on the site of our familiar old Hornsey steam shed with a southward extension which swallowed up a large part of Ferme Park up yard.

The 312s with their 'slam doors' are now long gone but the 313s are now, in 2018, the oldest surviving EMUs still in regular service and they presently work their last year of faithful service between London and the Hertfordshire suburbs, the 'Northern Heights' of old G.N. days. In 2018 they will be replaced by new Siemens 6-car '717' EMUs, while Hornsey EMU depot, which has accommodated all subsequent Great Northern EMUs, is now further extended, northwards, to take in the site of the old Hornsey carriage sidings, also long gone of course, but for ever remembered.

During the 1970s, then, some two years after my untimely departure from King's Cross MPD and some

30 years after the formulation of the Modernisation Plan, 'modernisation' arrived with a vengeance; with new trains in fixed sets and units, with sliding doors, electric heating, trains which could be driven from either end: the slow and grossly uneconomic change which had necessitated working new modern traction to old steam methods was now suddenly streamlined, speeded up, and a new railway era started; the start of an era which Sim Harris has recently called "the era of changing trains" (16) in a farseeing feature article, *Changing Trains*, published in the December 2016 edition of the *Railnews*.

Electrification reached Peterborough in 1987 and Cambridge in 1988 while the East Coast Main Line renewal was completed in 1990/1 when electrification arrived at Newcastle then Edinburgh and my 'young drivers', now a little older and more senior, became the first drivers of the GEC 125m.p.h. class '91' electric

BREL York built '313' EMUs have worked the Great Northern outer-suburban services since the line was first electrified in 1976. Here two veteran 313s terminate at Welwyn Garden City. In 2019 they will be replaced by 6-car Siemens EMUs, class 717. (Author)

The 1988-91 class '91' 'Electra' locomotives rarely leave their Mk.4 coach sets, but in June 2009 91126 in GNER blue has received attention at WABTEC Doncaster and prepares to return 'light engine' to Bounds Green TMD, 'blunt' cab leading. (Author)

locomotives, a class of 31 Bo-Bo locomotives built under contract from GEC by British Rail Engineering at Crewe. The 'Electras' - a name which, unfortunately, doesn't seem to have caught on - were built specifically for the proud East Coast Route as had been the case with the English Electric 'Deltic' diesel-electric loco-motives before them. The '91's entered service in 1990 together with their matching fixed 9-car 'IC225' sets of Mark 4 coaches. The locomotive is complemented at the other end of the set by an 'alternative locomo-tive', the 'Driving Van Trailer' or 'Driving Brake Van', an empty and cunning reproduction of a '91', com-plete with driving cab and controls which are wired through to the true '91' locomotive at the other end of the set. The DVTs contain a guard's compartment at the train end while the empty space between – passengers could not, in the 1980s, be conveyed in the end vehi-cles of trains travelling in excess of 100m.p.h. - is used to carry buffet-restaurant car product storage mod-ules – but not passengers' luggage! 'DVT's are mar-shalled at the south or London end of the rake, thus obviating the need for 'run-rounds' or engine change at termini. The 'IC225' electric locomotives and sets are now maintained at Bounds Green TMD while the ECML's remaining 32 'HST' sets and a variable 50 class '43' diesel locomotives (power cars) are looked after at the other end of the ECML at Edinburgh Craigentinny TMD. The 'IC225's and 'HST's are all now nearing the end of their useful lives and are all to be replaced in 2019 by new class 800 and 801 'bi-mode' five and nine-car electro-diesels, essentially EMUs, but also fit-ted with diesel engines which will allow them to go to places 'IC225's cannot reach, notably Inverness and Aberdeen, presently still served by the faithful, much rebuilt and re-engined, but now 40 years old 'HST's.

The 2010s, therefore, find the ECML in much the same optimistic situation that looked ahead in the 1970s, with brand new power arriving for both suburban and long-distance services. But the changes of the 1960s and 1970s can be seen in retrospect as little short of a rail-way revolution, finally seeing the end of some 150 years and more of steam locomotive working, but, with the essential continuation of the accompanying steam oper-ating practices for the next decade; practices which had powered the railways of the world since that first, much greater railway revolution, the actual birth of railways as a most essential part of Britain's burgeoning Industrial Revolution in the first decade of the nineteenth century, practices not easily dispensed with.

The proud drivers who at first suffered that slow transition from steam to diesel traction during the 1960s, then the more comfortable change to the revolutionary new electric trains and the operating divisions of priva-tisation in 1993, can now look on as the railway which they pioneered into the new era is taken forward once more by a new generation of railway locomotive people.

Back in the 1960s, assisted by we second-men, those drivers worked what may surely now be seen as the 'classic British diesel locomotives' which, in turn, in the 1970s gave way to the 'classic British diesel trains', the HSTs, shortly followed by the first electric trains, and now, in the 2010s we are about to see these 'British classics' replaced by a new generation of 'Globally produced' electric and electro-diesel trains which will be the ECML's share of the 5,693 new railway vehicles due to be delivered to the train operating companies throughout the British railway system over the next five years under the current Railway Upgrade Plan. The RUP is coordinated by the Rail Delivery Group, yet another new railway steering body which has recently replaced the Association of Train Operating Companies. The RDG tells us that this is the "highest sustained rate" of rail vehicles deliveries for the last 50 years - i.e. since the 1970s 'revolution' – and is the very latest in the long and complex line of modernisation planning groups, commissions and committees which have attempted to improve British railways over the last 60/70 years, sequels to the 1955 Modernisation Plan.

And the importance of these new train deliveries and, indeed, the complete £11.6billion Railway Upgrade Plan is summed up in the article mentioned above; *Changing Trains*, published in the December 2016 edition of the *Railnews* by Sim Harris who points out that,

"We are living in a period when decisions being made now about new trains will have a profound effect for decades to come." (16)

Surely this same sentiment was just as relevant in the revolutionary '50s when the hasty construction of too many untried diesel locomotives had an initially profoundly negative and uneconomic effect on railway modernisation and which increased the railway deficit for a decade and more. It is to be hoped that the "pro-found effect" of today's new trains will be more positive over the coming decades.

Unlike the revolutionary new locomotives, sets and units which appeared in the 1950 and 1960s, the 'twenty-first century trains are no longer entirely British products built in the remaining railway workshops of the pre-nationalisation 'Big Four' railways. Then, Crewe, Derby, Swindon, Eastleigh and our own ECML Darlington and Doncaster still turned out the new loco-motion, but were now joined by independent purveyors of the new traction such as 'Brush Electrical', 'English Electric' 'Cravens/Metropolitan Cammell', etc. while a sure sign of approaching modern times was the supply of Swiss 'Sulzer' and German 'Maybach' diesel engines. In 1969/70 British Railways' workshops were combined into British Rail Engineering Ltd. which concern was

allowed (by the government!) to "seek outside con-tracts." By 1992 BREL belonged to ABB (ASEA-Brown Boveri) Transportation Ltd and so started a long and increasingly complex family tree journey into today's brave new global world of multinational corpora-tions where its remains are interred in the ex-Midland Railway, ex-BREL works site at Litchurch Lane, Derby, now the UK base of the huge Canadian conglomerate known as 'Bombardier Transportation', the largest rail equipment manufacturer in the world.

'Bombardier Derby' has supplied new 'Electrostar' EMUs to Southern and South Eastern railways since the beginning of the new millennium and are due to provide much needed new trains for 'Abellio Greater Anglia'

The class 365 'Networker Express' 'EMU's were the last trains to be built by BREL/ABB at York 1994-5 and are in 2018 last to work Great Northern outer suburban services from King's Cross in company with 'new' Bombardier 'Electrostar's. 365507 is at Cambridge in 2011 when the new island platform was building on the right on the site of long gone Cambridge goods yard which I visited with night freight trains in the 1960s. (Author)

Second-hand from 'Thameslink', the 2015 build Bombardier 'Electrostar's share Great Northern outer suburban services with the 1995 BREL 'Network Express' EMUs until the 'new' railway runs in 2018. 387110 stands at Cambridge's south end in bay platform 2. (Author)

services from Liverpool Street from 2019. Meanwhile King's Cross outer suburban 'Great Northern' services have recently been enhanced by the re-allocation of some 29 'Bombardier' class '387' 'Electrostar' units from 'Thameslink' which will work alongside the last twenty year old BREL 'Networker' 365s as an interim measure before the complete renewal of services in 2018. In this renewal 'Great Northern's 'Electrostars' and 'Networkers' will be replaced by class '700' 'Desiro City' EMUs, many already working 'Thameslink' services, while the venerable 'BREL' 313s will be replaced by 6-car 'Desiro' '717's, equipped with end-doors, for working the inner suburban, Moorgate, services.

The 'Desiros' are manufactured by 'Siemens', another multinational concern, now a huge global organisation,

initially a small ambitious German firm, formed by brothers Werner and Wilhelm Siemens. Wilhelm came to England in 1843, developed the Siemens interests in telegraphy in England and steel works in South Wales, became naturalised as William, and was finally Sir William Siemens. The brothers made the firm into an early multinational concern and today 'Siemens UK Rails Systems' likes to emphasise Siemens' 170 year connection with Britain. The first British Siemens trains were 14 four and five car EMUs for the new 1998 Paddington based 'Heathrow Express' service, while from 2002 'SRS' replaced South West Trains' Waterloo outer-suburban and express services with a big order for 'Desiro' D.C. EMUs; 127 4-car '450's and 45 5-car '444's. By this time Siemens were successfully supplying locomotives and

A preview of the 'new' Great Northern railway; Siemens 'Desiro City' EMU 700015 calls at Hitchin on a driver training run on 27th June 2017. One 'Desiro' 700/0 unit consists of eight coaches, 700/1 of 12 coaches to one unit, considerably increasing Great Northern suburban capacity. (Author)

units, diesel and electric, d.c. and a.c, world-wide, and several varieties of Siemens' 'Desiro' can now be found throughout British railways.

The new '700' class 'Desiro Cities' are the first Siemens products to grace East Coast lines and will also be the first to connect the two 'Thameslink Railway' components physically when the new tunnel link opens in 2018. This new two road link leaves 'Great Northern' lines between Gasworks and Copenhagen tunnels, dives down under the old goods yard and 'Top Shed' site and so reaches the 'Thameslink' lines on the approach to 'St. Pancras Thameslink' station where they will join 'Thameslink' trains from Bedford to South London and Brighton, reviving a connection opened over 150 years ago; but the new wide and airy 'Great Northern' 'way to The South', turning west between the tunnels, is a vast change from the formidable, always steep – and in steam days suffocating

- descent from York Road and the corresponding climb through 'Hotel Curve' back into platform 16. 2018 will indeed show us a new suburban Great Northern Railway linked again to the South.

But 'Virgin Trains East Coast' are also to replace their 'HST's and '91's in 2018 and yet another now global, multi-industry 'conglomerate' – i.e. involved in just about everything! - is to provide the new stock. Hitachi ('Sunrise') was founded in Japan in 1910 by Namihei Odaira, an ambitious electrical engineer whose huts produced early electric motors and equipment, but soon became the leader in Japan's new electrical industry. In 1924 Hitachi produced Japan's first electric locomotive and by 1959 approached multinational days by opening 'Hitachi America Ltd.' and really joined the global movement in 1982 when 'Hitachi Europe Ltd.' was formed. 'Hitachi Rail' was the power behind the 'Tokaido

The ageing East Coast diesel HSTs share duties with the 91 'Electra's and are also able to go where electrics can't. A HST train-set, still in 'East Coast' livery, is headed by 'Virgin' liveried 'power car' (locomotive) 43274, coming up through Potters Bar in September 2015; a sister '43' assists (tails) at the back of the train. (Author)

Still 'state of the East Coast art' in 2018, 'Electra' 91131 and train were in 'East Coast' company livery throughout in April 2013, coming down the main between Potters Bar and Brookmans Park beside the hallowed line-path which I first trod round about 1950. (Author)

Shinkansen' 'bullet' trains which run 16 coach rush hour trains between Tokyo and Osaka at 150-200m.p.h – with a three minute headway! From the humbler Hitachi general purpose 'A-Train' concept came Britain's first Hitachis in 2006, 'Southeastern's 6-car '395' units which run at a stately 140m.p.h. between St. Pancras and south-east coast destinations. In 2008 Hitachi formed 'Agility Trains' in partnership with Britain's 'John Laing Group' and in 2012 the 'Agility Trains' consortium signed a contract with the Department for Transport for the 'Intercity Express Programme' (IEP), planned completely to replace the ECML and Great Western Railway 'HST' fleets with new EMUs, classes '800' (Bi-mode) and '801' (EMU) based on the "Hitachi Super Express Train".

Currently Hitachi are to supply 70 three and four car class '385' EMUs for ScotRail, six being built in Japan while the rest will be built in the new 'Agility Trains' 'rail vehicle manufacturing facility' at Newton Aycliffe in County Durham, United Kingdom, which will then proceed with the IEP '800' and '801' fleet renewal; 65 5-car and 9-car units will replace ECML '91's and HSTs. The newly electrified GWR will be similarly equipped with 57 units.

In the old days this fleet renewal would have been met from the various workshops of the pre-1923 independent railways or, after 1948, B.R. regions - Doncaster and Darlington for the ECML. But modernisation has seen most of these old and obsolete works closed or replaced by the new railway's 'rail vehicle manufacturing facility' – in today's world a simple word like 'works' or 'factory' is inadequate - and while Britain can no longer claim to be the 'workshop of the world',

A preview of the 'new' Virgin ECML railway; Hitachi IEP 5-car EMUs 802001 and 802002 come up through Welwyn North station on their delivery run from Tokyo to Acton via Doncaster on 6th August 2017. They are the first arrivals for Great Western Railway electric services from Paddington to Bristol; the ECML variation will be made up to 9-cars and known as the 'Azuma'. (Revd. Tom Gladwin)

29 British 'conglomerates' are listed currently, and Britain's share in global industry is summed up by the Hitachi partnership who point out that their trains are "DESIGNED IN JAPAN MADE IN BRITAIN."

The four road 'Agility Trains' factory at Newton Aycliffe is connected to the national system by a cross-over from 'The Bishop Line', the line which continues the Tees Valley Line from Saltburn to Darlington on to Bishop Auckland, following the exact route of the 1825 Stockton and Darlington Railway, the world's first public railway; indeed at the next station from Newton Aycliffe station, Heighington, is the unspoiled level crossing, the very spot, where George Stephenson's 1825 'Locomotion No.1', arrived in parts in horse-drawn carts from Newcastle, was assembled and set onto S&DR rails for the first time. The adjacent 'Locomotion No.1' pub was built as a combined pub and station in 1827 and incorporates parts of the original building. The next 'Bishop Line' station is Shildon - which surely warranted a mention in the railway's original name – 'The Stockton, Darlington and Shildon Railway' - where locomotives took over the haulage of the S&DR coal trains from the West Auckland pits. Little remains today of the huge railway complex of exchange sidings and locomotive works which Shildon became; but the site of one of the biggest marshalling yards in the world is now happily commemorated by the presence since 2004 of the National Railway Museum's 'sub-shed', the 'Locomotion' museum, actually built on the site of Shildon's considerable S&DR down-side or 'empty' sidings which were opened in 1870 and busy for just a century.

So Hitachi have brought Britain's railways full-circle, establishing the twenty-first century's 'new railway' 'rail vehicle manufacturing facility' in the very heart-land of the world's first railways, barely five miles from Shildon, the colliery village which became Timothy Hackworth's Stockton and Darlington Railway nineteenth century locomotive works, proudly self-styled today as 'The Cradle of the Railways'.

Sim Harris finished his article in the December 2016 *Railnews* with the observation that, "One thing is certain: our era of changing trains is just another staging point – not the end of the journey." And indeed this is so. Since the great acceptance point and subsequent proliferation of public railways in the 1830s we see several 'organisational' staging points throughout railway history;

perhaps the first, 'The Grouping' of 1923, the amalgamation of the many independent railway companies into just four geographical railways, 'The Big Four'; then, in 1948, 'Nationalisation' when 'The Big Four' became but one, 'British Railways'; then 'Privatisation' – a return to independent railways in 1993 - but the way to 'Privatisation' was marked by the great mid- twentieth century 'operational' staging point – the replacement of the original nineteenth century steam powered locomotive engine by the diesel-oil and electrically powered locomotive engines; the real outset of that innovative railway time which Sim Harris so aptly terms as the "era of changing trains" which has subsequently seen the replacement of the traditional locomotive engine at the head of a train by the incorporation of a relay of small static diesel engines or electric motors integral to, usually beneath, the very train vehicles themselves, the 'unit train' which can be driven from either end and where the complete train is now the locomotive.

And now the ECML, which approached "the era of changing trains" with the dieselisation of the late 1950s, the unique 'Deltic' diesel locomotives of the 1960s, and continued, upon electrification in the 1980s, with the unique 'Electra' (91) electric locomotives, is, in the early twenty-first century, to be completely renewed with 'state of the art' unit trains; Siemens 'Desiro City' and Hitachi 'Super Express'. Perhaps this renewal, taken across the whole of British railways, can be seen as the full realisation of this latest railway 'staging point' but, as Sim Harris points out – it will not be the end of the journey.

My own memories belong just after that time between 1959-1962 when R.H.N. Hardy could say, "we achieved the impossible." The steadying years just after that achievement included the few years during which I served my short term as drivers' assistant or 'second-man', and during those few years I was fortunate enough to work in the company of an exceptional railwayman on examples of all the then new, now 'classic', diesel-electric locomotive types which regularly worked the East Coast Main Line, notably the mighty 'Deltics', now the stuff of legend.

The diesel 1960s led the new 'era of changing trains' into the great electric railway revolution of the 1970s and 1980s, and then on to the present Railway Upgrade Plan which will soon provide the East Coast Main Line with a brand new railway.

CHAPTER 14

GREAT NORTHERN THAMESLINK 2018

On page 159 I expressed the hope that the 'profound effect' of today's new trains as envisaged by Sim Harris would be more positive than the initial effects experienced by the new diesel railway era of the 1960s. Unfortunately the introduction of the new Great Northern timetable can only, in June 2018, be described as chaotic. The first weekday implementation of the new timetable was Monday, May 21st and that first week resulted in swathes of cancellations and long delays bringing misery to thousands of King's Cross commuters. The major causes of this failure at the very outset of the new timetable would appear to be an insufficient amount of drivers trained on the new '700' units and on the linking route through the new tunnel.

Since that first week things have improved, initially with few Great Northern trains making the journey through the new tunnel link to St. Pancras and on to the South. The quantity of available trains is now adequate, but they can't be said to run reliably even to the temporary timetable now introduced.

On Tuesday, 26th June I arrived at Hitchin station at about 13.00 to go to London; the departure boards did not seem promising, trains marked as cancelled or delayed throughout. However, the 12.11 from Peterborough to Horsham stood out as being 'on time' and – I must admit to my surprise – it was! At London Bridge I left 12 car 700151 at 13.59 – exactly as advertised! On return at 16.00 London Bridge services were running like clockwork, one southbound Thameslink cancelled in the half hour during which I risked waiting for the 16.31 from Horsham to Peterborough – which rolled in at 16.30, 700151 returning; we arrived at Hitchin as booked at 17.19, a comfortable two-way journey which could not be faulted.

The performance of the 'new railway' is, therefore, improving, and while the initial working has been unquestionably negative, there is no doubt, looking to the future, that the final result will achieve Sim Harris's positive "profound effect for decades to come", with the Great Northern Railway successfully serving the London suburban needs at the south end of the ECML with, once again, a convenient connection to the South of the country, and running alongside an equally successful main line to the North and Scotland.

New in 1957, and immediately successful; the very first of the 'Brush' 'Type 2's which I came to know at King's Cross better than any other type, is most fortunately preserved in York NRM but unfortunately in her later anonymous TOPS 'BR blue' livery as 31018. (Author)

New in 1958, the 2.000h.p. 'English Electric' Type 4s were also a successful 'pilot' design; the first B.R. 'big' diesel type and predecessor to the unique Type 5 'Deltic'. D213 became TOPS 40013, but is thankfully preserved in original livery at Barrow Hill where she majestically greeted visitors to the April 2012 gala. I 'ferried' Gateshead '2,000's at Kings Cross. (Author)

New in 1961, the 'Type-5' 'English Electric' 3,300h.p. 'Deltic's replaced their 'Type-4' cousins on the ECML's best trains and soon became legendary locomotives. 34G was allocated eight of these 22 diesel thoroughbreds and I 'ferried' them to and from the 'Passenger Loco' and Finsbury Park - 34G - TMD. D9009 'Alycidon' was a 34G loco and still works for the Deltic Preservation Society who keep three of the surviving seven 'Deltics' at Barrow Hill where I found D9009 posing magnificently on 23rd August 2008. (Author)

New in 1975, the revolutionary HST heralded a new 'staging point' in the 'era of changing trains'; a fixed set of coaches is marshalled between two uniform 2,000h.p. locomotives, obviating the need for locomotive changes at termini. Here 43300 has arrived at platform 5 King's Cross as the leading, driven, locomotive – 'power-car' - of an up ECML train and will provide trailer power when that train returns northwards, controlled from a driven sister at the north end of the set. (Author)

New in 1988, 91001 was the first of 31 unique ECML 6,500h.p. electric locomotives which introduced electric motive power onto the ECML; the '91's work fixed sets of 9 Mark-4 coaches, hauling northbound trains and propelling southbound, when control is from a 'driving van trailer' – class '82' 'DVT' - a basic '91' shaped bodyshell equipped with a duplicate driving-cab, complementing the locomotive powered north end of the train. 91001 became 91101 when overhauled and now wears a special livery and bears a famous ECML name - 'Flying Scotsman', seen here calling at York. (Author)

'DVT' 82205 heads an up afternoon 'Virgin East Coast' train through Potters Bar in April 2016. Externally a sister to the '91' locomotive which is propelling at the rear of the train, the '82's are but empty 'driving trailer' shells which usually carry buffet/restaurant supplies. 82205 also complements '91' locomotive 91001 externally by carrying the famous 'Flying Scotsman' name. (Author)

D5683 was originally an Immingham engine built in 1961; withdrawn in 1999, she was painted into EWS colours in preservation on the Colne Valley Railway where I had a nostalgic day in August 2009. Now with 'Harry Needle Rail Services', her future is doubtful. (Dickie Pearce, Colne Valley Railway)

In the 'Deltic' seat again as a volunteer at 'Locomotion', Shildon NRM, in 2010 but going nowhere. DP1, the prototype 'Deltic', was withdrawn from B.R. service in 1961 and has recently returned to NRM Shildon after a visit to the Ribble Valley Railway. (NRM Shildon)

NOTES

1. Clough, David N. *The Modernisation Plan: British Railways' blueprint for the future.* p.135-136.
2. Clough op. cit. p.14.
3. Hardy, R.H.N. *'Beeching – Champion of the Railway?'* p.21.
4. Clough op. cit. p.125.
5. Clough op.cit. p.128.
6. Hardy op.cit. p.21
7. Hardy op.cit. Chapter 2
8. Hardy op.cit. ps.19/20
9. Hardy op.cit. ps. 23/24
10. Hardy op.cit. p.17
11. Hardy op.cit. p.23
12. Hardy op.cit. p21
13. Hardy op.cit. ps.23/24
14. Clough op.cit. p.166
15. Hardy op.cit. p.13
16. Harris, Sim. *'Changing Trains' Railnews* Feature Article, p.15ff. December 2016.

BIBLIOGRAPHY

British Railways Illustrated, Station Survey Finsbury Park, Chris Hawkins, Irwell Press, Vol.1 No.2, 1991/2.

Clough, David N., *'The Modernisation Plan – British Railways' Blueprint for the Future',* Ian Allan, 2014.

Connor, Charlie and Jim, King's Cross to Potters Bar, Middleton Press, 2009.

'Diesel Depot – B.R's Unsung Workhorses – 'Finsbury Park', Alex Fisher; published by 'Railways Illustrated', Mark Nicholls, editor, Key Publishing Ltd., 2017.

Hardy, R.H.N., *'Beeching – Champion of the Railway?',* Ian Allan, 1989.

Hawkins, Chris, *The Great British Railway Station King's Cross,* Irwell Press, 1990.

Kay, Peter. *'The Great Northern Main Line in London – Finsbury Park, Parts 1-3' - 'The London Railway Record',* numbers 41-43, 2004-2005.

Nock, O.S. *'Great Northern Suburban'.*

Railnews – 'Changing trains', Sim Harris, Railnews Ltd., December 2016.

Young, John N., *'Great Northern Suburban',* David & Charles, 1977.

INDEX